GREAT JOY
in
GREAT TRIBULATION

SIMPLIFIED PROPHECY
FOR THE LAST DAYS

by
Jim Searcy

Preface by John Hagee

GREAT JOY
in
GREAT TRIBULATION

SIMPLIFIED PROPHECY
FOR THE LAST DAYS

by
Jim Searcy

Preface by John Hagee

(QUESTIONS, COMMENTS, ORDERS 1-800-731-7545)

Companion Press
P.O. Box 310
Shippensburg, PA 17257-0310

"Good Stewards of the
Manifold Grace of God"

ISBN 1-56043-566-6

For Worldwide Distribution
Printed in the U.S.A.

TABLE OF CONTENTS

PREFACE..1

INTRODUCTION.............................6

MATTHEW.....................................10

MARK..38

LUKE...53

JOHN...65

PAUL...81

REVELATION..............................111

DANIEL...164

MOSES..218

ISAIAH...225

JEREMIAH....................................241

EZEKIEL..255

HOSEA..286

JOEL..291

AMOS...299

JONAH...308

NAHUM..313

HABAKKUK...................................317

ZEPHANIAH..................................323

HAGGAI...328

ZECHARIAH..................................332

PETER..347

Dedicated To:

Robin & Lizzie

To God be the Glory!

PREFACE

In the United States there are preachers, and teachers who are saying there is no reason for you to study prophecy. Let me give you 4 very valid bible reasons why you should know and study bible prophecy.

<u>One - Prophecy proves the authority of the word of God.</u>   The Bible is different from every other book. Certainly different from every other religious book. The books written by false religions or cults, try to explain the past. They try to explain the present. But all of them are silent about the future. Twenty-five per cent of the word of God, when it was written, predicted the future; and, it has come to pass with 100% accuracy. Consider the birth of Christ. The time of His birth is given in Daniel 9. The fact of His birth is given in Isaiah 7. The Place of His birth is given in Micah 5. The details of His life, His death, and His resurrection, are given in Psalms 22 and Isaiah 53. The fact of His resurrection is given in Psalm 16. One mathematician has figured out that there is 1 chance in 87E93 or 87 followed by 93 zeroes -(here is how the number looks regular, instead of scientific notation -
87,000,000,000,000,000,000,000,000,000,000,000,000, 000,000,000,000,000,000,000,000,000,000,000,000,000, 000,000,000,000,000,000.)- that the Bible could be

right on guess alone. It has to be supernaturally inspired.

Two - Prophecy demonstrates the ability of God to know the future; and to control kings, and to control kingdoms, and to see it come to pass. Consider Daniel's writings in Daniel 2 and 7. Daniel was given the panorama of the nations that were to come upon the face of the earth after his generation. He said to Nebuchadnezar, "you are the head of gold." And after you shall come the breastplate of silver, which was the Medes and the Persians. And then he said there shall be the belly of brass which represented Alexander the Great. And then he told of the iron legs, representing both eastern and western divisions of the Roman empire. And then he said that in the final generation, are the feet, having 10 toes representing 10 kingdoms. And there would be a stone cut without hands, speaking of Jesus Christ, the Cornerstone, precious and elect in Zion. That would come and crush the image, and make it fine as powder of the threshing floor and throw it into the wind. How could anyone know that future except it was God. Who, but God, could predict the future of kings and kingdoms with 100% accuracy. Bible prophecy proves beyond the shadow of a doubt, that God is in control, that He is in charge. The bible says that He puts one king up and He puts another down. Proverbs 21:1 says "The king's heart is in the hand of the LORD, as the rivers of water: he

turneth it whithersoever he will." Please understand
that the United States government, and the United
Nations, and the Soviet Union, and the European
Common Market, are no challenge for God. He
changes their hearts like He changes the course of a
stream. He is in total charge.

<u>Three - Prophecy reveals the purposes of God.</u>
God lets us see the future clearly and with
confidence. When you understand what is going to
happen, you have assurance and you have peace in
the present. God told Abraham the future of Sodom
and Gomorrah. In prophecy He tells us the future of
the world. We are not at the mercy of CNN, or CBS,
or ABC, or NBC. God's word has the answer about
tomorrow.

<u>Four - Prophecy is absolutely accurate.</u> 2 Peter
1:16 says "For we have not followed cunningly
devised fables, when we made known unto you the
power and coming of our Lord Jesus Christ, but
were eyewitnesses of his majesty." Peter said that
we, as followers of Jesus Christ, have not followed
after what we have heard people say about Jesus
Christ and His resurrection; but, we are eye
witnesses of His majesty. His majesty refers to the
eye witness of the Ascension of Jesus Christ.
2 Peter 1:19 says "We have also a more sure word
of prophecy; whereunto ye do well that ye take heed,
as unto a light that shineth in a dark place, until the

day dawn, and the day star arise in your hearts:" A more sure word of prophecy? More sure than what? More sure than our eyewitness account. Peter is saying that prophecy is more accurate than their eyewitness account of the resurrection of Jesus Christ. And then he said , secondly, we do well to take heed. Meaning there is a great benefit to knowing the future. Thirdly, as a light that shines in a dark place. I assure you that America is in a dark place. I assure you that the world is in spiritual darkness. But, I assure you that prophecy is the light that shows us the future so that we know where America is going. And we know where the world is going. And we have peace, and confidence knowing that God reigns. And that Jesus Christ is Lord, and that He sits at the right hand of God the Father. And everything is going to be all right; because, King Jesus is Lord of all.

Give Him Praise and Glory!!!

The above Preface is an excerpt from a sermon preached by Pastor John Hagee, Cornerstone Church, in San Antonio, TX. Pastor Hagee boldly and powerfully affirms the absolute inerrant truth of every word in the Bible. Pastor Hagee has kindly given his permission to use this sermon excerpt to encourage you to study prophecy. It does not mean that Pastor Hagee would necessarily agree with any of the interpretations in this book. The excerpt is taken from his opening remarks of a sermon titled "Apple

of God's Eye." May I encourage you to obtain a copy of
this important, bold, message regarding the Christian's
relationship to Israel and the Jewish people. To obtain this
important message "Apple of God's Eye," Write: Global
Evangelism Television, Inc., John Hagee Ministries, P.O.
Box 1400, San Antonio, TX, 78295 - 1400.

INTRODUCTION

Daniel 12:4 But thou, O Daniel, shut up the words, and seal the book, [even] to the time of the end: many shall run to and fro, and knowledge shall be increased.

Daniel was told to shut up the words and seal the book even to the time of the end. At the time of the end, when many shall run to and fro, and knowledge shall increase, we would then be able to understand Daniel's prophecy. If Daniel's prophecy is opening up, we need to know it. When Daniel's prophecy opens up we will see tremendous simplicity in understanding many end time prophecies that have historically frustrated or confused some brilliant scholars. The assumption that the time of the end is at hand, is a key to understanding those things which may have frustrated the scholar. The greatest credential of the bible student is to have the greatest teacher.

John 14:26 But the Comforter, [which is] the Holy Ghost, whom the Father will send in my name, <u>he shall teach you all things</u>, and bring all things to your remembrance, whatsoever I have said unto you.

If we are indeed at the time of the end, we may be confident that the Comforter, and greatest teacher, the Holy Ghost will let us see with beautiful simplicity how all of the prophecies of Daniel, Revelation, and Last Days Prophecy may be understood by all. Let us agree to disagree with anything that is not an essential doctrine of salvation by faith in the Lord Jesus Christ.

The essential doctrines of Christ and the faith which He delivered by the apostles and prophets must not be compromised. All of the other discussions must follow the instructions that the Apostle James gave us: **1:5 - If any of you lack wisdom, let him ask of God, that giveth to all [men] liberally, and upbraideth not; and it shall be given him. 3:13 - Who [is] a wise man and endued with knowledge among you? let him shew out of a good conversation his works with meekness of wisdom. 3:17 But the wisdom that is from above is first pure, then peaceable, gentle, [and] easy to be intreated, full of mercy and good fruits, without partiality, and without hypocrisy.**

To understand end time prophecy, just ask God, in faith, believing. Unless it is still to be sealed, by His Holy Spirit, He will give the understanding. We can be absolutely sure on the integrity of His word in James 1:5 that He will give us the wisdom we seek. It is good to seek confirmation and share what we have received with other believers.

What is the quality to look for when we want to find someone to help with our understanding of prophecy? In a word, it is MEEKNESS, according to James 3:13.

James 3:17 But the wisdom that is from above is first pure, then peaceable, gentle, [and] easy to be intreated, full of mercy and good fruits, without partiality, and without hypocrisy.

By all means do not seek to understand end times prophecy by discussing it with someone like James describes in 3:14-16 **But if ye have bitter envying and strife in your hearts, glory not, and lie not against the truth. This wisdom descendeth not from above, but [is] earthly, sensual, devilish. For where envying and strife [is], there [is] confusion and every evil work.** We may be able to discuss the fundamental doctrines of the Faith with such people but it is unwise to try to discuss prophecy interpretation with them. All we will come out with is confusion and strife and be further away from understanding then when we started.

There are a number of purposes for this book. One of the main ones is that my children have a clear understanding of end time prophecy. This is the reason for the simple personal style. In the study of the end times, most of the books and teaching available take a much different approach. Many of the books on the subject of end time prophecy are either complex scholarly works or else look at very few of the scriptures that only reinforce the popular escapist opinions. The purpose of this work is to present a simple and yet more thorough collection of the scriptures. Very heavy emphasis is given to the scriptures rather than sophisticated scholarly discussion. It is hoped that the Holy Spirit will clarify the truths regarding the end times if enough of the scriptures themselves are presented. Many people today sense the urgency of understanding end time prophecy. In their hearts, many people know that they are not being given the full council of God on this important subject from pulpits, radio, and TV. Few have the time to wade through the many escapist books to glean the little bits of new truth to increase their understanding of end time prophecy. Bibles don't come with all the end time prophecies underlined and highlighted.

Great Joy and Great Tribulation may sound like mutually exclusive terms. However, when one understands Who walks with us through these things it will bring great joy. Knowing the truth not only sets you free; it keeps you free. We have always been called to live by faith. Soon the supernatural living by faith will become increasingly more important. We are being called to the most exciting times ever in all history. We are being called to supernatural living for the glory of God. Even today the call remains rather optional. Soon, very soon perhaps, it will be the only way for saints to live. Don't let the strong meat scare or deter your search for truth. The truth is that we are living in the most exciting and glorious time of all history. Break up the fallow ground and pull all the stops. Cause your faith and love to grow as much as possible. You will find joy as you seek the truth, Jesus Christ, as your highest priority.

MATTHEW

The right place to begin any study of end time or last days prophecy is to see how Our Lord answered His apostles when they asked Him about these things. Matthew was the only gospel writer besides John who heard the words directly from the Lord. John's record is not included in his gospel account; however, in Revelation, the Lord gave John much more detail on what He had told them in the Olivet Discourse. It is good to remember that John likely wrote the Revelation after Rome had destroyed Jerusalem. Mark likely received his account from Peter. Luke likely used the accounts of Matthew and Mark to prepare his account of the Olivet Discourse. Of the three accounts in the gospels, Matthew's account not only is most detailed but likely most literal. It is often said that Matthew was writing to the Jews. He was writing to the Church, which with very few exceptions such as Luke, was almost all Jews at the time when he wrote it. Matthew wanted to make it clear that faith in Jesus involved no departure from the Old Testament, but was the goal to which the Old Testament pointed.

It can not be over emphasized how important the Olivet Discourse is to a solid understanding of end time prophecy. Study it carefully. Seek an understanding of the order of events that the Lord gives. Refer often to what Jesus answers as his apostles ask:

Matthew 24:3 And as he sat upon the mount of Olives, the disciples came unto him privately, saying,

Tell us, when shall these things be? and what [shall be] the sign of thy coming, and of the end of the world?

Luke 21:7 And they asked him, saying, Master, but when shall these things be? and what sign [will there be] when these things shall come to pass?

Mark 13:3-4 And as he sat upon the mount of Olives over against the temple, Peter and James and John and Andrew asked him privately,

Tell us, when shall these things be? and what [shall be] the sign when all these things shall be fulfilled?

We are asking just what the apostles asked. Lord, tell us when shall these things be? Lord, what shall be the sign of thy coming? Daniel and the other prophets who have spoken of the end of the world have left us confused. Lord, help us to understand as we look at what You had Matthew record for us.

Matthew 24:4 - 25:46

And Jesus answered and said unto them, Take heed that no man deceive you. For many shall come in my name, saying, I am Christ; and shall deceive many. And ye shall hear of wars and rumours of wars: see that ye be not troubled: for all [these things] must come to pass, but the end is not yet. For nation shall rise against nation, and kingdom against kingdom: and there shall be famines, and pestilences, and earthquakes, in divers places. All these [are] the beginning of sorrows. Then shall they deliver you up to be afflicted, and shall kill you:

and ye shall be hated of all nations for my name's sake. And then shall many be offended, and shall betray one another, and shall hate one another. And many false prophets shall rise, and shall deceive many. And because iniquity shall abound, the love of many shall wax cold. But he that shall endure unto the end, the same shall be saved. And this gospel of the kingdom shall be preached in all the world for a witness unto all nations; and then shall the end come. When ye therefore shall see the abomination of desolation, spoken of by Daniel the prophet, stand in the holy place, (whoso readeth, let him understand:)   Then let them which be in Judaea flee into the mountains: Let him which is on the housetop not come down to take any thing out of his house: Neither let him which is in the field return back to take his clothes. And woe unto them that are with child, and to them that give suck in those days! But pray ye that your flight be not in the winter, neither on the sabbath day: For then shall be great tribulation, such as was not since the beginning of the world to this time, no, nor ever shall be. And except those days should be shortened, there should no flesh be saved: but for the elect's sake those days shall be shortened.

Then if any man shall say unto you, Lo, here [is] Christ, or there; believe [it] not. For there shall arise false Christs, and false prophets, and shall shew great signs and wonders; insomuch that, if [it were]

possible, they shall deceive the very elect.
Behold, I have told you before. Wherefore if they
shall say unto you, Behold, he is in the desert; go
not forth: behold, [he is] in the secret chambers;
believe [it] not. For as the lightning cometh out of
the east, and shineth even unto the west; so shall
also the coming of the Son of man be. For
wheresoever the carcase is, there will the eagles be
gathered together.

Immediately after the tribulation of those days
shall the sun be darkened, and the moon shall not
give her light, and the stars shall fall from heaven,
and the powers of the heavens shall be shaken:

And then shall appear the sign of the Son of man in
heaven: and then shall all the tribes of the earth
mourn, and they shall see the Son of man coming
in the clouds of heaven with power and great glory.
And he shall send his angels with a great sound of a
trumpet, and they shall gather together his elect
from the four winds, from one end of heaven to the
other.

Now learn a parable of the fig tree; When his branch
is yet tender, and putteth forth leaves, ye know that
summer [is] nigh: So likewise ye, when ye shall see
all these things, know that it is near, [even] at the
doors. Verily I say unto you, This generation shall
not pass, till all these things be fulfilled. Heaven

and earth shall pass away, but my words shall not pass away.

But of that day and hour knoweth no [man], no, not the angels of heaven, but my Father only. But as the days of Noe [were], so shall also the coming of the Son of man be. For as in the days that were before the flood they were eating and drinking, marrying and giving in marriage, until the day that Noe entered into the ark, And knew not until the flood came, and took them all away; so shall also the coming of the Son of man be. Then shall two be in the field; the one shall be taken, and the other left. Two [women shall be] grinding at the mill; the one shall be taken, and the other left.

Watch therefore: for ye know not what hour your Lord doth come. But know this, that if the goodman of the house had known in what watch the thief would come, he would have watched, and would not have suffered his house to be broken up. Therefore be ye also ready: for in such an hour as ye think not the Son of man cometh. Who then is a faithful and wise servant, whom his lord hath made ruler over his household, to give them meat in due season? Blessed [is] that servant, whom his lord when he cometh shall find so doing. Verily I say unto you, That he shall make him ruler over all his goods. But and if that evil servant shall say in his heart, My lord delayeth his coming; And shall begin to smite [his]

fellowservants, and to eat and drink with the
drunken; The lord of that servant shall come in a day
when he looketh not for [him], and in an hour that he
is not aware of, And shall cut him asunder, and
appoint [him] his portion with the hypocrites: there
shall be weeping and gnashing of teeth.

Note that the parable of the talents is not included here.
Not because it is not important. We must be working for
the Lord with all of the talents He gives us. May we agree
that the parable of the talents was not part of the answer
given to the specific question raised in the Olivet Discourse?

Then shall the kingdom of heaven be likened
unto ten virgins, which took their lamps, and went
forth to meet the bridegroom. And five of them were
wise, and five [were] foolish. They that [were]
foolish took their lamps, and took no oil with them:
But the wise took oil in their vessels with their
lamps. While the bridegroom tarried, they all
slumbered and slept. And at midnight there was a
cry made, Behold, the bridegroom cometh; go ye out
to meet him. Then all those virgins arose, and
trimmed their lamps. And the foolish said unto the
wise, Give us of your oil; for our lamps are gone out.
But the wise answered, saying, [Not so]; lest there
be not enough for us and you: but go ye rather to
them that sell, and buy for yourselves. And while
they went to buy, the bridegroom came; and they that
were ready went in with him to the marriage: and the

door was shut. Afterward came also the other virgins, saying, Lord, Lord, open to us. But he answered and said, Verily I say unto you, I know you not. Watch therefore, for ye know neither the day nor the hour wherein the Son of man cometh.

When the Son of man shall come in his glory, and all the holy angels with him, then shall he sit upon the throne of his glory: And before him shall be gathered all nations: and he shall separate them one from another, as a shepherd divideth [his] sheep from the goats: And he shall set the sheep on his righthand, but the goats on the left. Then shall the King say unto them on his right hand, Come, ye blessed of my Father, inherit the kingdom prepared for you from the foundation of the world: For I was an hungred, and ye gave me meat: I was thirsty, and ye gave me drink: I was a stranger, and ye took me in: Naked, and ye clothed me: I was sick, and ye visited me: I was in prison, and ye came unto me. Then shall the righteous answer him, saying, Lord, when saw we thee an hungred, and fed [thee]? or thirsty, and gave [thee] drink? When saw we thee a stranger, and took [thee] in? or naked, and clothed [thee]? Or when saw we thee sick, or in prison, and came unto thee? And the King shall answer and say unto them, Verily I say unto you, Inasmuch as ye have done [it] unto one of the least of these my brethren, ye have done [it] unto me. Then shall he say also unto them on the left hand, Depart from me, ye cursed, into everlasting fire, prepared for the devil and his angels: For I was an hungred, and ye gave me no meat: I was thirsty, and ye gave me no drink: I was a stranger, and ye took me not in: naked, and ye clothed me not: sick, and in prison, and ye visited me not. Then shall they also answer him, saying, Lord, when saw we thee an hungred, or athirst, or a stranger, or naked, or sick, or in prison, and did not minister unto thee? Then shall he answer them, saying, Verily I say unto you, Inasmuch as ye did [it] not to one of the least of these, ye did [it] not to me. And these shall go away into everlasting punishment: but the righteous into life eternal.

The above account of the Olivet Discourse recorded by Matthew is more detailed than that of Luke and Mark. It would be good to reread the full context of Matthew's account of the Olivet Discourse before we look at the details.

Matthew 24:4 And Jesus answered and said unto them, Take heed that no man deceive you.
This is so very important. Jesus begins His answer this same way in all accounts. Take heed - pay attention, this is important. Take heed that no man deceive you. The Holy Spirit is your teacher. Don't take any man's word for the answer to the very important question of when shall these things be. Take heed - pay attention to the only absolutely reliable teacher you have. The word of God is absolutely true and the Holy Spirit is your only absolutely reliable teacher. Don't trust any man to answer these important

questions. Don't trust the televangelists. Don't trust your friends. Don't trust me. Don't even trust your pastor. Don't even trust your family.

How you answer the question of when the rapture will occur is so important that it will affect most of the decisions that you make including how diligently you seek God and how righteously you live. The great New Testament heroes of the faith lived expecting the Lord to return in great power and glory to deliver them from the great tribulation which they either were in, or were expecting to experience. May I suggest that you take a new look at how you answer this question laying aside all preconceptions, and everything that you have been taught, looking only at the scriptures, and trusting the Spirit of Truth to give you the truth you seek. May I also suggest that one looses nothing by preparing to live supernaturally in great tribulation. May I also suggest that when antichrist is given full power to wage war on the saints, that supernatural living by faith will no longer be optional. It will be the only way for the saints to live.

Matthew 24:5 For many shall come in my name, saying, I am Christ; and shall deceive many.
What are names of some false christs? Years ago people were pretty much limited to Satan, or Lucifer, and Antichrist. Today we have Sun Young Moon, Djwhal Khul, Lord Maitreya, thousands of "Ascended Masters," thousands of "Spirit Guides," Masters of Wisdom, the Master Mind, Krishna, Dalai Lama, Joseph Smith, Buddha,

Gaia, Zen, Tao, The Force, Yin/Yang, Sanat, and thousands
more. No previous generation has had as many false christs
from which to choose. The New Age Movement is a return
to dark age mystic occultism and its thousands of false
christs and its philosophy that "ye shall be
as god," in fact, makes everyone a false christ unto
themselves and to each other. The New Age Movement and
New World Order is the end time movement of Satan, the
Antichrist, and his False Prophet.

**Matthew 24:6 And ye shall hear of wars and
rumours of wars: see that ye be not troubled: for all
[these things] must come to pass, but the end is not
yet.**
There are more wars going on today than can hardly be
counted, more than ever in recorded history. They are small
scale but some of them will surely escalate. Watch out when
Vladimir Zhirinovsky takes control in Russia. His speeches
are Russian translations of those used by Hitler. Russia still
has over 20,000 strategic nuclear weapons. Peace, peace,
they say yet the world has never been in more perilous
threat of total destruction. How could Jesus tell us not to let
it trouble us? The key is where your affections are set.
**Colossians 3:1 If ye then be risen with Christ, seek
those things which are above, where Christ sitteth
on the right hand of God.
Colossians 3:2 Set your affection on things above,
not on things on the earth.
Colossians 3:14 And above all these things [put on]
charity, which is the bond of perfectness.**

I John 2:15 Love not the world, neither the things [that are] in the world. If any man love the world, the love of the Father is not in him.

I John 4:18 There is no fear in love; but perfect love casteth out fear: because fear hath torment. He that feareth is not made perfect in love.

The true Christian sees the effect of a strategic nuclear blast as identical to the Rapture. Either means to be instantly with the Lord. Only Christians can look squarely at the true peril that exists in the world today without fear.

Matthew 24:7 - 8 For nation shall rise against nation, and kingdom against kingdom: and there shall be famines, and pestilences, and earthquakes, in divers places. All these [are] the beginning of sorrows.

Here are some interesting and sobering statistics on earthquakes. There was only 1 major earthquake recorded world-wide between 1900 - 1910 which was the San Francisco quake of 1906. In the next 2 decades there were 4 major quakes. There were 5 in the 1940's. There were 13 in the 1960's. There were 56 in the 1970's. Between 1980 and 1989 there were 74 major earthquakes. The earthquakes, floods, hurricanes, famines, and pestilences are the beginning.

Matthew 24:9 Then shall they deliver you up to be afflicted, and shall kill you: and ye shall be hated of all nations for my name's sake.

This is one of the verses which make it almost impossible for many Christians to consider the possibility of a post tribulation rapture. Most Christians in America have no idea how Christians have been and are being persecuted around the world. Everyone should be aware of the antichristian bias growing in America. Since Jesus returned to the right hand of the Father, starting with Stephen, Christians have suffered and been killed for Jesus name's sake. Is it settled in your mind and heart that you will be hated by the majority of people? Do you know you are called to suffer and possibly be killed for being a Christian? Many Christians who believe the rapture occurs before the tribulation will be taken by surprise by this truth. Jesus was faithful to give the warning us; but, most of us just plain don't want to hear it. We want to heap to ourselves teachers who will tickle our ears by telling us what we want to hear. We need to hear the truth. Don't let hard truth discourage you. Maranatha! - the Lord Jesus Christ is coming.

Matthew 24:10 And then shall many be offended, and shall betray one another, and shall hate one another.
Does it offend you when someone tries to tell you to get prepared for tribulation? Corrie ten Boom said, "There are some among us teaching there will be no tribulation, that the Christians will be able to escape all this. These are the false teachers Jesus was warning us to expect in the latter days. Most of them have little knowledge of what is already going on across the world." There should be an overwhelming compulsion for teachers, preachers, and

pastors to tell people to prepare for tribulation. You lose nothing by being prepared. Praise God if you are raptured first; but, don't fail to be prepared. How do you prepare for tribulation? The answer is faith, and faith cometh by hearing, and hearing by the word of God. We need to make the study of the word of God high priority.

Matthew 24:11 And many false prophets shall rise, and shall deceive many.
There are indeed more false prophets today than at any other time in history. How do you tell a false prophet? The false prophet will contradict the word of God, or glorify himself rather than God. Many false prophets will display supernatural power; however, if Jesus is not clearly glorified by any apparent miracle have no part of it.

Matthew 24:12 And because iniquity shall abound, the love of many shall wax cold.
Do we see iniquity abounding? How could it get so bad so fast? Do we see the love of many growing cold? Is much of the love in the church feigned affection? Love and truth go together. Would you be acting in love to know that the church will go through the great tribulation and not say anything about it because you knew people did not want to think about such a possibility? Is your popularity more important than the truth?

Matthew 24:13 But he that shall endure unto the end, the same shall be saved.
What does it mean to endure to the end? Does this mean to

endure the rapture? Will you consider that the end, the Lord's return, and the rapture are simultaneous events which occur at the end of great tribulation? If you will consider this you will then see it the same way that the apostles understood it to be. The earliest date of pre-tribulation rapture teaching is the mid 19th century. Paul and all of the apostles believed the rapture would occur at the end of great tribulation simultaneous with the Lord's return in great power and glory. The Lord's return will not be a secret. Every eye shall see Him.

Matthew 24:14 And this gospel of the kingdom shall be preached in all the world for a witness unto all nations; and then shall the end come.
Do you know that satellite communication technology has made this a reality in our generation?

Matthew 24:15 When ye therefore shall see the abomination of desolation, spoken of by Daniel the prophet, stand in the holy place, (whoso readeth, let him understand:)
The abomination of desolation is something which we need to try to understand. Daniel speaks of it in chapters 9 and 12. The abomination of desolation will likely be when Antichrist goes to Jerusalem and proclaims himself to be god and demands worship as god from everyone in the world including Jews, Christians and Moslems.

Matthew 24:16 Then let them which be in Judaea flee into the mountains:

When we do see Antichrist proclaiming himself to be god
and demanding worship, then if we are in the cities we
should flee to the low population areas. The wilderness is
the place to be when Antichrist demands that the world
worship him as god.

Matthew 24:17 Let him which is on the housetop
not come down to take any thing out of his house:
Matthew 24:18 Neither let him which is in the field
return back to take his clothes.
Matthew 24:19 And woe unto them that are with child,
and to them that give suck in those days!
Matthew 24:20 But pray ye that your flight be not in
the winter, neither on the sabbath day:

Get out of the cities quickly and don't take time to pack
anything. At this time you will have to live by faith totally
trusting God to meet your every need. Why should this
frighten us? Why could we not view this with excitement
and joy knowing that God will provide for our needs
supernaturally and that He will soon be returning in great
power and glory? When is the last time that you heard
anyone in any church prayer meeting praying that our
flight not be in the winter? Why would Jesus say such a
thing if we were to be raptured before the tribulation?
One might say this all pertains to the Jews when Rome sent
Titus to destroy the Jerusalem in 70AD. That is true, but
like so much of prophecy, there are former and latter
fulfillments. Jesus was speaking to the Church as it was
then and as it is now. This will become more clear as we
look at subsequent scriptures here and in Daniel.

Matthew 24:21 For then shall be great tribulation, such as was not since the beginning of the world to this time, no, nor ever shall be.

This is great tribulation. It applied in 70AD; however, it is more applicable to us when we see Antichrist proclaiming himself to be god and demanding to be worshipped as god.

Matthew 24:22 And except those days should be shortened, there should no flesh be saved: but for the elect's sake those days shall be shortened.

This verse strongly indicates strategic nuclear warfare.

Matthew 24:23 Then if any man shall say unto you, Lo, here [is] Christ, or there; believe [it] not. Matthew 24:24 For there shall arise false Christs, and false prophets, and shall shew great signs and wonders; insomuch that, if [it were] possible, they shall deceive the very elect. Matthew 24:25 Behold, I have told you before. Matthew 24:26 Wherefore if they shall say unto you, Behold, he is in the desert; go not forth: behold, [he is] in the secret chambers; believe [it] not. Matthew 24:27 For as the lightning cometh out of the east, and shineth even unto the west; so shall also the coming of the Son of man be. Matthew 24:28 For wheresoever the carcase is, there will the eagles be gathered together.

Antichrist will have power to wage war on the saints. Christians will be deceived and misled by people who claim to know that Christ has returned. <u>The Lord's return will</u>

not be in secret. The Lord's return will be in great power
and glory. Do not follow anyone doing miracles who does
not do them in the name of the Lord Jesus Christ for the
glory of God.

**Matthew 24:29 Immediately after the tribulation
of those days shall the sun be darkened, and the
moon shall not give her light, and the stars shall fall
from heaven, and the powers of the heavens shall be
shaken:
Matthew 24:30 And then shall appear the sign of the
Son of man in heaven: and then shall all the tribes of
the earth mourn, and they shall see the Son of man
coming in the clouds of heaven with power and
great glory.
Matthew 24:31 And he shall send his angels with a
great sound of a trumpet, and they shall gather
together his elect from the four winds, from one end
of heaven to the other.**

Remember the questions which Jesus was answering. Tell
us, when shall these things be? and what [shall be] the sign
of thy coming, and of the end of the world? Master, but
when shall these things be? and what sign [will there be]
when these things shall come to pass? when shall these
things be? and what [shall be] the sign when all these things
shall be fulfilled?

1) After the tribulation of those days the sun and moon will
be darkened and the powers of the heavens shall be shaken.
2) Then shall appear the sign of the Son of man in heaven
causing everyone but those who know Messiah Jesus Christ

to mourn as everyone sees the Lord returning with power and great glory.

3) He shall send His angels with a great sound of a trumpet to gather the Christians to join in His glorious parade to put an end to the armies of Antichrist who have been waging war on His saints. RAPTURE TIME! There are quite a number of events which are to happen before we get to this RAPTURE TIME.

Matthew 24:32 Now learn a parable of the fig tree; When his branch is yet tender, and putteth forth leaves, ye know that summer [is] nigh:

Matthew 24:33 So likewise ye, when ye shall see all these things, know that it is near, [even] at the doors.

Matthew 24:34 Verily I say unto you, This generation shall not pass, till all these things be fulfilled.

Matthew 24:35 Heaven and earth shall pass away, but my words shall not pass away.

We find fig tree parables in Judges 9:10-11 and Proverbs 27:18. There is general agreement that the fig tree symbolizes the nation of Israel. Israel once again became a nation in 1948. End time prophecy revolves around the nation of Israel. This does not mean that the Church or the Holy Spirit will not be present during the great tribulation. Paul and the other apostles were Jews but they were also part of the Church. When any Jew comes to know Messiah Yeshua as Lord and Savior that Jew becomes part of the Church. When Israel blossoms as a nation; however, has tremendous end time prophetic significance. The generation to witness this event is the generation to witness the fulfillment of all end time prophecy. How many years are represented by a bible generation? The year of Jubilee was every 50 years and other scriptures would indicate a bible generation to be 40 years. If one were to assign 1948 as the blossoming of the fig tree, Israel, adding 40 gives significance to 1988 or adding 50 gives significance to 1998. Fixing dates is not what we are to do. However, the Lord has told us to take heed, to watch, to know that His return is near. Without fixing any specific dates, we still have every reason to believe that we are the generation to witness the fulfillment of all end time prophecy and witness the Lord's return in great power and glory. Heaven and earth shall pass away but the word of God shall not pass away. No generation in history has ever had as much incentive to search the scriptures and study His word as our generation.

Matthew 24:36 But of that day and hour knoweth no [man], no, not the angels of heaven, but my Father only.

Here is why we are not to fix specific dates. However, since almost 20% of the New Testament is devoted to this subject we must know that it is extremely important. Jesus wanted His Church, the saints, to know various signs during the great tribulation which would encourage them to endure to the end while Antichrist was waging war on them. These various signs would let His Church know that they had less then 7 years in which to endure this war of Antichrist. If you hear anyone fixing a specific day or hour steer clear of such a person. The tribulation will begin so gradually that no one will know when it started. However, we have many signs which will let us know we are well into the great tribulation. It is quite possible that the great tribulation has already started.

Matthew 24:37 But as the days of Noe [were], so shall also the coming of the Son of man be. Matthew 24:38 For as in the days that were before the flood they were eating and drinking, marrying and giving in marriage, until the day that Noe entered into the ark, Matthew 24:39 And knew not until the flood came, and took them all away; so shall also the coming of the Son of man be.

How were things in the days of Noah?

1) There were demonic unions of fallen angels and humans. (Gen. 6:2-4)

The core of the New Age Movement is demonic. Most of the people who are sucked into the connections with their "Ascended Master," "Spirit Guide" or whatever else they want to call it do not realize they are demons.

2) Great wickedness to the point that every imagination of the thoughts of his heart was only evil continually. (Gen. 6:5) It would seem that we are rapidly approaching this way of evil again.

3) They were marrying and giving in marriage. The marriage rate equaled the divorce rate. Musical partners without commitment. Except for Noah and his family no one was aware of God's imminent judgment. This is how it will be at the Lord's return. Noah was a preacher of righteousness and was ridiculed and persecuted by all as he

prepared the ark. Noah endured 100 years of persecution
and ridicule and tribulation while completing the ark. So
will the Christians and Jews be ridiculed and persecuted as
they prepare for the Lord's return during the
great tribulation. Did Noah escape the flood or did God
tell him how to prepare to be protected through it? The
Christians and Jews will be the only people who will not go
along with the demonic evil of the New World Order under
Antichrist.

**Matthew 24:40 Then shall two be in the field; the
one shall be taken, and the other left.
Matthew 24:41 Two [women shall be] grinding at the
mill; the one shall be taken, and the other left.
Matthew 24:42 Watch therefore: for ye know not
what hour your Lord doth come.**
The Lord is returning in great power and glory.
Conditions in the world are as it was in the days of Noah;
unrestrained evil, with Antichrist waging total war on the
saints. The saints should be watching and doing what the
Lord tells them. Noah was a great example for us. Noah
worked building the ark for 100 years suffering
tremendous ridicule and persecution. Jesus is giving
important instruction to His Church as it was then and is
now. Tribulation has been great, however it had started so
gradually no one knew for sure when it had actually
started. Now it is time for His return. In speaking to His
Church, He tells us that one will be taken and the other left.
Why? There is a sad truth that there are people in the
Church who have not been saved. How can this be? There

are hypocrites and pretenders in the church. There are
people in the church who are there because that is what
good people do. There are those in the church who think if
they do enough good works they will be acceptable to God.
Why are you acceptable to God?   Do you know absolutely
that you are going to be one of those who goes up to be part
of the Lord's parade returning in great power and glory?
He is returning to destroy the armies of Antichrist and
confine the Antichrist and the False Prophet to the Lake of
Fire. Are you going to be one of those who are taken up to
meet Him and be in His powerful glorious parade? What is
it that makes you certain of your place in the parade? Have
you been born again? Will you endure to the end? If you
are not absolutely certain, what will you do? Watch
therefore: for ye know not what hour your Lord doth come.

Matthew 24:43 But know this, that if the
goodman of the house had known in what watch the
thief would come, he would have watched, and
would not have suffered his house to be broken up.
Matthew 24:44 Therefore be ye also ready: for in
such an hour as ye think not the Son of man cometh.
Matthew 24:45 Who then is a faithful and wise
servant, whom his lord hath made ruler over his
household, to give them meat in due season?
Matthew 24:46 Blessed [is] that servant, whom his
lord when he cometh shall find so doing.
Matthew 24:47 Verily I say unto you, That he shall
make him ruler over all his goods.
Matthew 24:48 But and if that evil servant shall say

in his heart, My lord delayeth his coming;
Matthew 24:49 And shall begin to smite [his]
fellowservants, and to eat and drink with the
drunken;
Matthew 24:50 The lord of that servant shall come in
a day when he looketh not for [him], and in an hour
that he is not aware of,
Matthew 24:51 And shall cut him asunder, and
appoint [him] his portion with the hypocrites: there
shall be weeping and gnashing of teeth.

The great tribulation will test the faith of believers. The
believers will have to live by faith and their love for one
another will be tested as well as their faith. We are called
to endure to the end. Will the saints hoard or share? Will
brother betray brother? Those who are living in faith and
love, as they should be, will be very happy when the Lord
returns. Those who smite and hurt and betray their
brothers during the war on the saints will not be happy
when the Lord returns. God hates hypocrisy. If you are a
hypocrite you would be better off getting out of the church.

Matthew 25:1 Then shall the kingdom of heaven
be likened unto ten virgins, which took their lamps,
and went forth to meet the bridegroom.
Matthew 25:2 And five of them were wise, and five
[were] foolish.
Matthew 25:3 They that [were] foolish took their
lamps, and took no oil with them:
Matthew 25:4 But the wise took oil in their vessels
with their lamps.

Matthew 25:5 While the bridegroom tarried, they all slumbered and slept.

Matthew 25:6 And at midnight there was a cry made, Behold, the bridegroom cometh; go ye out to meet him.

Matthew 25:7 Then all those virgins arose, and trimmed their lamps.

Matthew 25:8 And the foolish said unto the wise, Give us of your oil; for our lamps are gone out.

Matthew 25:9 But the wise answered, saying, [Not so]; lest there be not enough for us and you: but go ye rather to them that sell, and buy for yourselves.

Matthew 25:10 And while they went to buy, the bridegroom came; and they that were ready went in with him to the marriage: and the door was shut.

Matthew 25:11 Afterward came also the other virgins, saying, Lord, Lord, open to us.

Matthew 25:12 But he answered and said, Verily I say unto you, I know you not.

Matthew 25:13 Watch therefore, for ye know neither the day nor the hour wherein the Son of man cometh.

An oil lamp is useless without oil. A Christian without the Holy Spirit is useless. An oil lamp with or without the oil looks good until it is time to give light in the darkness. Churches are full of people who may appear to be holy. In the darkness of the great tribulation the people in the church who do not have the Holy Spirit will be useless. How do we get filled with the Holy Spirit? Get filled with the word of God. The Holy Spirit is the Spirit of Holiness and the Spirit of Truth. We are called to holiness and truth. The bible is our best source of truth and the ways of holiness. God knows the true conditions of our heart. What motivates us to do whatever we do? Our motives are more important than our actions or appearance. If our motives are right our actions and appearance will be right. Are you motivated to do what you do for the Glory of God or for your own vain glory? We need to seek the fullness of the Holy Spirit and we all leak a lot. Holiness is a personal thing. We can not give or share holiness. Each must pursue holiness himself. We can encourage others to pursue holiness but it is a matter of the heart. Only God knows the heart of anyone. What is the condition of my heart? I don't like to look because Jeremiah 17:9 says **"The heart is deceitful above all things, and desperately wicked: who can know it?"** Yet a true mark of holiness is recognizing this deceitful and desperately wicked condition of the heart. The pursuit of holiness is personal and internal. It is what keeps us hunting the beam in our own eyes rather than trying to help our brother to take the speck out of his eye. However, the more we submit to the convicting work of the Holy Spirit and agree with God regarding the sinful state of our heart motives the more freedom the Holy Spirit has to work His mighty powerful works through us. This is the way of the overcomer when Antichrist wages total war on the saints during the great tribulation. One will put a thousand to flight and two will put ten thousand to flight. The victory is sure.

Matthew 25:31 When the Son of man shall come in his glory, and all the holy angels with him, then shall he sit upon the throne of his glory:

Matthew 25:32 And before him shall be gathered all nations: and he shall separate them one from another, as a shepherd divideth [his] sheep from the goats:

Matthew 25:33 And he shall set the sheep on his right hand, but the goats on the left.

Maranatha!   The Lord Jesus Christ is coming to judge the living and the dead. Our Blessed Hope is His return. The war that Antichrist wages on the saints is won by the saints because Our King Jesus wins it for us single handed. Blessed is he that endures to the end. The following verses instruct us in how to endure to the end. We must be careful to pay attention to what our King wants us to do.

Matthew 25:34 Then shall the King say unto them on his right hand, Come, ye blessed of my Father, inherit the kingdom prepared for you from the foundation of the world:

Matthew 25:35 For I was an hungered, and ye gave me meat: I was thirsty, and ye gave me drink: I was a stranger, and ye took me in:

Matthew 25:36 Naked, and ye clothed me: I was sick, and ye visited me: I was in prison, and ye came unto me.

Matthew 25:37 Then shall the righteous answer him, saying, Lord, when saw we thee an hungred, and fed [thee]? or thirsty, and gave [thee] drink?

Matthew 25:38 When saw we thee a stranger, and took [thee] in? or naked, and clothed [thee]?

Matthew 25:39 Or when saw we thee sick, or in prison, and came unto thee?

Matthew 25:40 And the King shall answer and say unto them, Verily I say unto you, Inasmuch as ye have done [it] unto one of the least of these my brethren, ye have done [it] unto me.

Many church people will have their love grow cold during the great tribulation. Many church people will have been so deluded expecting to be raptured without any suffering that they will have taken the mark of the beast and actually joined the world ecumenical religion of the Antichrist in the war on those narrow-minded fundamentalists who refuse to go along with all the good programs of the New World Order. The true church of Jesus in the great tribulation will have nothing but their faith in Jesus. They will have been stripped of all their possessions. Many will have been imprisoned. Since they will not be able to buy and sell they will have need of food, clothing, and shelter. The wise Christians who have been preparing for the tribulation must also be prepared to share. How compassionate are you? We are to be known by the love we have for one another. If you are preparing for tribulation, the most important part of your preparation is the preparation of a tender compassionate heart for those in need. Anything that you do for someone less fortunate, you do for King Jesus.

Matthew 25:41 Then shall he say also unto them on the left hand, Depart from me, ye cursed, into everlasting fire, prepared for the devil and his angels:

Matthew 25:42 For I was an hungred, and ye gave me no meat: I was thirsty, and ye gave me no drink:

Matthew 25:43 I was a stranger, and ye took me not in: naked, and ye clothed me not: sick, and in prison, and ye visited me not.

Matthew 25:44 Then shall they also answer him, saying, Lord, when saw we thee an hungred, or athirst, or a stranger, or naked, or sick, or in prison, and did not minister unto thee?

Matthew 25:45 Then shall he answer them, saying, Verily I say unto you, Inasmuch as ye did [it] not to one of the least of these, ye did [it] not to me.

Matthew 25:46 And these shall go away into everlasting punishment: but the righteous into life eternal.

If we are preparing to take care of ourselves in the great tribulation we are making the wrong preparations. If our faith grows, our love will grow. Practice giving. Practice caring. We must be preparing to take care of others. Study the bible every day. We are to be the Church, the body of Christ. The body of Christ should have the eyes and heart of Christ to see those in need and minister to them. Who is hungry? Who is thirsty? Who is in need of a place to stay? There will be many such people in the great tribulation. Our hearts must be prepared to share with those in need. Many souls will be won for the Lord Jesus Christ when the Church shares with the many who will be in need of the basic necessities of life during the great tribulation. Anything we do for anyone less fortunate than ourselves we do for King Jesus. Anything we fail to share with someone in need we refuse to share with King Jesus.

MARK

Mark was closely associated with Peter. Irenaeus, one of the early church fathers, says "Mark, the disciple and interpreter of Peter, also handed down to us in writing what had been preached by Peter." That Peter was a primary source of Mark's gospel account may be seen where Peter calls him his son in 1 Peter 5:13. Mark also traveled with Paul and Barnabas in the first missionary journey. Paul asked Timothy to bring Mark with him to Rome during Paul's second imprisonment in Rome (2 Timothy 4:11). Even the hyper-dispensational (tell them what they want to hear) teachers, would agree that Mark's gospel was written to appeal to the Roman mindset. Was the Roman mindset Gentile or Jewish? This is pointed out with the hope that you may see that all scripture is for the Church past, present, and future, whether the individual Church member be Jew or Gentile, bond or free, male or female. It is time for reconciliation and restoration in the Church. It is time for the Jews to become part of the Church and for the Church to recognize its Jewish roots. It is time for the gospel to be preached and received by the Jew first. Can you consider that the times of the gentiles have been fulfilled because the Jews again possess Jerusalem?

If the Olivet Discourse was only given to Peter, James, John, and Andrew then it perhaps should be placed before Matthew as we look for an understanding of End Time Prophecy. It is likely that Peter, James, John and Andrew posed the question, and likely that Matthew and the other apostles heard the answer which Jesus gave. While some might argue that Matthew's gospel was written for the Jews, it would be very difficult to argue, at the same time, that Mark's gospel was not written to the Gentiles. They were both written for the Church. The Jew who trusts Messiah Yeshua (Christ Jesus) for his salvation is part of the Church. He will stand with his Gentile brother in tribulation. Any church member who does not love and bless the Jew is a questionable Church member indeed. It is time for reconciliation and restoration in the Church. It is not quite rapture time yet.

No matter what the circumstances, it is well to look at Mark's account of how Jesus explains End Time prophecy and events.

Mark 13:1-37 And as he went out of the temple, one of his disciples saith unto him, Master, see what manner of stones and what buildings [are here]! And Jesus answering said unto him, Seest thou these great buildings? there shall not be left one stone upon another, that shall not be thrown down. And as he sat upon the mount of Olives over against the temple, Peter and James and John and Andrew asked him privately,
Tell us, when shall these things be? and what [shall be] the sign when all these things shall be fulfilled? And Jesus answering them began to say, Take heed lest any [man] deceive you:
For many shall come in my name, saying, I am [Christ]; and shall deceive many.

And when ye shall hear of wars and rumours of wars, be ye not troubled: for [such things] must needs be; but the end [shall] not [be] yet.
For nation shall rise against nation, and kingdom against kingdom: and there shall be earthquakes in divers places, and there shall be famines and troubles: these [are] the beginnings of sorrows.

But take heed to yourselves: for they shall deliver you up to councils; and in the synagogues ye shall be beaten: and ye shall be brought before rulers and kings for my sake, for a testimony against them.
And the gospel must first be published among all nations.
But when they shall lead [you], and deliver you up, take no thought beforehand what ye shall speak, neither do ye premeditate: but whatsoever shall be given you in that hour, that speak ye: for it is not ye that speak, but the Holy Ghost.
Now the brother shall betray the brother to death, and the father the son; and children shall rise up against [their] parents, and shall cause them to be put to death.
And ye shall be hated of all [men] for my name's sake: but he that shall endure unto the end, the same shall be saved.

But when ye shall see the abomination of desolation, spoken of by Daniel the prophet, standing where it ought not, (let him that readeth understand,) then let them that be in Judaea flee to the mountains:
And let him that is on the housetop not go down into

the house, neither enter [therein], to take any thing
out of his house:
And let him that is in the field not turn back again for
to take up his garment.
But woe to them that are with child, and to them that
give suck in those days!
And pray ye that your flight be not in the winter.
For [in] those days shall be affliction, such as was
not from the beginning of the creation which God
created unto this time, neither shall be.
And except that the Lord had shortened those days,
no flesh should be saved: but for the elect's sake,
whom he hath chosen, he hath shortened the days.
And then if any man shall say to you, Lo, here [is]
Christ; or, lo, [he is] there; believe [him] not:
For false Christs and false prophets shall rise, and
shall shew signs and wonders, to seduce, if [it were]
possible, even the elect.
But take ye heed: behold, I have foretold you all
things.
        But in those days, after that tribulation, the sun
shall be darkened, and the moon shall not give her
light,
And the stars of heaven shall fall, and the powers
that are in heaven shall be shaken.
And then shall they see the Son of man coming in
the clouds with great power and glory.
And then shall he send his angels, and shall gather
together his elect from the four winds, from the
uttermost part of the earth to the uttermost part of

heaven.

Now learn a parable of the fig tree; When her branch
is yet tender, and putteth forth leaves, ye know that
summer is near:

So ye in like manner, when ye shall see these things
come to pass, know that it is nigh, [even] at the
doors. Verily I say unto you, that this generation
shall not pass, till all these things be done.

Heaven and earth shall pass away: but my words
shall not pass away.

   But of that day and [that] hour knoweth no man,
no, not the angels which are in heaven, neither the
Son, but the Father.

Take ye heed, watch and pray: for ye know not when
the time is.

[For the Son of man is] as a man taking a far journey,
who left his house, and gave authority to his
servants, and to every man his work, and
commanded the porter to watch.

Watch ye therefore: for ye know not when the master
of the house cometh, at even, or at midnight, or at
the cockcrowing, or in the morning:

Lest coming suddenly he find you sleeping.

And what I say unto you I say unto all, Watch.

   It would be good to reread Mark's short Chapter 13
account of the Olivet Discourse before looking at the
details.

Mark 13:1 And as he went out of the temple, one of his disciples saith unto him, Master, see what manner of stones and what buildings [are here]! Mark 13:2 And Jesus answering said unto him, Seest thou these great buildings? there shall not be left one stone upon another, that shall not be thrown down.

The disciples were marveling at the magnificence of the temple. Jesus then told them that the great temple which Herod had built would be so totally destroyed that there would not be one stone left on another. When Rome destroyed Jerusalem in 70 A.D. they burned the temple. Some of the gold in the temple melted and they disassembled the foundation stones to remove the melted gold.

Mark 13:3 And as he sat upon the mount of Olives over against the temple, Peter and James and John and Andrew asked him privately, Mark 13:4 Tell us, when shall these things be? and what [shall be] the sign when all these things shall be fulfilled?

Jesus got the full attention of His disciples when He told them the temple was going to be destroyed. When shall these things be? What shall be the sign? How shall we know when all these things shall be fulfilled? "What shall be the sign of thy coming and of the end of the world?" (Matthew 24:3)

The destruction of the temple foreshadowed the time of the end. The destruction of the temple marked with certainty the beginning of the "Times of the Gentiles."

From this event, Israel would not again possess Jerusalem
until the times of the Gentiles be fulfilled. God allowed the
apparent total destruction of Israel in judgment because of
their rejection of Messiah. God would never forget
Israel. When the times of the Gentiles were fulfilled, God
would reestablish and regather Israel. Jerusalem was part
of Jordan until Jordan invaded Israel in 1967. In 1917
Britain took Palestine from the Turks. Because of the
tension between Jews and Arabs, the land was divided
between the Jewish section (Palestine) and the Arab section
(Jordan). The proper name of the Palestinian State should
be Jordan. Jordan is the Palestinian State. The West Bank
was part of Jordan until Jordan attacked Israel in 1967.
Jordan lost the war that they started. Israel again took
possession of Jerusalem. There is good reason to believe
that this marked the end of the "Times of the Gentiles."
God has obviously been on the side of Israel. If you support
Israel you will be on God's side in the continuing turmoil of
the Middle East. The powers of the world want the wealth
of the Middle East oil and it is just a matter of time until
Russia goes after it under the guise of attacking Israel. The
large Moslem population of Russia and economics will
make this a popular move for some Russian leader such as
Vladimir Zhirinovsky.

Mark 13:5 And Jesus answering them began to
say, Take heed lest any [man] deceive you:
Mark 13:6 For many shall come in my name, saying,
I am [Christ]; and shall deceive many.
Mark 13:7 And when ye shall hear of wars and

rumours of wars, be ye not troubled: for [such things] must needs be; but the end [shall] not [be] yet.

We know from verse 7 that the Lord has finished talking about the destruction of Herod's temple and is talking about the end times. Take heed, pay attention, this is important. Don't be deceived. You will be deceived if you listen to men. Seek truth from the Word of God by His Holy Spirit. Don't trust anyone. Measure everything you are told by what the scriptures say. Let the bible be your source of truth. There has been much false teaching and deceptive teaching will increase as an end time sign. Remain teachable; but, let the Holy Spirit be your teacher.

Mark 13:8 For nation shall rise against nation, and kingdom against kingdom: and there shall be earthquakes in divers places, and there shall be famines and troubles: these [are] the beginnings of sorrows.

The wars, rumors of wars, earthquakes, famines, and troubles are just the beginning. But what about the rapture?

Mark 13:9 But take heed to yourselves: for they shall deliver you up to councils; and in the synagogues ye shall be beaten: and ye shall be brought before rulers and kings for my sake, for a testimony against them.

Mark 13:10 And the gospel must first be published among all nations.

Mark 13:11 But when they shall lead [you], and deliver you up, take no thought beforehand what ye shall speak, neither do ye premeditate: but whatsoever shall be given you in that hour, that speak ye: for it is not ye that speak, but the Holy Ghost.

Take heed! Satellite communication technology has made possible the publishing of the gospel among all nations. The Lord is describing the conditions at the time of the end. He is speaking to His Church. We don't want to hear this; however, in verse 5 and again here in verse 9 He says "Take heed." Even if it is not what we want to hear we must have ears to hear what the Lord is trying to tell His Church of the end time. He is not talking to the Jews. He is talking to His Church of the end time, both Jews and Gentiles. The blindness of the Jews is lifting. They are recognizing Messiah Jesus Christ in exponentially increasing numbers. His Church will be hated by all at the time of the end. At the time of the end, Antichrist will be waging war on the ******? The missing word is Saints. That means both Jew and Gentile believers. The believers will be outlaws in the New World Order of Antichrist. Revelation 19:10 tells us that the testimony of Jesus is the spirit of prophecy. What are you prepared to suffer for your testimony of Jesus Christ as Lord? The Lord tells us not to worry because the Holy Spirit will speak for us and through us. If God is for you who can be against you? The problem is that no one wants to suffer. We need our faith to grow if we may be called to suffer for our testimony of Jesus. Faith cometh by hearing and hearing by the Word of God. What

about the Rapture? The Lord has not gotten to the Rapture
yet. Let us TAKE HEED to what He said regardless of
what we have been taught or the way we want it to be. The
way He said it will be is the way it will be. He will give us
the answer if we will have ears to hear.

**Mark 13:12 Now the brother shall betray the
brother to death, and the father the son;
and children shall rise up against [their] parents, and
shall cause them to be put to death.
Mark 13:13 And ye shall be hated of all [men] for my
name's sake: but he that shall endure unto the end,
the same shall be saved.**
When Antichrist wages war on the saints, we will be
reported to officials by our brothers. The pretenders in the
church will report the true believers to the government.
Everyone wants to have the favor of the people we know
and love. Jesus tells us that we should take heed and know
that we will be hated of all except true Jew and Gentile
believers for His name's sake. He tells us that those who
endure to the end shall be saved. Do we endure the
Rapture? He has not gotten to the Rapture yet.

**Mark 13:14 But when ye shall see the
abomination of desolation, spoken of by Daniel the
prophet, standing where it ought not, (let him that
readeth understand,) then let them that be in Judaea
flee to the mountains:
Mark 13:15 And let him that is on the housetop not
go down into the house, neither enter [therein], to**

take any thing out of his house:

Mark 13:16 And let him that is in the field not turn back again for to take up his garment.

Mark 13:17 But woe to them that are with child, and to them that give suck in those days!

Mark 13:18 And pray ye that your flight be not in the winter.

Mark 13:19 For [in] those days shall be affliction, such as was not from the beginning of the creation which God created unto this time, neither shall be.

What is the abomination of desolation of which Daniel spoke? It will be when we see Antichrist standing in the temple in Jerusalem proclaiming himself to be god and demanding to be worshipped as god by everyone. At this time the speculation and guessing about who the Antichrist is, will be ended. At this time we will not want to be downtown in any big city. We will need to be in Goshen. None of the plagues of Egypt had any effect on the Jews in Goshen. Faithful Christians will be safe in their occupied territories. Is our church strong enough in faith and the power of the Holy Spirit to make it safe like Goshen? What can be done to make it so? Where would we go, because we have not gotten to the rapture yet?

Mark 13:20 And except that the Lord had shortened those days, no flesh should be saved: but for the elect's sake, whom he hath chosen, he hath shortened the days.

Mark 13:21 And then if any man shall say to you, Lo, here [is] Christ; or, lo, [he is] there; believe [him] not:

Mark 13:22 For false Christs and false prophets shall rise, and shall shew signs and wonders, to seduce, if [it were] possible, even the elect.
Mark 13:23 But take ye heed: behold, I have foretold you all things.

Again we hear the Lord telling us that we are to TAKE HEED. Will we hear Him saying - Look, pay attention to the warnings I am giving you in advance? If we are going to be raptured out why would He be telling us to TAKE HEED to His warnings, or why would He even be giving us the warnings in the first place? The rapture is not yet.

Mark 13:24 But in those days, after that tribulation, the sun shall be darkened, and the moon shall not give her light,
Mark 13:25 And the stars of heaven shall fall, and the powers that are in heaven shall be shaken.
Mark 13:26 And then shall they see the Son of man coming in the clouds with great power and glory.

Let us recap and list His warnings:

1. Many false teachers.
2. Many false christs.
3. Wars and rumors of wars.
4. Nation against nation and kingdom against kingdom.
   (Ethnic Cleansing)
5. Earthquakes
6. Famines
7. Troubles (pestilence, plagues, AIDS,)
8. Believers in Jesus will be persecuted
9. Gospel published among all nations

10. Believers to be taken by the government to prison and beatings and to testify against the wicked rulers of the New World Order.

11. Brother will betray brother.

12. Children will rise up against their parents and cause them to be put to death. (outcome based education, and solution to social security crisis)

13. Believers hated by all for Jesus name's sake.

14. The abomination of desolation.

15. Flight from the cities.

16. Greater affliction than ever seen on earth.

17. False christs showing great signs.

18. Sun and moon darkened.

19. Stars falling and the powers of heaven shaken.

20. Appearing of Jesus coming in the clouds in great power and glory.

21. NOW IT IS RAPTURE TIME!

Mark 13:27 And then shall he send his angels, and shall gather together his elect from the four winds, from the uttermost part of the earth to the uttermost part of heaven.

After the sun and moon are darkened, with stars falling from heaven, and every eye sees Jesus coming in great power and glory then He raptures His elect to join in His parade to victory. This may not be the order of events we have been taught. It may not be the order of events that we want. But if this is the order of events that Jesus said would be, it would be wise to prepare for this order of events. We lose nothing by preparing for the events as

Jesus told us, which is sort of a worst case scenario. We
could lose a great deal if we fail to TAKE HEED to what
He said. Wishing and hoping and listening to false
teachers will not make it so. The Word of God makes it so.

Mark 13:28 Now learn a parable of the fig tree;
When her branch is yet tender, and putteth forth
leaves, ye know that summer is near:
Mark 13:29 So ye in like manner, when ye shall see
these things come to pass, know that it is nigh,
[even] at the doors.
Mark 13:30 Verily I say unto you, that this generation
shall not pass, till all these things be done.
Israel, the fig tree, is the key to end time prophecy. Israel
again took possession of Jerusalem in 1967. If a
bible generation is 40 years, everything including the
tribulation and the Lord's return should be done by 2007.
Please note that we are not telling anyone the day or the
hour. We could be several years into the 7 years of final
great tribulation and very few of us would know it. We
have reason to expect the end to be before the end of 2007.

Mark 13:31 Heaven and earth shall pass away:
but my words shall not pass away.
Mark 13:32 But of that day and [that] hour knoweth
no man, no, not the angels which are in heaven,
neither the Son, but the Father.
No one knows the day or hour. TAKE HEED - again the
Lord tells us to pay attention. Get to know the order of
end time events from the Word of God and not a false

teacher or a wishful thinking process. Know the great tribulation sign posts. TAKE HEED. If heaven and earth are soon to pass away but the Word of God endures forever, should we not give higher priority to the Word of God?

Mark 13:33 Take ye heed, watch and pray: for ye know not when the time is.
Mark 13:34 [For the Son of man is] as a man taking a far journey, who left his house, and gave authority to his servants, and to every man his work, and commanded the porter to watch.
Mark 13:35 Watch ye therefore: for ye know not when the master of the house cometh, at even, or at midnight, or at the cockcrowing, or in the morning:
Mark 13:36 Lest coming suddenly he find you sleeping.
Mark 13:37 And what I say unto you I say unto all, Watch.

TAKE HEED, watch and pray. We don't know the day or the hour but we know it is nearer than it has been for any previous generation. Nothing can put a believer to sleep or get him distracted better than a pre-tribulation rapture belief. Nothing will keep a believer on the watch, and taking heed, and better focused than a post tribulation rapture belief. Watch. TAKE HEED.

LUKE

Luke is the Gentile doctor and companion of Paul. He was the last friend to stay with Paul in the second imprisonment in Rome (2 Timothy 2:11). Luke was an eye witness of the events which he recorded in the book of Acts. He would have relied heavily on the accounts of Matthew and Mark for his gospel. It is quite possible that Mark's gospel record was part of Paul's request to Timothy for the books and parchments. **II Timothy 4:11-13 Only Luke is with me. Take Mark, and bring him with thee: for he is profitable to me for the ministry. And Tychicus have I sent to Ephesus. The cloke that I left at Troas with Carpus, when thou comest, bring [with thee], and the books, [but] especially the parchments.**

This second letter to Timothy could possibly have been written only 3 - 5 years before Rome destroyed Jerusalem. Luke was still with Paul in Rome at this time. By way of the Praetorian guards Paul and Luke may have even had some knowledge of the planning of the destruction of Jerusalem. It should be given some consideration that Luke's record of the Olivet Discourse may have focused almost entirely on the destruction of Jerusalem and very little on the Lord's end time prophecy. He and Paul were in Rome at the time under Roman Praetorian guard. Matthew heard directly from the Lord the Olivet Discourse. Mark heard the Olivet Discourse from Peter. Luke was informed about the Olivet Discourse from Mark's report. It would seem that if one wanted

information on the destruction of Jerusalem one would go
first to Luke, then Mark, and then Matthew. If on the
other hand, if one wanted information on end time
prophecy one would go first to Matthew, then Mark, and
then Luke. Luke's gospel account to his faithful friend
Theophilus may have saved the lives of many of the saints
in the Jerusalem Church who were warned to flee the city
before it was destroyed by Rome.

Luke 21:5 -36 And as some spake of the temple,
how it was adorned with goodly stones and gifts, he
said, [As for] these things which ye behold, the days
will come, in the which there shall not be left one
stone upon another, that shall not be thrown down.
And they asked him, saying, Master, but when shall
these things be? and what sign [will there be] when
these things shall come to pass?
And he said, Take heed that ye be not deceived: for
many shall come in my name, saying, I am [Christ];
and the time draweth near: go ye not therefore after
them.
But when ye shall hear of wars and commotions, be
not terrified: for these things must first come to
pass; but the end [is] not by and by.
Then said he unto them, Nation shall rise against
nation, and kingdom against kingdom:
And great earthquakes shall be in divers places, and
famines, and pestilences; and fearful sights and
great signs shall there be from heaven.
But before all these, they shall lay their hands on

you, and persecute [you], delivering [you] up to the synagogues, and into prisons, being brought before kings and rulers for my name's sake.

And it shall turn to you for a testimony.

Settle [it] therefore in your hearts, not to meditate before what ye shall answer:

For I will give you a mouth and wisdom, which all your adversaries shall not be able to gainsay nor resist.

And ye shall be betrayed both by parents, and brethren, and kinsfolks, and friends; and [some] of you shall they cause to be put to death.

And ye shall be hated of all [men] for my name's sake.

But there shall not an hair of your head perish.

In your patience possess ye your souls.

And when ye shall see Jerusalem compassed with armies, then know that the desolation thereof is nigh.

Then let them which are in Judaea flee to the mountains; and let them which are in the midst of it depart out; and let not them that are in the countries enter thereinto.

For these be the days of vengeance, that all things which are written may be fulfilled.

But woe unto them that are with child, and to them that give suck, in those days! for there shall be great distress in the land, and wrath upon this people.

And they shall fall by the edge of the sword, and

shall be led away captive into all nations: and
Jerusalem shall be trodden down of the Gentiles,
until the times of the Gentiles be fulfilled.

And there shall be signs in the sun, and in the
moon, and in the stars; and upon the earth distress
of nations, with perplexity; the sea and the waves
roaring;
Men's hearts failing them for fear, and for looking
after those things which are coming on the earth: for
the powers of heaven shall be shaken.
And then shall they see the Son of man coming in a
cloud with power and great glory.
And when these things begin to come to pass, then
look up, and lift up your heads; for your redemption
draweth nigh.
And he spake to them a parable; Behold the fig tree,
and all the trees;
When they now shoot forth, ye see and know of your
own selves that summer is now nigh at hand.
So likewise ye, when ye see these things come to
pass, know ye that the kingdom of God is nigh at
hand.
Verily I say unto you, This generation shall not pass
away, till all be fulfilled.
Heaven and earth shall pass away: but my words
shall not pass away.
And take heed to yourselves, lest at any time your
hearts be overcharged with surfeiting, and
drunkenness, and cares of this life, and [so] that day
come upon you unawares.

For as a snare shall it come on all them that
dwell on the face of the whole earth.
Watch ye therefore, and pray always, that ye may be
accounted worthy to escape all these things that
shall come to pass, and to stand before the Son of
man.

It is good to reread Luke's account in full context. While
his gospel was reaching to the Gentiles it is quite possible
that this particular part was to warn of Rome's destruction
of Jerusalem more so than Matthew or Mark's account.

Luke 21:5 And as some spake of the temple,
how it was adorned with goodly stones and gifts, he
said,
Luke 21:6 [As for] these things which ye behold, the
days will come, in the which there shall not be left
one stone upon another, that shall not be thrown
down.
Luke 21:7 And they asked him, saying, Master, but
when shall these things be? and what sign [will
there be] when these things shall come to pass?
The setting and the question is the same. When shall these
things be and what sign will there be when these things
shall come to pass?

Luke 21:8 And he said, Take heed that ye be not
deceived: for many shall come in my name, saying, I
am [Christ]; and the time draweth near: go ye not
therefore after them.

TAKE HEED. All accounts have the TAKE HEED, pay attention, this is important warning from the Lord. We are warned not to be deceived. Carefully test by the Spirit and the Word of God what any man tells you regarding end time prophecy. We are open to deception even from Christian teachers, coming and saying their words are from the Lord regarding end times prophecy. The Holy Spirit and the Word of God must be our teacher in regard to end time prophecy.

Luke 21:9 But when ye shall hear of wars and commotions, be not terrified: for these things must first come to pass; but the end [is] not by and by.
Luke 21:10 Then said he unto them, Nation shall rise against nation, and kingdom against kingdom:
Luke 21:11 And great earthquakes shall be in divers places, and famines, and pestilences; and fearful sights and great signs shall there be from heaven.
Our generation has seen these signs more clearly than any previous generation. The Lord's return is nearer than when we first believed. What about the fearful sights and great signs from heaven? Satan is referred to as the prince of the power of the air in Ephesians 2:2. This may refer to mass extra terrestrial sightings. Be informed that the extra terrestrials are demons. We may know this because of the consistency of the Luciferian gospel that they all preach. The lie is consistent and always essentially the same - "ye shall be as god." Know that extra terrestrials will be subject to you in the name of Jesus if you are covered by the blood of the Lamb.

Luke 21:12 But before all these, they shall lay their hands on you, and persecute [you], delivering [you] up to the synagogues, and into prisons, being brought before kings and rulers for my name's sake.
Luke 21:13 And it shall turn to you for a testimony.
Luke 21:14 Settle [it] therefore in your hearts, not to meditate before what ye shall answer:
Luke 21:15 For I will give you a mouth and wisdom, which all your adversaries shall not be able to gainsay nor resist.

The concept of persecution and suffering is a foreign concept to the Church in America. The highest calling of God in Christ Jesus is to be counted worthy to suffer for Him. It is almost impossible for Americans to hear or understand this. Nobody wants to suffer. Are we not in the age of grace? The government annihilation of the people at Waco may have marked the beginning of the persecution of the church in America. Let's hope that at least the Christian and Jewish people do not rationalize or forget the massacre of 79 American men, women, and children at Waco, Texas. These people were Americans who had no trial to prove them guilty of anything. The message of Waco is that no person or group, especially religious fanatics, will stand against the almighty power of the almighty government. It is not a question of if bible believing people can expect such treatment, so much as when. God's grace is infinite, His mercy endures forever. Freedom from persecution is the exception rather than the rule for the true Church of Jesus Christ. America has been so blessed by God for their support of missions and especially for the national support of Israel.

Luke 21:16 And ye shall be betrayed both by parents, and brethren, and kinsfolks, and friends; and [some] of you shall they cause to be put to death.
Luke 21:17 And ye shall be hated of all [men] for my name's sake.
Luke 21:18 But there shall not an hair of your head perish.
Luke 21:19 In your patience possess ye your souls.
To whom does this apply? In the end times Christians will be blamed for every problem and catastrophe. The New Age Movement and New World Order of Antichrist will have everyone going along with the program except the true Church. It is natural to be hated for Jesus name's sake. Expect it. Glory in your persecution that you were counted worthy to suffer for His name's sake.

Luke 21:20 And when ye shall see Jerusalem compassed with armies, then know that the desolation thereof is nigh.
Luke 21:21 Then let them which are in Judaea flee to the mountains; and let them which are in the midst of it depart out; and let not them that are in the countries enter thereinto.
Luke 21:22 For these be the days of vengeance, that all things which are written may be fulfilled.
Luke 21:23 But woe unto them that are with child, and to them that give suck, in those days! for there shall be great distress in the land, and wrath upon

this people.

Luke 21:24 And they shall fall by the edge of the sword, and shall be led away captive into all nations: and Jerusalem shall be trodden down of the Gentiles, until the times of the Gentiles be fulfilled.

Was Luke warning the Church in Jerusalem of the soon coming destruction of the nation of Israel by Rome? There is no abomination of desolation. He warns of armies surrounding Jerusalem. "Jerusalem shall be trodden down by the Gentiles until the times of the Gentiles be fulfilled." Luke helps define the "Times of the Gentiles." The times of the Gentiles extended from 70 to 1967 AD. Doctor Luke's warning saved many lives in the Jerusalem church.

Luke 21:25 And there shall be signs in the sun, and in the moon, and in the stars; and upon the earth distress of nations, with perplexity; the sea and the waves roaring;

Luke 21:26 Men's hearts failing them for fear, and for looking after those things which are coming on the earth: for the powers of heaven shall be shaken.

Luke 21:27 And then shall they see the Son of man coming in a cloud with power and great glory.

Luke 21:28 And when these things begin to come to pass, then look up, and lift up your heads; for your redemption draweth nigh.

Now we are back to end time prophecy. It is so important to recognize what we are being told in verse 28. When we see these things begin to come to pass we should be joyful because our Blessed Hope of the Lord's return is near. Is

this rapture time? The following is a recap of the order of
end time events that Luke has recorded for us:

1. Worldwide persecution of the Church (Luke 21:12)

2. Many false teachers and false christs.

3. Terrifying wars and commotions.

4. Nation rising against nation and kingdom against
   kingdom.

5. Earthquakes.

6. Famines.

7. Pestilences (plagues, AIDS)

8. Fearful and great signs from heaven.

9. Worldwide hatred of Christians (Luke 21:17 all men).

10. Israel possessing Jerusalem.

11. Signs in the sun, moon, and stars.

12. Distress of nations (world economic depression and
    political chaos)

13. Mens hearts failing for fear.

14. Powers of heaven shaken.

15. Then Jesus comes in great power and glory and its
    RAPTURE TIME.

Luke 21:29 And he spake to them a parable; Behold
the fig tree, and all the trees;
Luke 21:30 When they now shoot forth, ye see and
know of your own selves that summer is now nigh
at hand.
Luke 21:31 So likewise ye, when ye see these things
come to pass, know ye that the kingdom of God is
nigh at hand.
Luke 21:32 Verily I say unto you, This generation

shall not pass away, till all be fulfilled.

Luke 21:33 Heaven and earth shall pass away: but my words shall not pass away.

Often, head knowledge of the word of God is derided. No one knows the condition of anyone's heart. Faith comes by hearing and hearing by the word of God. We should do everything to encourage each other to get more knowledge of the word of God. Hosea 4:6 says "My people are destroyed for lack of knowledge:". Were the times of the Gentiles fulfilled in 1967 when Israel again possesses Jerusalem? If this be true, without fixing any specific day or hour, and assuming a bible generation to be 40 years, it will all be done including the tribulation, rapture and the Lord's return by 2007. Israel is the key to understanding end time prophecy. Heaven and earth will soon pass away but the Word of God endures forever. Let us all give higher priority to the study of the Word of God. Let us hide it in our hearts and let it show in our life. D. L. Moody wrote in the front of his bible "This Book will keep you from sin. Sin will keep you from this book."

Luke 21:34 And take heed to yourselves, lest at any time your hearts be overcharged with surfeiting, and drunkenness, and cares of this life, and [so] that day come upon you unawares.

Luke 21:35 For as a snare shall it come on all them that dwell on the face of the whole earth.

Luke 21:36 Watch ye therefore, and pray always, that ye may be accounted worthy to escape all these things that shall come to pass, and to stand before the Son of man.

TAKE HEED! Do not let your heart be concerned with the things of this world. Surfeiting is the pursuit of excess, being consumed with acquiring more than you need. This can allow you to be caught in the web of the New Age Movement and New World Order of Antichrist. Watch. Pray always that you may be counted worthy to escape all these things and be able to stand before the Lord. Does this mean to pray to be raptured? The Greek word translated escape is ekpheugo, meaning to flee out of so as not to be caught in the web. It is the love, faith, courage, and endurance of the saints in tribulation which will have them standing confidently at the Lord's return. The desire to escape tribulation and suffering is not what will give confidence to stand before the Lord. Noah faithfully endured 100 years of ridicule, persecution, and tribulation while he constructed the ark which allowed him to ekpheugo the flood. The 3 friends of Daniel were able to ekpheugo the fiery furnace with Jesus. God could have raptured them; but, He received more glory by having them remain faithful witnesses in the trial. How can we best give glory to God?

JOHN

John certainly heard the Olivet discourse; however, he did not verbatim record it in his gospel account. He gives great detail on the things of the Olivet Discourse and much more in Revelation. Something is however very important in his gospel account as we study end time prophecy. Jesus gives His Church timeless instructions in Chapters 14, 15, and 16. Jesus prays for His Church in Chapter 17. We must be born again by the Holy Spirit. We need to know how the Holy Spirit will lead, guide, teach, keep and protect us in tribulation.

John 14:1 Let not your heart be troubled: ye believe in God, believe also in me.

John 14:2 In my Father's house are many mansions: if [it were] not [so], I would have told you. I go to prepare a place for you.

John 14:3 And if I go and prepare a place for you, I will come again, and receive you unto myself; that where I am, [there] ye may be also.

John 14:4 And whither I go ye know, and the way ye know.

John 14:5 Thomas saith unto him, Lord, we know not whither thou goest; and how can we know the way?

John 14:6 Jesus saith unto him, I am the way, the truth, and the life: no man cometh unto the Father, but by me.

John 14:7 If ye had known me, ye should have known my Father also: and from henceforth ye know him, and have seen him.

John 14:8 Philip saith unto him, Lord, shew us the Father, and it sufficeth us.

John 14:9 Jesus saith unto him, Have I been so long time with you, and yet hast thou not known me, Philip? he that hath seen me hath seen the Father; and how sayest thou [then], Shew us the Father?

John 14:10 Believest thou not that I am in the Father, and the Father in me? the words that I speak unto you I speak not of myself: but the Father that dwelleth in me, he doeth the works.

John 14:11 Believe me that I [am] in the Father, and the Father in me: or else believe me for the very works' sake.

John 14:12 Verily, verily, I say unto you, He that believeth on me, the works that I do shall he do also; and greater [works] than these shall he do; because I go unto my Father.

John 14:13 And whatsoever ye shall ask in my name, that will I do, that the Father may be glorified in the Son.

John 14:14 If ye shall ask any thing in my name, I will do [it].

John 14:15 If ye love me, keep my commandments.

John 14:16 And I will pray the Father, and he shall give you another Comforter, that he may abide with you for ever;

John 14:17 [Even] the Spirit of truth; whom the world

cannot receive, because it seeth him not, neither knoweth him: but ye know him; for he dwelleth with you, and shall be in you.

John 14:18 I will not leave you comfortless: I will come to you.

John 14:19 Yet a little while, and the world seeth me no more; but ye see me: because I live, ye shall live also.

John 14:20 At that day ye shall know that I [am] in my Father, and ye in me, and I in you.

John 14:21 He that hath my commandments, and keepeth them, he it is that loveth me: and he that loveth me shall be loved of my Father, and I will love him, and will manifest myself to him.

John 14:22 Judas saith unto him, not Iscariot, Lord, how is it that thou wilt manifest thyself unto us, and not unto the world?

John 14:23 Jesus answered and said unto him, If a man love me, he will keep my words: and my Father will love him, and we will come unto him, and make our abode with him.

John 14:24 He that loveth me not keepeth not my sayings: and the word which ye hear is not mine, but the Father's which sent me.

John 14:25 These things have I spoken unto you, being [yet] present with you.

John 14:26 But the Comforter, [which is] the Holy Ghost, whom the Father will send in my name, he shall teach you all things, and bring all things to your remembrance, whatsoever I have said unto you.

John 14:27 Peace I leave with you, my peace I give unto you: not as the world giveth, give I unto you. Let not your heart be troubled, neither let it be afraid.
John 14:28 Ye have heard how I said unto you, I go away, and come [again] unto you. If ye loved me, ye would rejoice, because I said, I go unto the Father: for my Father is greater than I.
John 14:29 And now I have told you before it come to pass, that, when it is come to pass, ye might believe.
John 14:30 Hereafter I will not talk much with you: for the prince of this world cometh, and hath nothing in me.
John 14:31 But that the world may know that I love the Father; and as the Father gave me commandment, even so I do. Arise, let us go hence.

This would be a great Chapter to memorize. This is great tribulation preparation. Don't worry. Trust God. Trust Jesus. He has prepared a place for us and He is coming back for us. Jesus is the way, the truth, and the life. The miracles that Jesus did, we will be able to do. We may not be able to buy or sell but we will live supernaturally in the great tribulation. The fulfillment of the greater works mentioned in verse 12 will likely be in the great tribulation. WE MUST NEVER FORGET THAT IT IS GOD WHO DOES THE MIRACLES IN THE NAME OF JESUS SO THAT GOD GETS ALL THE GLORY. God delights to do miracles for us if we ask as Jesus would ask. That the Father may be glorified. Who would want to be able to buy or sell when we can just ask God to glorify Himself with a miracle to meet our need? Who would want government health care if we could simply lay on hands asking for healing in the name of Jesus for the glory of God? Why does everyone want to miss such a time? If we love Jesus we will prove it by the way we love, care, and share with the other believers in tribulation. We have The Comforter in great tribulation. The great tribulation will provide the Church with its greatest opportunity to glorify God. Why does everybody want to miss it? What is our highest reason for being other than to glorify God? Do you really believe or do you just have fire insurance? How do we come to be able to live such a supernatural life of faith? The answers are in chapter 15 and 16.

John 15:1 I am the true vine, and my Father is the husbandman.
John 15:2 Every branch in me that beareth not fruit he taketh away: and every [branch] that beareth fruit, he purgeth it, that it may bring forth more fruit.
John 15:3 Now ye are clean through the word which I have spoken unto you.
John 15:4 Abide in me, and I in you. As the branch cannot bear fruit of itself, except it abide in the vine; no more can ye, except ye abide in me.
John 15:5 I am the vine, ye [are] the branches: He that abideth in me, and I in him, the same bringeth forth much fruit: for without me ye can do nothing.
John 15:6 If a man abide not in me, he is cast forth as a branch, and is withered; and men gather them,

and cast [them] into the fire, and they are burned.
John 15:7 If ye abide in me, and my words abide in you, ye shall ask what ye will, and it shall be done unto you.
John 15:8 Herein is my Father glorified, that ye bear much fruit; so shall ye be my disciples.

Here is great tribulation preparation. We must draw our life from Jesus the true vine not from our own self efforts. We can bear fruit only if we find our life is in Jesus. The pruning of the great tribulation will help us branches bear much more fruit. We will ask for a miracle and it shall be done for the glory of God and to bring many souls to faith in Him.

John 15:9 As the Father hath loved me, so have I loved you: continue ye in my love.
John 15:10 If ye keep my commandments, ye shall abide in my love; even as I have kept my Father's commandments, and abide in his love.
John 15:11 These things have I spoken unto you, that my joy might remain in you, and [that] your joy might be full.
John 15:12 This is my commandment, That ye love one another, as I have loved you.
John 15:13 Greater love hath no man than this, that a man lay down his life for his friends.
John 15:14 Ye are my friends, if ye do whatsoever I command you.
John 15:15 Henceforth I call you not servants; for the servant knoweth not what his lord doeth: but I

have called you friends; for all things that I have
heard of my Father I have made known unto you.
John 15:16 Ye have not chosen me, but I have
chosen you, and ordained you, that ye should go
and bring forth fruit, and [that] your fruit should
remain: that whatsoever ye shall ask of the Father
in my name, he may give it you.
John 15:17 These things I command you, that ye
love one another.

Here is great tribulation preparation. We are called to
holiness. The law is made perfect in love. If you love
someone you will not lie to them. If you love someone you
will not steal from them. If you love someone you are
happy to share with them. If you love someone their well
being is as important as your own well being. We are to
love one another as Jesus has loved us. It is sad today how
churches are often known for their unkindness and
hypocrisy more than they are for their love and truth. We
must love one another in deed and in truth. It may now be
somewhat optional but it will not be optional in great
tribulation. King Jesus commands us to love one another.

John 15:18 If the world hate you, ye know that it
hated me before [it hated] you.
John 15:19 If ye were of the world, the world would
love his own: but because ye are not of the world,
but I have chosen you out of the world, therefore the
world hateth you.
John 15:20 Remember the word that I said unto you,
The servant is not greater than his lord. If they have

persecuted me, they will also persecute you; if they
have kept my saying, they will keep yours also.
John 15:21 But all these things will they do unto you
for my name's sake, because they know not him that
sent me.
John 15:22 If I had not come and spoken unto them,
they had not had sin: but now they have no cloke for
their sin.
John 15:23 He that hateth me hateth my Father also.
The New World Order of Antichrist will blame every
problem and catastrophe on those narrow-minded, bible
believing, Jesus people.

John 15:24 If I had not done among them the works
which none other man did, they had not had sin: but
now have they both seen and hated both me and my
Father.
John 15:25 But [this cometh to pass], that the word
might be fulfilled that is written in their law, They
hated me without a cause.
John 15:26 But when the Comforter is come, whom I
will send unto you from the Father, [even] the Spirit
of truth, which proceedeth from the Father, he shall
testify of me:
John 15:27 And ye also shall bear witness, because
ye have been with me from the beginning.
If the world hated Jesus than it will hate His followers.
Does the world hate your church? Maybe it is not
following Jesus closely enough to be hated by the world?
The world hates holiness. Is there enough holiness in your

church to make the world hate it?

John 16:1 These things have I spoken unto you, that ye should not be offended.

John 16:2 They shall put you out of the synagogues: yea, the time cometh, that whosoever killeth you will think that he doeth God service.

John 16:3 And these things will they do unto you, because they have not known the Father, nor me.

John 16:4 But these things have I told you, that when the time shall come, ye may remember that I told you of them. And these things I said not unto you at the beginning, because I was with you.

John 16:5 But now I go my way to him that sent me; and none of you asketh me, Whither goest thou?

John 16:6 But because I have said these things unto you, sorrow hath filled your heart.

John 16:7 Nevertheless I tell you the truth; It is expedient for you that I go away: for if I go not away, the Comforter will not come unto you; but if I depart, I will send him unto you.

John 16:8 And when he is come, he will reprove the world of sin, and of righteousness, and of judgment:

John 16:9 Of sin, because they believe not on me;

John 16:10 Of righteousness, because I go to my Father, and ye see me no more;

John 16:11 Of judgment, because the prince of this world is judged.

John 16:12 I have yet many things to say unto you, but ye cannot bear them now.

John 16:13 Howbeit when he, the Spirit of truth, is

come, he will guide you into all truth: for he shall not speak of himself; but whatsoever he shall hear, [that] shall he speak: and he will shew you things to come.

John 16:14 He shall glorify me: for he shall receive of mine, and shall shew [it] unto you.

John 16:15 All things that the Father hath are mine: therefore said I, that he shall take of mine, and shall shew [it] unto you.

John 16:16 A little while, and ye shall not see me: and again, a little while, and ye shall see me, because I go to the Father.

John 16:17 Then said [some] of his disciples among themselves, What is this that he saith unto us, A little while, and ye shall not see me: and again, a little while, and ye shall see me: and, Because I go to the Father?

John 16:18 They said therefore, What is this that he saith, A little while? we cannot tell what he saith.

John 16:19 Now Jesus knew that they were desirous to ask him, and said unto them, Do ye enquire among yourselves of that I said, A little while, and ye shall not see me: and again, a little while, and ye shall see me?

John 16:20 Verily, verily, I say unto you, That ye shall weep and lament, but the world shall rejoice: and ye shall be sorrowful, but your sorrow shall be turned into joy.

John 16:21 A woman when she is in travail hath sorrow, because her hour is come: but as soon as she is delivered of the child, she remembereth no more the anguish, for joy that a man is born into the world.

John 16:22 And ye now therefore have sorrow: but I will see you again, and your heart shall rejoice, and your joy no man taketh from you.

John 16:23 And in that day ye shall ask me nothing. Verily, verily, I say unto you, Whatsoever ye shall ask the Father in my name, he will give [it] you.

John 16:24 Hitherto have ye asked nothing in my name: ask, and ye shall receive, that your joy may be full.

John 16:25 These things have I spoken unto you in proverbs: but the time cometh, when I shall no more speak unto you in proverbs, but I shall shew you plainly of the Father.

John 16:26 At that day ye shall ask in my name: and I say not unto you, that I will pray the Father for you:

John 16:27 For the Father himself loveth you, because ye have loved me, and have believed that I came out from God.

John 16:28 I came forth from the Father, and am come into the world: again, I leave the world, and go to the Father.

John 16:29 His disciples said unto him, Lo, now speakest thou plainly, and speakest no proverb.

John 16:30 Now are we sure that thou knowest all things, and needest not that any man should ask thee: by this we believe that thou camest forth from God.

John 16:31 Jesus answered them, Do ye now

believe?

John 16:32 Behold, the hour cometh, yea, is now come, that ye shall be scattered, every man to his own, and shall leave me alone: and yet I am not alone, because the Father is with me.

John 16:33 These things I have spoken unto you, that in me ye might have peace. In the world ye shall have tribulation: but be of good cheer; I have overcome the world.

It is true that much of what Jesus said here was to prepare His disciples for His death, burial, and resurrection. There is also much encouragement for His Church then, now, and especially at the time of the end. He told us that a time would come when people would think they were serving God by killing His people because they do not really know God or Jesus. Jesus had to return to be with the Father so that we could have the Holy Spirit. He told us these things to encourage us to hang in there and endure to the end. The world hates the Spirit of Holiness because He makes everyone aware that they are sinners and need a Savior. The prince of this world is judged. Our victory in the war that Antichrist wages on the saints is absolutely certain. The Spirit of Truth must be our teacher and guide. The Holy Spirit will show us how we may give God the most glory. The Holy Spirit will show us what is coming and the way we need to go. The Holy Spirit will manifest the power and glory of Jesus through us. That should cause us to shout with joy. However, for a short time, the world will be doing the rejoicing while we are sorrowful. Our sorrow for the short time will be turned into great joy forever. This joy will be so great that we will not remember any of the sorrow. Whatever we ask of God, in the name of Jesus, we shall have that we may be full of joy. Do you believe? Do you just have fire insurance? God loves you. Why? Because, you love His Son Jesus, and you believe that God the Father sent Him to solve your sin problem. You believe that Jesus died to pay the required price for your sins and the sins of all the world. Jesus asks, "Do you now believe?" Jesus tells us, "In the world ye shall have tribulation: but be of good cheer; I have overcome the world."

John 17:1 These words spake Jesus, and lifted up his eyes to heaven, and said, Father, the hour is come; glorify thy Son, that thy Son also may glorify thee:

John 17:2 As thou hast given him power over all flesh, that he should give eternal life to as many as thou hast given him.

John 17:3 And this is life eternal, that they might know thee the only true God, and Jesus Christ, whom thou hast sent.

John 17:4 I have glorified thee on the earth: I have finished the work which thou gavest me to do.

John 17:5 And now, O Father, glorify thou me with thine own self with the glory which I had with thee before the world was.

John 17:6 I have manifested thy name unto the men which thou gavest me out of the world: thine they were, and thou gavest them me; and they have kept thy word.

John 17:7 Now they have known that all things whatsoever thou hast given me are of thee.

John 17:8 For I have given unto them the words which thou gavest me; and they have received [them], and have known surely that I came out from thee, and they have believed that thou didst send me.

John 17:9 I pray for them: I pray not for the world, but for them which thou hast given me; for they are thine.

John 17:10 And all mine are thine, and thine are mine; and I am glorified in them.

John 17:11 And now I am no more in the world, but these are in the world, and I come to thee. Holy Father, keep through thine own name those whom thou hast given me, that they may be one, as we [are].

John 17:12 While I was with them in the world, I kept them in thy name: those that thou gavest me I have kept, and none of them is lost, but the son of perdition; that the scripture might be fulfilled.

John 17:13 And now come I to thee; and these things I speak in the world, that they might have my joy fulfilled in themselves.

John 17:14 I have given them thy word; and the world hath hated them, because they are not of the world, even as I am not of the world.

John 17:15 I pray not that thou shouldest take them out of the world, but that thou shouldest keep them from the evil.

John 17:16 They are not of the world, even as I am not of the world.

John 17:17 Sanctify them through thy truth: thy word is truth.

John 17:18 As thou hast sent me into the world, even so have I also sent them into the world.

John 17:19 And for their sakes I sanctify myself, that they also might be sanctified through the truth.

John 17:20 Neither pray I for these alone, but for them also which shall believe on me through their word;

John 17:21 That they all may be one; as thou, Father, [art] in me, and I in thee, that they also may be one in us: that the world may believe that thou hast sent me.

John 17:22 And the glory which thou gavest me I have given them; that they may be one, even as we are one:

John 17:23 I in them, and thou in me, that they may be made perfect in one; and that the world may know that thou hast sent me, and hast loved them, as thou hast loved me.

John 17:24 Father, I will that they also, whom thou hast given me, be with me where I am; that they may behold my glory, which thou hast given me: for thou lovedst me before the foundation of the world.

John 17:25 O righteous Father, the world hath not known thee: but I have known thee, and these have known that thou hast sent me.

John 17:26 And I have declared unto them thy name, and will declare [it]: that the love wherewith thou hast loved me may be in them, and I in them.

The purpose of prayer is to glorify God. How God may be glorified should be the roots of our prayer. His Church has nothing to fear knowing that Jesus is at the right hand of the Father continuing to pray like this for us. In verse 15, John uses a peculiar combination of Greek words that are found only here, and in Revelation 3:10. No one seems to have much trouble understanding the meaning John tried to express with *tereo ek* here in verse 15. There is general misunderstanding of *tereo ek* in Revelation 3:10. This will be discussed as we study Revelation. It would be great to memorize this complete prayer that Jesus continues to pray for us. It is most uplifting to think about Jesus being at the right hand of the Father continuing to pray like this for us! Jesus has given us eternal life. If we are killed, our eternal life continues with Jesus. He has given us the power and authority to use His name. We belong to Him and He is well able to take care of us. We are with Him, and He is with us, in the presence and power of His Holy Spirit. Jesus wants His joy to be in us in fullness. The world hates us because of His Spirit of Holiness being in us. The world hates holiness. He may not take us out of this world that hates us. He will take care of us and keep us until we come to Him at our death, or He sends His angels to bring us up into His victory parade at the Rapture.

PAUL

It was Paul who opened the doors of the Church to the
Gentiles. Before Paul began his ministry only Jews were in
the Church. In his missionary work, when Paul would go
to a city, he would go to the synagogue. In Corinth he spent
18 months ministering in the synagogue in Corinth while
working with Aquila and Pricilla. Usually when Paul would
preach Jesus of Nazareth as the fulfillment of Messianic
prophecy he did not last 18 months before he was run out of
the synagogue. There would always be at least a handful of
Jews who knew Paul was speaking the truth about Messiah
Jesus. They would follow Paul out of the synagogue where
they would establish a new synagogue or a Church that
would welcome Gentiles who believed in the God of Israel.
Most of the elders and deacons in the Churches Paul
established were probably Jews. In the last days we should
see a restoration of the Church with both Jew and Gentile,
bond and free, male and female worshipping God together
in Spirit and in Truth. Jews and Gentiles will be together
in love, faith, truth, and power. Jews and Gentiles will be
standing together in the great tribulation war of Antichrist
against the saints. Paul preached Jesus to the Jew first and
also to the Gentile. Paul's intention was that the Lord
Jesus, by His Holy Spirit, would confirm us to the end, that
we may be blameless in the day of our Lord Jesus Christ (1
Corinthians 1:8). In studying Paul's letters for end times
prophecy we will focus on 1 Corinthians 15, I Thessalonians
chapters 3 - 5, II Thessalonians chapters 2 - 3, I Timothy 4,

and II Timothy 3.

I Corinthians 15:1 Moreover, brethren, I declare unto you the gospel which I preached unto you, which also ye have received, and wherein ye stand;
I Corinthians 15:2 By which also ye are saved, if ye keep in memory what I preached unto you, unless ye have believed in vain.
I Corinthians 15:3 For I delivered unto you first of all that which I also received, how that Christ died for our sins according to the scriptures;
I Corinthians 15:4 And that he was buried, and that he rose again the third day according to the scriptures:
I Corinthians 15:5 And that he was seen of Cephas, then of the twelve:
I Corinthians 15:6 After that, he was seen of above five hundred brethren at once; of whom the greater part remain unto this present, but some are fallen asleep.
I Corinthians 15:7 After that, he was seen of James; then of all the apostles.
I Corinthians 15:8 And last of all he was seen of me also, as of one born out of due time.
I Corinthians 15:9 For I am the least of the apostles, that am not meet to be called an apostle, because I persecuted the church of God.
I Corinthians 15:10 But by the grace of God I am what I am: and his grace which [was bestowed] upon me was not in vain; but I laboured more abundantly than

they all: yet not I, but the grace of God which was with me.

I Corinthians 15:11 Therefore whether [it were] I or they, so we preach, and so ye believed.

I Corinthians 15:12 Now if Christ be preached that he rose from the dead, how say some among you that there is no resurrection of the dead?

I Corinthians 15:13 But if there be no resurrection of the dead, then is Christ not risen:

I Corinthians 15:14 And if Christ be not risen, then [is] our preaching vain, and your faith [is] also vain.

I Corinthians 15:15 Yea, and we are found false witnesses of God; because we have testified of God that he raised up Christ: whom he raised not up, if so be that the dead rise not.

I Corinthians 15:16 For if the dead rise not, then is not Christ raised:

I Corinthians 15:17 And if Christ be not raised, your faith [is] vain; ye are yet in your sins.

I Corinthians 15:18 Then they also which are fallen asleep in Christ are perished.

I Corinthians 15:19 If in this life only we have hope in Christ, we are of all men most miserable.

I Corinthians 15:20 But now is Christ risen from the dead, [and] become the firstfruits of them that slept.

I Corinthians 15:21 For since by man [came] death, by man [came] also the resurrection of the dead.

I Corinthians 15:22 For as in Adam all die, even so in Christ shall all be made alive.

I Corinthians 15:23 But every man in his own order:
Christ the firstfruits; afterward they that are Christ's
at his coming.

I Corinthians 15:24 Then [cometh] the end, when he
shall have delivered up the kingdom to God, even
the Father; when he shall have put down all rule
and all authority and power.

I Corinthians 15:25 For he must reign, till he hath put
all enemies under his feet.

I Corinthians 15:26 The last enemy [that] shall be
destroyed [is] death.

I Corinthians 15:27 For he hath put all things under
his feet. But when he saith all things are put under
[him, it is] manifest that he is excepted, which did
put all things under him.

I Corinthians 15:28 And when all things shall be
subdued unto him, then shall the Son also himself
be subject unto him that put all things under him,
that God may be all in all.

I Corinthians 15:29 Else what shall they do which are
baptized for the dead, if the dead rise not at all? why
are they then baptized for the dead?

I Corinthians 15:30 And why stand we in jeopardy
every hour?

I Corinthians 15:31 I protest by your rejoicing which I
have in Christ Jesus our Lord, I die daily.

I Corinthians 15:32 If after the manner of men I have
fought with beasts at Ephesus, what advantageth it
me, if the dead rise not? let us eat and drink; for to
morrow we die.

I Corinthians 15:33 Be not deceived: evil
communications corrupt good manners.

I Corinthians 15:34 Awake to righteousness, and sin
not; for some have not the knowledge of God: I
speak [this] to your shame.

I Corinthians 15:35 But some [man] will say, How are
the dead raised up? and with what body do they
come?

I Corinthians 15:36 [Thou] fool, that which thou
sowest is not quickened, except it die:

I Corinthians 15:37 And that which thou sowest, thou
sowest not that body that shall be, but bare grain, it
may chance of wheat, or of some other [grain]:

I Corinthians 15:38 But God giveth it a body as it
hath pleased him, and to every seed his own body.

I Corinthians 15:39 All flesh [is] not the same flesh:
but [there is] one [kind of] flesh of men, another flesh
of beasts, another of fishes, [and] another of birds.

I Corinthians 15:40 [There are] also celestial bodies,
and bodies terrestrial: but the glory of the celestial
[is] one, and the [glory] of the terrestrial [is] another.

I Corinthians 15:41 [There is] one glory of the sun,
and another glory of the moon, and another glory of
the stars: for [one] star differeth from [another] star
in glory.

I Corinthians 15:42 So also [is] the resurrection of
the dead. It is sown in corruption; it is raised in
incorruption:

I Corinthians 15:43 It is sown in dishonour; it is
raised in glory: it is sown in weakness; it is raised in

power:

I Corinthians 15:44 It is sown a natural body; it is raised a spiritual body. There is a natural body, and there is a spiritual body.

I Corinthians 15:45 And so it is written, The first man Adam was made a living soul; the last Adam [was made] a quickening spirit.

I Corinthians 15:46 Howbeit that [was] not first which is spiritual, but that which is natural; and afterward that which is spiritual.

I Corinthians 15:47 The first man [is] of the earth, earthy: the second man [is] the Lord from heaven.

I Corinthians 15:48 As [is] the earthy, such [are] they also that are earthy: and as [is] the heavenly, such [are] they also that are heavenly.

I Corinthians 15:49 And as we have borne the image of the earthy, we shall also bear the image of the heavenly.

I Corinthians 15:50 Now this I say, brethren, that flesh and blood cannot inherit the kingdom of God; neither doth corruption inherit incorruption.

I Corinthians 15:51 Behold, I shew you a mystery; We shall not all sleep, but we shall all be changed,

I Corinthians 15:52 In a moment, in the twinkling of an eye, at the last trump: for the trumpet shall sound, and the dead shall be raised incorruptible, and we shall be changed.

I Corinthians 15:53 For this corruptible must put on incorruption, and this mortal [must] put on immortality.

I Corinthians 15:54 So when this corruptible shall
have put on incorruption, and this mortal shall have
put on immortality, then shall be brought to pass the
saying that is written, Death is swallowed up in
victory.
I Corinthians 15:55 O death, where [is] thy sting? O
grave, where [is] thy victory?
I Corinthians 15:56 The sting of death [is] sin; and
the strength of sin [is] the law.
I Corinthians 15:57 But thanks [be] to God, which
giveth us the victory through our Lord Jesus Christ.
I Corinthians 15:58 Therefore, my beloved brethren,
be ye stedfast, unmoveable, always abounding in
the work of the Lord, forasmuch as ye know that
your labour is not in vain in the Lord.

This long passage is all great tribulation preparation. It is
important to know what you believe regarding the
Resurrection. For if we have hoped in Christ in this life
only, we are of all men most to be pitied. Nothing in first
century history is more well documented than the death
and resurrection of Jesus Christ.   The specific end time
passages are :22 -24 and 50-52.

I Corinthians 15:22 For as in Adam all die, even so in
Christ shall all be made alive.
i Corinthians 15:23 But every man in his own order:
Christ the firstfruits; afterward they that are Christ's
at his coming.
I Corinthians 15:24 Then [cometh] the end, when he
shall have delivered up the kingdom to

God, even the Father; when he shall have put down all rule and all authority and power.

The rapture is somewhere in these verses. Where? Christ rose from the dead and ascended into heaven. He is coming back and the dead will be raised incorruptible with bodies similar to the one Christ displayed in the 40 days between His resurrection and ascension. Does this mean that the rapture occurs when the dead are raised at the end of the tribulation when the Lord returns with great power and glory? It is difficult to dismiss this possibility in light of the further explanation Paul gives in verses 50 - 52.

I Corinthians 15:50 Now this I say, brethren, that flesh and blood cannot inherit the kingdom of God; neither doth corruption inherit incorruption.
I Corinthians 15:51 Behold, I shew you a mystery; We shall not all sleep, but we shall all be changed,
I Corinthians 15:52 In a moment, in the twinkling of an eye, at the last trump: for the trumpet shall sound, and the dead shall be raised incorruptible, and we shall be changed.

We shall not all sleep but we shall all be changed. We can be certain that this is the rapture. In a moment, in the twinkling of an eye, the dead in Christ shall be raised and we shall be changed. This is the rapture for sure and it occurs at the ____ ____? First trumpet? Sixth trumpet? LAST TRUMP! The Seventh Trumpet of Revelation is the last trumpet. The following is a list of all New Testament verses with the word trump, trumpet or trumpets: I Corinthians 15:52, I Thessalonians 4:16, Matthew 6:2,

Matthew 24:31, I Corinthians 14:8, Hebrews 12:19,
Revelation 1:10, Revelation 4:1, Revelation 8:2,
Revelation 8:6, Revelation 8:13, Revelation 9:14, and
Revelation 10:7.

The following apply to the last trump reference to
I Corinthians 15:52:

Matthew 24:31 And he shall send his angels with a great sound of a trumpet, and they shall gather together his elect from the four winds, from one end of heaven to the other.

I Thessalonians 4:16 For the Lord himself shall descend from heaven with a shout, with the voice of the archangel, and with the trump of God: and the dead in Christ shall rise first:

Revelation 8:2 And I saw the seven angels which stood before God; and to them were given seven trumpets.

Revelation 8:6 And the seven angels which had the seven trumpets prepared themselves to sound.

Revelation 9:14 Saying to the sixth angel which had the trumpet, Loose the four angels which are bound in the great river Euphrates.

Revelation 10:7 But in the days of the voice of the seventh angel, when he shall begin to sound, the mystery of God should be finished, as he hath declared to his servants the prophets.

The last trump is the trumpet to sound when the Lord returns to put down the armies of Antichrist. <u>The Lord's return in great power and glory, the resurrection of those who have died in Christ, and the rapture, is a single event.</u>

THE LORD'S RETURN, THE RESURRECTION, AND
THE RAPTURE ALL HAPPEN IN THE TWINKLING OF
AN EYE. Maybe that is not the way we would like it to be;
but, that is the way we should prepare and plan for it to be.
Praise God if it happens before the tribulation; but, if the
scriptures tell us it happens at the end, let us plan to live
supernaturally in Christ during the great tribulation. Let
us rejoice if we are counted worthy to suffer for Him.

I Thessalonians 3:2 And sent Timotheus, our
brother, and minister of God, and our
fellowlabourer in the gospel of Christ, to establish
you, and to comfort you concerning your faith:
I Thessalonians 3:3 That no man should be moved
by these afflictions: for yourselves know that we are
appointed thereunto.
I Thessalonians 3:4 For verily, when we were with
you, we told you before that we should suffer
tribulation; even as it came to pass, and ye know.
I Thessalonians 3:5 For this cause, when I could no
longer forbear, I sent to know your faith, lest by
some means the tempter have tempted you, and our
labour be in vain.

Paul sent Timothy from Athens to check on the faith of the
believers in the church in Thessalonica. He had established
it on his second missionary journey. Timothy would rejoin
Paul with a good report in Corinth. Paul was concerned to
know if the believers would depart from the faith because
of afflictions. True faith grows in affliction and tribulation.

Feigned or pretended faith often is lost in tribulation.
Pretended love will also disappear in tribulation. True
faith and love will grow in tribulation. This has been
proven during the history of the church. An apostate
church will promote hypocrisy, deny the power of God, soft
peddle the truth, and quench the Spirit of Holiness. Such a
church will disappear and fall apart in tribulation. Paul
was much more bold than the typical evangelist. He made
it perfectly clear that believers are called to affliction. Paul
told the truth with no concern for whether it was what his
audience wanted to hear. His popularity was of no concern
to Paul. He knew that people who would reject the hard
truth of the call to affliction, would not be able to endure to
the end of tribulation. He told the Thessalonians, truly, and
face to face, before it came to pass, that "we should suffer
tribulation." Not many preachers in America can deliver
this kind of strong meat.

**I Thessalonians 3:12 And the Lord make you to
increase and abound in love one toward another,
and toward all [men], even as we [do] toward you:
I Thessalonians 3:13 To the end he may stablish your
hearts unblameable in holiness before God, even our
Father, at the coming of our Lord Jesus Christ with
all his saints.**

Paul's prayer was that we increase and abound in love
toward one another. Love may be soft or tough but it must
be solidly founded in truth. He prayed that our hearts
would be established unblamable in holiness. That means
truth. No difference found between what you think inside

and how you act before your brothers. That we would hide nothing from God or our brothers for which we would be ashamed when the Lord returns with all his saints.

I Thessalonians 4:7 For God hath not called us unto uncleanness, but unto holiness.
I Thessalonians 4:8 He therefore that despiseth, despiseth not man, but God, who hath also given unto us his holy Spirit.
I Thessalonians 4:9 But as touching brotherly love ye need not that I write unto you: for ye yourselves are taught of God to love one another.

Holiness is great tribulation preparation. Holiness is acting outwardly as you think inwardly. Holiness is being real. Feigned affection is common in the church today. When the church is in tribulation those with feigned affection will get real or get out. King Jesus commands us to love one another.

I Thessalonians 4:13 But I would not have you to be ignorant, brethren, concerning them which are asleep, that ye sorrow not, even as others which have no hope.
I Thessalonians 4:14 For if we believe that Jesus died and rose again, even so them also which sleep in Jesus will God bring with him.
I Thessalonians 4:15 For this we say unto you by the word of the Lord, that we which are alive [and] remain unto the coming of the Lord shall not prevent them which are asleep.

I Thessalonians 4:16 For the Lord himself shall descend from heaven with a shout, with the voice of the archangel, and with the trump of God: and the dead in Christ shall rise first:
I Thessalonians 4:17 Then we which are alive [and] remain shall be caught up together with them in the clouds, to meet the Lord in the air: and so shall we ever be with the Lord.
I Thessalonians 4:18 Wherefore comfort one another with these words.

Regarding death or dying, we do not have to be sorrowful as those who do not have faith in Jesus Christ. Without Jesus we have no hope. With Jesus we have hope no matter what happens. Even if we are to be killed we have hope. We don't die. Our bodies will die but we go to be with Jesus. We will get new glorified bodies when He returns. Every saint will be in the great victory parade of King Jesus. When He returns we don't have to worry about whether the believers who have died will be in the parade. King Jesus will have all His saints witness Him single-handedly destroy the armies of Antichrist who had been waging war on the living saints. He will do it with a shout. We who are alive at the return of King Jesus will join in the glorious victory parade. We join the parade immediately after those who have died in Christ receive their glorified bodies at the resurrection. They will already be there. King Jesus returns from heaven with the voice of the archangel and with the trump of God. That trump of God is the last trumpet as we have seen in Matthew 24:30-31 and I Corinthians 15:50-52. The dead in Christ

shall rise first. Then those who are still enduring
Antichrist's war on the saints shall be caught up to meet
the Lord in the air. We who are alive will witness, with all
the saints and angels, as He single-handedly has victory
over the armies of Antichrist. This is great comfort for
great tribulation. This is our blessed hope.

**I Thessalonians 5:1 But of the times and the
seasons, brethren, ye have no need that I write
unto you.**
**I Thessalonians 5:2 For yourselves know perfectly
that the day of the Lord so cometh as a thief in the
night.**
**I Thessalonians 5:3 For when they shall say, Peace
and safety; then sudden destruction cometh upon
them, as travail upon a woman with child; and they
shall not escape.**

We are not to know the day or the hour. We are to take
heed and watch and be doing what King Jesus commands.
We are to love one another no matter how great the
tribulation that we are to endure. One of the signs will
be that the world will be saying "Peace and safety." This is
the political platform upon which Antichrist will come to
power. The world has never been in greater peril with the
proliferation of nuclear weapons now getting into the hands
of many small countries with unstable governments. There
is even some possibility of terrorists getting weapons of mass
destruction. The "break up" of the Soviet Union bringing
peace is a myth which borders on insanity. It illustrates the
extremes to which wishful thinking can take us, if we choose

to ignore or twist the truth to our liking.

I Thessalonians 5:4 But ye, brethren, are not in darkness, that that day should overtake you as a thief.
I Thessalonians 5:5 Ye are all the children of light, and the children of the day: we are not of the night, nor of darkness.
I Thessalonians 5:6 Therefore let us not sleep, as [do] others; but let us watch and be sober.
I Thessalonians 5:7 For they that sleep sleep in the night; and they that be drunken are drunken in the night.
I Thessalonians 5:8 But let us, who are of the day, be sober, putting on the breastplate of faith and love; and for an helmet, the hope of salvation.
I Thessalonians 5:9 For God hath not appointed us to wrath, but to obtain salvation by our Lord Jesus Christ,
I Thessalonians 5:10 Who died for us, that, whether we wake or sleep, we should live together with him.

If we are taking heed to the signs and end time prophecies we will not be surprised when the day of the Lord occurs. What about those who think they are going to be raptured before any of these things happen? Could they be lulled into sleeping while the many webs of the New Age, New World Order, of Antichrist are being put in place? If it is said that post tribulation rapture doctrine gives rise to fanaticism, it should also be considered that the pre tribulation rapture doctrine may give rise to complacency or sleep. We must be about putting on the breastplate of faith and love. Faith cometh by hearing and hearing by the word of God. Faith to move mountains will be quite handy in the war with Antichrist. However it will not be worth a rip without love. The helmet of salvation is the key. When one focuses on the love of God expressed by Jesus at Calvary, it will bring fourth love. Love rejoices in the truth. Love will not dismiss hard truth out of hand. Love and truth must go together or feigned affection results.

What about the truth that God has not appointed us to wrath? The rest of the verse is that we obtain salvation. Just as God protected the Jews in the Exodus plagues on Egypt, we may be confident of His presence and protection by the Holy Spirit during great tribulation. We are sealed by God from the wrath of the plagues God sends during tribulation. The war of Antichrist is not the wrath of God. The lake of fire is the ultimate expression of the wrath of God. We are free of such wrath through our faith in Jesus. King Jesus commands that we love one another. The wrath of Antichrist in his war on the saints is something totally different from the wrath of God. If Antichrist wins some battles it is not the wrath of God. We have certain ultimate victory in our blessed hope when King Jesus returns. In the mean time, we are to love one another and bring the good news of our blessed hope to those who will otherwise join the war on the side of Antichrist.

I Thessalonians 5:16 Rejoice evermore.
I Thessalonians 5:17 Pray without ceasing.
I Thessalonians 5:18 In every thing give thanks: for

this is the will of God in Christ Jesus concerning you.
I Thessalonians 5:19 Quench not the Spirit.
I Thessalonians 5:20 Despise not prophesyings.
I Thessalonians 5:21 Prove all things; hold fast that which is good.
I Thessalonians 5:22 Abstain from all appearance of evil.
I Thessalonians 5:23 And the very God of peace sanctify you wholly; and [I pray God] your whole spirit and soul and body be preserved blameless unto the coming of our Lord Jesus Christ.
I Thessalonians 5:24 Faithful [is] he that calleth you, who also will do [it].

Here is Paul's checklist for great tribulation. Here is how to be more than a conqueror. This is worth memorizing.

1. Rejoice evermore.
2. Pray without ceasing.
3. In everything give thanks.
4. Quench not the Spirit.
5. Despise not prophesying.
6. Prove all things.
7. Hold fast that which is good.
8. Abstain from all appearance of evil.
9. Wholly set your life to the Glory of God.
10. He who has called us is faithful to help us do whatever we must.

Thinking on these 10 principles will help you rejoice evermore. Constant communion with the Lord in thanksgiving and praise is the way to joy regardless of circumstances. The Spirit of Holiness and Truth is

quenched when we want to hide our sins instead of
confessing them. Do we despise the preacher who preaches
hell fire and brimstone or confronts us with the desperately
wicked conditions of the human heart? The testimony of
Jesus is the spirit of prophecy. The only way of proving
things should be by testing them with the absolute truth of
the word of God. We must spend time reading and studying
the word of God with the Holy Spirit as our teacher. It is
not the pastor's job to feed us unless we are still a baby
Christian. Do we despise strong meat referred to in
Hebrews 5:8-14? We are called to holiness and to rejoice if
we are counted worthy to suffer for Him.

II Thessalonians 2:1 Now we beseech you, brethren,
by the coming of our Lord Jesus Christ, and [by] our
gathering together unto him,
II Thessalonians 2:2 That ye be not soon shaken in
mind, or be troubled, neither by spirit, nor by word,
nor by letter as from us, as that the day of Christ is
at hand.
II Thessalonians 2:3 Let no man deceive you by any
means: for [that day shall not come], except there
come a falling away first, and that man of sin be
revealed, the son of perdition;
II Thessalonians 2:4 Who opposeth and exalteth
himself above all that is called God, or that is
worshipped; so that he as God sitteth in the temple
of God, shewing himself that he is God.
II Thessalonians 2:5 Remember ye not, that, when I
was yet with you, I told you these things?

Paul gives us some very detailed end time prophecy along with the same type of encouragement and warning that Our Lord gave us in the Olivet Discourse. Don't be troubled by the nearness of the Day of Christ. Rejoice and look up for our blessed hope of the return of King Jesus. Let no man deceive you by any means. Get your information straight from the word of God by the Holy Spirit. Trust no man in regard to the end time events. Is the "falling away" the rapture? The word Paul used for "falling away" is *apostasia*. Apostasia means defection from the truth. It is the root from which we get the word apostasy. Many, perhaps even the majority of the people, in churches today will defect from true faith in Jesus Christ to follow Antichrist. There is more apostasy in the Church today than there ever has been. Have we already witnessed the "falling away?" During great tribulation the love of many will grow cold. Many will depart from the faith and forsake the command of King Jesus to love one another. The identity of Antichrist will be made certain. What makes us certain of the identity of Antichrist? The abomination of desolation, where this powerful world ruler stands in the temple in Jerusalem claiming to be God and demanding worship as God will give certain identity of Antichrist. One should recognize the illogical nature of Paul giving such information to the Church, if the Church were to be raptured prior to the events. Remember the things about which he is telling the Church to be on watch. The positive identity of Antichrist occurs well into the final 7 years of tribulation. The identity of Antichrist will be made certain and many in the Church will defect from faith in Jesus Christ to follow Antichrist.

**II Thessalonians 2:6 And now ye know what
withholdeth that he might be revealed in his time.
II Thessalonians 2:7 For the mystery of iniquity doth
already work: only he who now letteth [will let], until
he be taken out of the way.**

Let or letteth means: to restrain, to limit, to resist, to
withstand, to retain, or to withhold. Who is "he who now
letteth?" Could it be the Church? It is not likely that the
Church, the "Bride of Christ," would be a he. Who is it
that is holding down and limiting the killing and destruction
that Satan wants to do on earth? Do you believe in angels?
The good angels are faithful and totally obedient to God.
They are protecting us and ministering to us by restraining
what the demon evil angels who follow Satan might
otherwise do to us. Do these good ministering angels have a
leader? This great angel who is leading the resistance to the
evil work of demons on earth is most likely the "he who now
letteth."

It could possibly be individual soverign nation governments.
If we have a global or one world government in the New
World Order, there would be no soverign nation opposition
to the world dictator. It was soverign nations such as the
United States and England who restrained and opposed
Hitler's attempt at world dictatorship. The Antichrist of
the New World Order will have no such opposition.

It most certainly could not be the Holy Spirit. It would not be possible for anyone to be able to say "Jesus is Lord" without the Holy Spirit. We should know the great tribulation will be the greatest time for glory and evangelism in the history of the Church. There was once war in heaven when the two thirds of the faithful angels had victory over Satan and his evil angel followers. There is coming another war in heaven in which "he who now letteth" will be called to heaven. When this war in heaven concludes, Satan and his evil angels will be permanently ejected and cast down to earth. God may not send the "he who now letteth" and his angels back to earth.

II Thessalonians 2:8 And then shall that Wicked be revealed, whom the Lord shall consume with the spirit of his mouth, and shall destroy with the brightness of his coming:
II Thessalonians 2:9 [Even him], whose coming is after the working of Satan with all power and signs and lying wonders,
II Thessalonians 2:10 And with all deceivableness of unrighteousness in them that perish; because they received not the love of the truth, that they might be saved.
When the second war in heaven is concluded, Satan and his demon evil angels will be cast out of heaven down to earth. Without the restraining work of the good angels, under the direction of "he who now letteth," it will most certainly be great tribulation on earth. The positive identity of Antichrist will be revealed with certainty. Our Blessed Hope, the return of King Jesus, will be in less than 7 years.

Antichrist will have established the New World Order, of the New Age Movement with all the power, signs, and lying wonders of Satan.

Many church members, who have not received the love of the truth, will defect from the truth of Jesus Christ and follow Antichrist in his war on the saints. Not to worry, we will have the greatest outpouring of Holy Spirit power ever in the history of the Church. All we need is faith and to keep the command of King Jesus to love one another. It will be the most glorious time ever for the Church and you should not want to miss it.

II Thessalonians 2:11 And for this cause God shall send them strong delusion, that they should believe a lie:
II Thessalonians 2:12 That they all might be damned who believed not the truth, but had pleasure in unrighteousness.

Why would anyone want to follow Antichrist? God shall send them strong delusion so that they should believe a lie. What could this strong delusion be, that they may believe a lie? What is the lie? The lie essentially has never changed. It may have a different sugar coating but the lie is still the same: "ye shall be as god." Are you aware that this is the common thread of the New Age Movement and is the gospel preached by the occult and all encounters with extra terrestrials? The lie is the gospel of Antichrist. The core of the lie does not change; but, we must know how to recognize the lie regardless of the deception in which it is cloaked.

The reason is always the same why anyone believes the lie.
They have pleasure in their unrighteousness of pride,
vanity, and licentiousness. They refuse to admit their need
for a savior. They want to do it their own way and will not
submit to the way of God, which is holiness.

II Thessalonians 3:6 Now we command you,
brethren, in the name of our Lord Jesus Christ, that
ye withdraw yourselves from every brother that
walketh disorderly, and not after the tradition which
he received of us.
II Thessalonians 3:7 For yourselves know how ye
ought to follow us: for we behaved not ourselves
disorderly among you;
II Thessalonians 3:8 Neither did we eat any man's
bread for nought; but wrought with labour and
travail night and day, that we might not be
chargeable to any of you:
II Thessalonians 3:9 Not because we have not power,
but to make ourselves an ensample unto you to
follow us.
II Thessalonians 3:10 For even when we were with
you, this we commanded you, that if any would not
work, neither should he eat.
II Thessalonians 3:11 For we hear that there are
some which walk among you disorderly, working
not at all, but are busybodies.
We are commanded, in the name of the Lord, to
disassociate from anyone who calls himself a Christian,
who will not commit himself to the way of holiness and

rejects the discipline of the church. We all sin. We all need to be beam hunters rather than mote hunters. We need to get the beam out of our own eye before we try to help our brother get the mote out of his eye. The church is required to have the discipline of holiness. We are to work. We are to be productive and busy so that we will have something to share with our brother who is in need. We are not to see the nearness of the return of King Jesus as an excuse to just sit and stop working. We are to keep working so that we will have something to share with our brothers in need. "Idleness is the devil's workshop." Paul says that "if any would not work, neither should he eat." If we are busy enough we will not have time to be a busybody, who finds faults with his brother.

II Thessalonians 3:12 Now them that are such we command and exhort by our Lord Jesus Christ, that with quietness they work, and eat their own bread.
II Thessalonians 3:13 But ye, brethren, be not weary in well doing.
II Thessalonians 3:14 And if any man obey not our word by this epistle, note that man, and have no company with him, that he may be ashamed.
II Thessalonians 3:15 Yet count [him] not as an enemy, but admonish [him] as a brother.

While we are to be busy and productively working, we must be careful not to forget the command of King Jesus to love one another. "Be not weary in well doing." Never tire of ministering to the needs of others. Have no company with any member of the church who will not turn away from his

sin. Don't count him an enemy but encourage him to make
the necessary changes in his life so that fellowship may be
restored. Don't compromise the standards of holiness; but,
don't shoot the wounded of the church. There is a balance
and sometimes tough love is required so that the standard
of holiness is not compromised. We will need the full power
and presence of the Holy Spirit to triumph and be more
than conquerors in great tribulation. The requisite for the
fullness of the HolySpirit's presence and power is holiness.
We must love one another; but, our very survival, and
victory, and joy in great tribulation requires that we not
compromise the standard of holiness.

I Timothy 1:5 Now the end of the commandment is
charity out of a pure heart, and [of] a good
conscience, and [of] faith unfeigned:
I Timothy 1:6 From which some having swerved have
turned aside unto vain jangling;
I Timothy 1:7 Desiring to be teachers of the law;
understanding neither what they say, nor whereof
they affirm.
I Timothy 1:8 But we know that the law [is] good, if a
man use it lawfully;
Is this book vain jangling or a wake up call to the church?
The end of the law is love from a pure heart, and faith that
is real, and not just for show. The law is good if it is
properly understood. We are called to holiness because
God wants to bless us. God must separate Himself from sin
because He is a holy God. We must have the Holy Spirit to
survive and be overcomers in great tribulation.

I Timothy 4:1 Now the Spirit speaketh expressly, that in the latter times some shall depart from the faith, giving heed to seducing spirits, and doctrines of devils;

I Timothy 4:2 Speaking lies in hypocrisy; having their conscience seared with a hot iron;

I Timothy 4:3 Forbidding to marry, [and commanding] to abstain from meats, which God hath created to be received with thanksgiving of them which believe and know the truth.

I Timothy 4:4 For every creature of God [is] good, and nothing to be refused, if it be received with thanksgiving:

I Timothy 4:5 For it is sanctified by the word of God and prayer.

I Timothy 4:6 If thou put the brethren in remembrance of these things, thou shalt be a good minister of Jesus Christ, nourished up in the words of faith and of good doctrine, whereunto thou hast attained.

Paul here gives us a perfect description of the New Age Movement. There are many who have already left true faith in Jesus Christ and plugged into the New Age Movement. Many churches are even bringing the New Age Movement into the church. What is the New Age Movement other than the total acceptance of the lie that "ye shall be as god." You get in touch with your "Ascended Master," or your "Spirit Guide," or your "Master of Wisdom," or even your "Visualization of Jesus," whatever you want to call the seducing spirit to whom you give heed. When you contact and pay attention to the guidance of a demon your conscience will be seared with a hot iron. You will no longer even have a conscience. Abstaining from meats, animal rights, and environmental extremism is part of the demon foolishness of the New Age Movement. Everyone does what is right in their own eyes as they are directed by the seducing spirit to whom they give heed.

II Timothy 2:2 And the things that thou hast heard of me among many witnesses, the same commit thou to faithful men, who shall be able to teach others also.
II Timothy 2:3 Thou therefore endure hardness, as a good soldier of Jesus Christ.
II Timothy 2:4 No man that warreth entangleth himself with the affairs of [this] life; that he may please him who hath chosen him to be a soldier.
Have you ever heard your preacher tell you that we are called to endure hardness as good soldiers of Jesus Christ? There will be hardness involved when the spiritual warfare becomes total warfare during the great tribulation. Be of good cheer. We will be more than conquerors, in the mighty power of His Holy Spirit. Be careful not to entangle yourself in the affairs of this life. Set your affection on things above where King Jesus is preparing to come and give all of His soldiers ultimate final victory.

II Timothy 2:10 Therefore I endure all things for the elect's sakes, that they may also obtain the salvation which is in Christ Jesus with eternal glory.
II Timothy 2:11 [It is] a faithful saying: For if we be dead with [him], we shall also live with [him]:

II Timothy 2:12 If we suffer, we shall also reign with [him]: if we deny [him], he also will deny us:
Setting our affection on things above means that we are called to endure tribulation and suffering. It may not be what we want to hear but it is something for which we must be prepared. We need to consider our self centered sin nature to be dead, and to have been raised in the new nature of selfless life in Christ. If we _____ , we shall also reign with Him. None of us likes to hear the word. The missing word is not rapture. It is suffer. If we deny Him, He also will deny us.

II Timothy 3:1 This know also, that in the last days perilous times shall come.
II Timothy 3:2 For men shall be lovers of their own selves, covetous, boasters, proud, blasphemers, disobedient to parents, unthankful, unholy,
II Timothy 3:3 Without natural affection, trucebreakers, false accusers, incontinent, fierce, despisers of those that are good,
II Timothy 3:4 Traitors, heady, highminded, lovers of pleasures more than lovers of God;
II Timothy 3:5 Having a form of godliness, but denying the power thereof: from such turn away.
Does this description fit the condition of the world today? When it fits, we may very well be in the last days. Do many churches have a form of godliness without preaching holiness or the power of the Holy Spirit?

II Timothy 3:12 Yea, and all that will live godly in

Christ Jesus shall suffer persecution.
II Timothy 3:13 But evil men and seducers shall wax
worse and worse, deceiving, and being deceived.
We need to know that all who will live godly in Christ Jesus
shall suffer persecution. Paul, by the inspiration of the Holy
Spirit, tells us not that we might suffer; but, all shall suffer
persecution who will live godly in Christ. It is the holiness
that the world hates and we shall be persecuted for it. This
same holiness is the means of survival and victory in great
tribulation. Without holiness the power of the Holy Spirit
is quenched. We need the fullness of the power and
presence of the Holy Spirit for victory and great joy in
great tribulation. **For the kingdom of God is not meat**
and drink; but, righteousness, and peace and joy in
the Holy Ghost. (Romans 14:7)

II Timothy 4:1 I charge [thee] therefore before God,
and the Lord Jesus Christ, who shall judge the quick
and the dead at his appearing and his kingdom;
II Timothy 4:2 Preach the word; be instant in season,
out of season; reprove, rebuke, exhort with all
longsuffering and doctrine.
II Timothy 4:3 For the time will come when they will
not endure sound doctrine; but after their own lusts
shall they heap to themselves teachers, having
itching ears;
II Timothy 4:4 And they shall turn away [their] ears
from the truth, and shall be turned unto fables.
II Timothy 4:5 But watch thou in all things, endure
afflictions, do the work of an evangelist, make full

proof of thy ministry.

What would happen to the preacher who continually reproved and rebuked his congregation with sound doctrine? Would he not likely be run out of the church. It seems that the time has come when they will not endure sound doctrine. Why is it, that the full gospel, of the call to holiness with the suffering of persecution that follows true holiness, is seldom heard? Everyone wants to be told what they want to hear. The pre tribulation rapture fable, which first surfaced in the mid nineteenth century, is taught as doctrine everywhere. Many who have been in American churches for 50 years have never heard it preached any other way. Many have never bothered to search the scriptures for themselves on these things. Having heard so many good preachers explain these difficult things, who needs to search the scriptures on the subject. If it is heard over and over, and its what one wants to hear, it is settled. No one wants to be instructed to endure to the end. Everyone wants to escape before the great tribulation starts. Truly we have a heap of teachers tickling the ears with the pre tribulation rapture fable. Check out what the scriptures say. We are not likely to hear this truth preached in our church.

REVELATION

This is the New Testament prophetic revelation of Jesus Christ which was given to John for the Church to be able to know of the certain victory which we have in Jesus.

The church is instructed regarding those things which will shortly (true meaning = suddenly) take place.

YOU WILL BE BLESSED IF YOU READ, HEAR, AND KEEP THAT WHICH IS WRITTEN IN THE BOOK OF REVELATION.

Of the 4 possible methods of interpretation the futurist interpretation is the most logical and best approach. The REVELATION is the New Testament book of Prophesy and Revelation of Jesus Christ. To say it has all happened (preterist = past) is nonsense. To say that nothing in the book of REVELATION is real (idealist) is just about as illogical. To say that REVELATION is a continuous history (historical) makes the book very symbolic and difficult to understand. The historical interpretation method brings about many cockeyed identifications of present personalities with those of the REVELATION. In the middle of such persecution as Luther and Wycliffe were in, it is understandable how they could lean toward such a method of interpretation. However, these 3 methods fail to fit the facts. The (futurist) interpretation is the only logical interpretation that is in line with the instruction given in the Scriptures themselves. Starting with chapter 4, and on through chapter 19, are likely still

future and deal with the period just before the Second
Coming of Jesus Christ in Great Power and Glory. Every
generation of the Church and ESPECIALLY OUR
GENERATION must seek to gain such an understanding
of chapters 4 - 19 so as to be able to KNOW WITH
CERTAINTY that we are the generation to witness these
things. Only such an interpretation will motivate us to do
what is necessary to be an overcomer and not capitulate or
be caught in the web of Antichrist.

Revelation 1:19 Write the things which thou hast seen, and the things which are, and the things which shall be hereafter;

This clearly tells us that there will be some past
information but it also tells us quite clearly that it is not all
past information. Most of the information is for the
present and the future. If we want to rightly divide the
word of truth in the book of revelation seek an
understanding which places us as a witness of the things
described in chapters 4 - 19 and pray for the Lord to show
us how we are to live and prepare to live during such
conditions. This is just what Luther and Wycliffe did.
They were thus motivated to be the best they could be for
the Glory of God. How much more reason do we have to
believe that we are the witnesses of the unfolding of
Revelation 4 - 19. We don't want to hear this but we must
test by the Spirit and the Word for ourselves to see if the
pre-tribulation rapture doctrine is not sound doctrine. We
must not play like an ostrich and stick our head in the
sand. We can understand these things. It is unwise to

totally avoid them or not even try to properly understand them.

Revelation 1:3 Blessed [is] he that readeth, and they that hear the words of this prophecy, and keep those things which are written therein: for the time [is] at hand.

Revelation 14:13 And I heard a voice from heaven saying unto me, Write, Blessed [are] the dead which die in the Lord from henceforth: Yea, saith the Spirit, that they may rest from their labours; and their works do follow them.

Revelation 16:15 Behold, I come as a thief. Blessed [is] he that watcheth, and keepeth his garments, lest he walk naked, and they see his shame.

Revelation 19:9 And he saith unto me, Write, Blessed [are] they which are called unto the marriage supper of the Lamb. And he saith unto me, These are the true sayings of God.

Revelation 20:6 Blessed and holy [is] he that hath part in the first resurrection: on such the second death hath no power, but they shall be priests of God and of Christ, and shall reign with him a thousand years.

Revelation 22:7 Behold, I come quickly: blessed [is] he that keepeth the sayings of the prophecy of this book.

Revelation 22:14 Blessed [are] they that do his commandments, that they may have right to the tree of life, and may enter in through the gates into the city.

Learn to let the scriptures interpret themselves. Look at <u>Revelation 1:20 The mystery of the seven stars which thou sawest in my right hand, and the seven golden candlesticks. The seven stars are the angels of the seven churches: and the seven candlesticks which thou sawest are the seven churches.</u> How is that for letting the scriptures interpret themselves? We can easily loose sight of the fact that the Bible is its own best source of insight regarding difficult passages.   Check out the margin references of a good old KJV. Check them out but be aware of possible human error in the margin references of good reference bibles like Ryrie, Scofield, Thompson, and Dake. Tools like Strongs concordance are most helpful. Pray and discuss it with others who have a peaceable and NOT a contentious spirit. The essential doctrines of Christ and the faith which He delivered by the apostles and prophets must not be compromised. To understand the book of Revelation just ask God. We can be absolutely sure on the integrity of His word in James 1:5 that He will give us the wisdom we seek. It is good to seek confirmation and share what we have received with other believers. What is the quality to look for when seeking to find someone to help in understanding Revelation? In a word it is MEEKNESS according to James 3:13.

CHAPTER 2

Here begins the messages to the 7 churches. Why 7? It is God's number because it signifies fullness or completeness. Which of the 7 churches describes your church? One of them will be an accurate description of your church. Pay close attention who is speaking, who is being spoken to, and what is being spoken about.

Jesus is doing the talking, so listen carefully. When He speaks to the angel of the respective church it is a message to the one who has been given authority over the church or the pastor. Is your pastor a good listener? Will your pastor have ears to hear if you tell him which REVELATION church describes your church and what you think needs to be done to make it a better church? There is no such thing as a perfect church because of the imperfect people like me and you who are part of it. Just as we can find the power in Christ to change ourselves for the better so can our church.

EPHESUS - "meaning desirable"
     Here is a church which was working hard for the Lord. It was a church that would not tolerate false teachers. It was a church that knew the truth and tested those who claimed they were sent or inspired by the Lord with the truth of His word. These people knew their Bible. They kept their swords sharp. They would not tolerate liars and hypocrites. This church had lost its first love. They were not on fire to win the lost for Jesus. Some leader in the church was quenching the Spirit. Others were complacent. This DESIRABLE church of Ephesus was being called to remember its first love. It was to fan the flames of the Holy Spirit. It was to evangelize not

socialize. It was to turn away from its desirable path of becoming a Christian social club and be the bold, powerful, witnessing body of Christ. This DESIRABLE church was in danger of being removed. They were a people's church. They hated the deeds of the Nicolaitanes (means = conquerors of the People) who thought there should be two classes of people in the church, clergy and laity or rule by a hierarchy.

SMYRNA - "meaning myrrh"

Jesus knew this church because it was being persecuted by the government. The persecution of the church of Jesus Christ by tyrannical government is to be expected. America's relative freedom from such persecution seems to rapidly be drawing to a close. Myrrh must be crushed to yield its sweet smelling savor. Every crushing blow of a tyrannical government on a church which is faithful and loyal to Jesus Christ produces a sweet smelling savor unto God that never fails to be appreciated and rewarded by God. Such churches are strengthened and become mighty in Holy Spirit power as long as they remain faithful and do not capitulate. They may become poor in worldly wealth but they will be rich in power.

PERGAMOS - "meaning marriage"

The devil and many governments learn that persecuting a true church of Jesus Christ is about as smart as trying to put out a fire by pouring gasoline on it. The smarter tyrannical governments try to "officially charter" the church. They try to protect the church and marry it to the government. The church's power is removed by the spiritual adultery of compromising the evangelical mission of the church. Such words as Pluralism, Ecumenical, Tolerant, are some key buzz words when the true church is being married to the government and not to Jesus Christ. The doctrine of Balaam is that of uniting the church with the world, compromising the standards of the church to bring it into conformity with the world in which it exists. It is a doctrine of lowering standards to become more appealing to a broader group of people. It is a doctrine of excusing and covering sin as opposed to confessing and exposing sin.

THYATIRA - "meaning continual sacrifice"

This church will put on a good show. It may even put on a great pompous show. It is a hotbed of hypocrites. It will bring in any teacher with a flare or pedigree to draw a crowd. It will bring in false teachers to spread false doctrines if they can draw a crowd. It will have few if any standards. It will take no stand. Its discipline could be stated - if it feels good do it. It could also be stated - anything is all right as long as you can keep it quiet and don't get caught. Corruption at the top will be evident to those who know their bible in such a church.

CHAPTER 3

SARDIS - "meaning remnant"

When there is sin it must be rooted out. Doesn't God know that the sin is present? This church has a name, it lives, yet it is dead. Most churches fit this description.

The dead body still has a name but it has no power.
The body of Christ is alive. A true church is the body of
Christ and can never be dead. Yet it will appear to be dead
without the power of the Holy Spirit, without growth, and
without good works. A church dies when the last true
believer leaves it. Yet a church becomes a true church and
body of Christ if it has ANY true born again believers.

No matter how small there is a remnant of true
believers. Jesus commands to be watchful and strengthen
the things that remain that are ready to die. People are
supposed to bloom in the church where they are planted.
When you see things that are not right in your church pray
and work to make them right. This will often involve
confrontation. Most people avoid confrontation because
confrontation requires courage. Most people would rather
backbite or find a new church.

We are not commanded to go to another church. We
are commanded to be watchful and strengthen the things
which remain. We must do all we can to bring revival to
our church. When a church is ready to die it doesn't need
the members to go church shopping. It needs its members
praying for revival and confronting sin. Unite in prayer
with the remnant. Get believers in other churches to join
you in prayer. Grit up your gut and confront sin. Take a
bold stand for righteousness and dare them to run you out
of the church. The church shopper will never know how it
feels to shake the dust from his feet when being run out of a
church.

He that overcometh will not have his name blotted out

from the Lamb's book of Life. Where is the sin in your church? Go beam hunting not mote hunting.

Matthew 7:3-5 And why beholdest thou the mote that is in thy brother's eye, but considerest not the beam that is in thine own eye? Or how wilt thou say to thy brother, Let me pull out the mote out of thine eye; and, behold, a beam [is] in thine own eye? Thou hypocrite, first cast out the beam out of thine own eye; and then shalt thou see clearly to cast out the mote out of thy brother's eye.

PHILADELPHIA - "meaning brotherly love"

There is nothing but good things that can be said about this church. They love one another. This is how all men will know that we are in a true church. To improve your understanding of love memorize 1 Corinthians 13 and meditate on what Jesus did for us at Calvary.

Many say this church description in verse 10 proves a pre-tribulation rapture. Actually it is one of the strongest proofs of the fact that the rapture occurs at the end of the tribulation. The only other place where the exact combination of these words occurs is in John 17:15 - **I pray not that thou shouldest take them out of the world, but that thou shouldest keep them from the evil.** To properly understand Rev 3:10 it should be compared with the only other text where John uses these very specific Greek words. The very careful choice and specific meaning of the words is that we not be taken out but that we be watched over, and guarded, and protected in the middle of the great tribulation.

Now this will help us to see why we must pull all the stops to become a church like the Philadelphia church. One of the main purposes of the tribulation is that the true believers will be shaken and separated from the pretenders. The Philadelphia church was being persecuted by the government as severely as any church. They loved one another in the middle of tremendous persecution. They did not let their love for one another grow cold. They did not allow the pressure of persecution to close the door of evangelism which Christ had opened for them. They kept sound doctrine. They did not quit, or back down, or ease off. They would die rather than to deny Jesus. Because of this they were guarded and kept safe by God in the middle of as great of a persecution as any church ever experienced. No one in this church was raptured, many were killed.

LAODICEA - "meaning the people's rights"

The problem in the Laodicean church was its lukewarmness. They were neither hot nor cold. They were not on fire to win souls for Jesus. Many, perhaps most churches, would be found in this classification. Within the body of Christ, people's rights cause lukewarm attitudes. What are our rights when we become a member of the body of Christ? We have a right to suffer, a right to be persecuted for righteousness, a right to tithe, a right to be humiliated, a right to confess our sins, and a right to be bold to witness for Jesus. Do people take over the church and refuse to let Christ be the Head? There are things that make God angry and there is something that makes Him feel like vomiting. The toughest nuts to crack are the hard shells of the self righteous and the hypocrite.

Isaiah 65:5 - Which say, Stand by thyself, come not near to me; for I am holier than thou. These [are] a smoke in my nose, a fire that burneth all the day. Laodicea was rich in worldly wealth. They did not need anything including the power of the Holy Spirit. They had been so blinded by their self-righteousness and their hypocrisy that they had no idea how spiritually wretched, and miserable, and poor, and blind, and naked they were. When will we stop covering our sins and be honest with God and ourselves? Those who are loved by the Lord are rebuked and chastened. Does this sound contrary to the name it and claim it, health and wealth gospel we have been hearing lately? Is Christ, the Head of your church or is He outside knocking on the door trying to have someone open the door and let Him in?

CHAPTER 4

Have you ever wondered what is going on in heaven? It is tough enough to figure out what is going on here on earth sometimes. Perhaps a trip to heaven will help us have a better perspective. God's throne is the main thing in heaven. **Hebrews 4:14-16 Seeing then that we have a great high priest, that is passed into the heavens, Jesus the Son of God, let us hold fast [our] profession. For we have not an high priest which cannot be touched with the feeling of our infirmities; but was in all points tempted like as [we are, yet]** without sin. Let us therefore come boldly unto the throne of grace, that we may obtain mercy, and find grace to help in time of need. Just as Jesus took John to the throne in heaven, we all can go BOLDLY, with Jesus to God's throne in prayer at any time. WOW! How about that?

When Jesus took John to heaven he saw God's power represented by the thunder and lightening about the throne. John also saw God's mercy represented by the rainbow.

CHAPTER 5

What was that scroll? It was the title deed to the universe. No man could be found worthy to redeem the world which Adam had lost to Satan by his sin in the garden. Only Jesus is worthy.

Revelation 5:11-13 And I beheld, and I heard the voice of many angels round about the throne and the beasts and the elders: and the number of them was ten thousand times ten thousand, and thousands of thousands; Saying with a loud voice, Worthy is the Lamb that was slain to receive power, and riches, and wisdom, and strength, and honour, and glory, and blessing. And every creature which is in heaven, and on the earth, and under the earth, and such as are in the sea, and all that are in them, heard I saying, Blessing, and honour, and glory, and power, [be] unto him that sitteth upon the throne, and unto the Lamb for ever and ever. Yes, He is worthy. Jesus paid it all. We have been redeemed. Glory to God and to the Lamb.

CHAPTER 6

The first seal discloses the white horse and its rider. This is not Jesus who now holds the scroll and will be found on a great white horse later in REVELATION. This white horse rider who is going forth to conquer is the impostor known as Antichrist. He comes in the name of Christ masquerading as Christ. He comes promising a peace. He promises world peace and a false Millennium. He is a great liar. "But when they say peace and safety then sudden destruction comes" and they that shall follow Antichrist shall not escape.

The second seal discloses the red horse with a very powerful weapon. The liar Antichrist who has come to world power on a lying peace platform now plunges the whole world into unprecedented bloodshed. Could the significance of the RED horse be the REDS. All of Russia's most powerful weapons are intact and aimed at the United States. As Russia grows more unstable and more desperate this could possibly be nuclear rapture time for the American Christians and nuclear hell for the other Americans. There is absolutely no difference for the true believer in Christ between the rapture and a strategic nuclear attack - both mean instantly with the Lord.

The black horse third seal of famine always comes on the heels of war. This will be the worst war ever, since the destruction this time is from the great sword of nuclear weapons. The whole world will be starving and rationing its food.

The pale, corpse colored, horse of Death indicates that

one fourth of the world's population will be destroyed by war, famine, and plagues. Hell always follows death for those who are not in Christ. However, Jesus told Martha just before He raised Lazarus, that those who live believing in Him never actually die. They have abundant eternal life because He is the resurrection and the life.

The fifth seal shows that many believers will be slain for the word of God and holding their faith in Jesus. Some say this proves the rapture is before the tribulation but it sounds more like a post tribulation rapture proof text. These saints had been martyred by the rule of Antichrist. They had obviously not been killed by a generation previous to that of the Antichrist's rule. Any previous generation shedding the blood of saints would already be in torment and there would be no cry for God's vengeance. They were told to be patient for a little season until their fellow servants and their brothers (the saints with whom Antichrist was still waging war) should also be killed. Assurance of final victory and of God's vengeance is given to the saints in heaven who had been martyred by Antichrist's war on the saints.

The sixth seal marks a cataclysmic earthquake. Earthquake frequency and amplitude are going off the record books. With such an earthquake, volcanic ash will darken all the skies and allow only the red light spectrum to penetrate this ash cloud causing the moon to turn blood red. The resulting panic and fear will cause many to try to hide in caves and want the rocks of the mountains to fall on them and hide them from the face of God and the wrath of the Lamb.

CHAPTER 7

This chapter gives us additional information about the great tribulation from a salvation perspective. Before any further destruction occurs as a result of God's wrath, angels are sent to seal the saints in their foreheads with the seal of God, not the mark of the beast. There were 144,000 Jewish members of the church who were sealed 12,000 from each of the 12 tribes. After this a great number which no man could number, of all nations, which had come out of great tribulation, were seen before the throne in heaven. They had not taken the mark of the beast and probably had been martyred for the testimony of Jesus. This could possibly indicate a mid-tribulation rapture but before jumping to any conclusions see what else is said about this innumerable bunch of saints.

Obviously people will be saved during the tribulation. That is why the church will go through the tribulation. Whoever is rejecting the gospel and God's grace today will become a victim of the strong delusion spread by Antichrist. Now is the day of salvation. Now is the time to be saved. Now is the time for repentance. Now if ye will hear His voice harden not your hearts. Rejecting the truth of the gospel today makes it almost certain that we will take the mark of the beast and buy the lies of the Antichrist.

CHAPTER 8

When the 7th seal is opened all heaven is silenced for about a half hour. How ominous, from loud resounding praise to sudden silence so intense we can almost feel it. We are now shifting into some heavy and possibly frightening things that we will seldom if ever hear preached in the end times because the churches of the last days will insist on having preachers tell them what they want to hear. Almost everyone will tell us that we don't have to worry about these things because we will be raptured out first. This is just plain wishful thinking and not what the scriptures clearly teach. If there was silence in heaven they were all ready to hear and we too must be ready to hear the truth. No one can ever tell us the day or the hour of the Lord's return. We must know full well all of the horrible judgments of REVELATION so that we can know when we find ourselves in the middle of tribulation that we have less than 7 years to hold. Much more importantly, we must know that there are things coming on this earth which are much worse than death for those who refuse to hear the truth.

If we will not stand to hear the truth of God's wrath and judgment then we will quite likely buy into the great lie and strong delusion being spread by Antichrist. If the coming judgment is such that the angels gasp in horror, how much more should we be alarmed and rush to be cleansed, covered, and protected by the blood of the Lamb? Pre tribulation rapture doctrine will not break through the hard shells of pride, self righteousness and hypocrisy. It is the knowledge of this horrible coming judgment that can break through these and other hard shells and lead to repentance.

<u>Verse 7 - The first angel sounded, and there followed hail and fire mingled with blood, and they</u>

were cast upon the earth: and the third part of trees was burnt up, and all green grass was burnt up.

Verse 8 - And the second angel sounded, and as it were a great mountain burning with fire was cast into the sea: and the third part of the sea became blood;

Verse 11 The third angel sounded - And the name of the star is called Wormwood: and the third part of the waters became wormwood; and many men died of the waters, because they were made bitter.

Verse 12 - And the fourth angel sounded, and the third part of the sun was smitten, and the third part of the moon, and the third part of the stars; so as the third part of them was darkened, and the day shone not for a third part of it, and the night likewise.

Verse 13 - And I beheld, and heard an angel flying through the midst of heaven, saying with a loud voice, Woe, woe, woe, to the inhabiters of the earth by reason of the other voices of the trumpet of the three angels, which are yet to sound!

It is very easy to see why these verses are not to be heard coming from the pulpit unless accompanied by a pre-tribulation rapture viewpoint. Otherwise it would literally scare the hell out of us. Could it possibly be that is why John wrote it? And woe, woe, woe, there are 3 angels still to sound.

CHAPTER 9
Revelation 9:4 And it was commanded them that

<u>they should not hurt the grass of the earth, neither any green thing, neither any tree; but only those men which have not the seal of God in their foreheads.</u> What is this seal of God? Could it be the mind of Christ as opposed to having bought into the Antichrist system that required the mark of the beast on the forehead or right wrist? What do you think?

<u>Revelation 9:5 And to them it was given that they should not kill them, but that they should be tormented five months: and their torment [was] as the torment of a scorpion, when he striketh a man. Revelation 9:6 And in those days shall men seek death, and shall not find it; and shall desire to die, and death shall flee from them.</u> If we are ever tempted to take the scanner symbol mark of the beast so that we will be able to buy or sell, we must think of this. The people who take the mark of the beast will not be protected from this plague which will cause people to be in such torment that they will try to commit suicide but the people with this plague will not be able to die.

<u>Revelation 9:16 And the number of the army of the horsemen [were] two hundred thousand thousand: and I heard the number of them.</u> The kings of the east will go on the march across the Euphrates. This is Red China. The time must be at hand. Today China boasts of the size of their standing army to be 200,000,000 men. This is the exact number that John heard. There were not 200,000,000 people on the planet when John wrote this! It is high time to get hold of a solid understanding of the book of Revelation.

Revelation 9:20 And the rest of the men which
were not killed by these plagues yet repented not of
the works of their hands, that they should not
worship devils, and idols of gold, and silver, and
brass, and stone, and of wood: which neither can
see, nor hear, nor walk:
Revelation 9:21 Neither repented they of their
murders, nor of their sorceries, nor of their
fornication, nor of their thefts. Here we see both the
infinite mercy of God and the blindness of men who rebel
against God. These judgments just keep coming in ever
increasing waves. The waves of judgment are call after call
to repentance. Just like Pharaoh they all harden their
hearts. It is also interesting to note the Greek word
translated sorceries is pharmakia or drugs.

CHAPTER 10

Revelation 10:6-7 And sware by him that liveth
for ever and ever, who created heaven, and the
things that therein are, and the earth, and the things
that therein are, and the sea, and the things which
are therein, that there should be time no longer: But
in the days of the voice of the seventh angel, when
he shall begin to sound, the mystery of God should
be finished, as he hath declared to his servants the
prophets.
This is very important because Paul in 1 Thessalonians
4, 1 Corinthians 15 and also the Lord Himself in Matthew
24, and Luke 21, and Mark 13 uses this LAST TRUMPET

angel sounding to give an absolute answer to whether the
rapture is pre-tribulation, mid tribulation, or
post-tribulation. When this LAST TRUMPET sounds is the
sign of the end of the age when time to repent, and time
itself will be no more. It marks the end of the age of Grace
and brings in the Millennial Kingdom of Jesus Christ. It
marks when the mystery of God should be finished. The
mystery of the ages is Christ in you the hope of glory.

I Corinthians 15:51-52 Behold, I shew you a
mystery; We shall not all sleep, but we shall all be
changed, In a moment, in the twinkling of an eye, at
the last trump: for the trumpet shall sound, and the
dead shall be raised incorruptible, and we shall be
changed.

At the LAST TRUMP we shall all be changed in a moment
and be raptured.

I Thessalonians 4:16-18 For the Lord himself shall
descend from heaven with a shout, with the voice of
the archangel, and with the trump of God: and the
dead in Christ shall rise first: Then we which are
alive [and] remain shall be caught up together with
them in the clouds, to meet the Lord in the air: and
so shall we ever be with the Lord. Wherefore
comfort one another with these words.

In the Olivette discourse the disciples asked Jesus what
would be the sign of His coming and of the end of the age.
The following words of Jesus give the timing of the rapture,
Matthew 24:30-31 also see Luke 21:25-28 and Mark
13:24-27. Even if we believe that it is scary, we must be
encouraged to prepare for tribulation. We loose nothing by

being prepared. Praise God if we are raptured out before the tribulation; but, the wise servant will be prepared, and be watching, and be looking up knowing that our blessed hope of the Lord's return in great power and glory is drawing near.

Matthew 24:30-31 And then shall appear the sign of the Son of man in heaven: and then shall all the tribes of the earth mourn, and they shall see the Son of man coming in the clouds of heaven with power and great glory. And he shall send his angels with a great sound of a trumpet, and they shall gather together his elect from the four winds, from one end of heaven to the other.

Mark 13:24-27 But in those days, after that tribulation, the sun shall be darkened, and the moon shall not give her light, And the stars of heaven shall fall, and the powers that are in heaven shall be shaken. And then shall they see the Son of man coming in the clouds with great power and glory. And then shall he send his angels, and shall gather together his elect from the four winds, from the uttermost part of the earth to the uttermost part of heaven.

Luke 21:25-28 And there shall be signs in the sun, and in the moon, and in the stars; and upon the earth distress of nations, with perplexity; the sea and the waves roaring; Men's hearts failing them for fear, and for looking after those things which are coming on the earth: for the powers of heaven shall be shaken. And then shall they see the Son of man coming in a cloud with power and great glory. And when these things begin to come to pass, then look up, and lift up your heads; for your redemption draweth nigh.

Look carefully at all 3 accounts of the complete Olivet discourse. You will see that the Lord's description of the end time scenario is exactly the same as the scenario of the seven trumpets.

CHAPTER 11

Revelation 11:3 And I will give [power] unto my two witnesses, and they shall prophesy a thousand two hundred [and] threescore days, clothed in sackcloth.
Revelation 11:5 And if any man will hurt them, fire proceedeth out of their mouth, and devoureth their enemies: and if any man will hurt them, he must in this manner be killed.
Revelation 11:6 These have power to shut heaven, that it rain not in the days of their prophecy: and have power over waters to turn them to blood, and to smite the earth with all plagues, as often as they will.
Revelation 11:7 And when they shall have finished their testimony, the beast that ascendeth out of the bottomless pit shall make war against them, and shall overcome them, and kill them.
Revelation 11:8 And their dead bodies [shall lie] in the street of the great city, which spiritually is called Sodom and Egypt, where also our Lord was crucified.
Revelation 11:9 And they of the people and kindreds

and tongues and nations shall see their dead bodies three days and an half, and shall not suffer their dead bodies to be put in graves.

Revelation 11:10 And they that dwell upon the earth shall rejoice over them, and make merry, and shall send gifts one to another; because these two prophets tormented them that dwelt on the earth.

Revelation 11:11 And after three days and an half the Spirit of life from God entered into them, and they stood upon their feet; and great fear fell upon them which saw them.

Revelation 11:12 And they heard a great voice from heaven saying unto them, Come up hither. And they ascended up to heaven in a cloud; and their enemies beheld them.

Revelation 11:13 And the same hour was there a great earthquake, and the tenth part of the city fell, and in the earthquake were slain of men seven thousand: and the remnant were affrighted, and gave glory to the God of heaven.

Revelation 11:14 The second woe is past; [and], behold, the third woe cometh quickly.

Revelation 11:15 And the seventh angel sounded; and there were great voices in heaven, saying, The kingdoms of this world are become [the kingdoms] of our Lord, and of his Christ; and he shall reign for ever and ever.

Many have speculated about who these 2 witness are. Since it is appointed unto all men once to die and there are only 2 men mentioned in scripture who did not die they may

be Enoch and Elijah. Since Elijah was doing this same sort
of work before God took him up in the fiery chariot we can
be fairly certain of him. Many say this proves a mid
tribulation rapture but since the tribulation begins so
gradually their ministry may not start until the middle of
the tribulation. The tribulation may have already begun
and we would not be certain of it until these 2 prophets
begin their ministry. The comforting thing is that we would
only have 3.5 years to hold on when these two mighty
prophets BEGIN their ministry. We will be raptured at the
END of their ministry. When you see these things come to
pass look up for your redemption draweth nigh.

Revelation 11:19 And the temple of God was
opened in heaven, and there was seen in his temple
the ark of his testament: and there were lightnings,
and voices, and thunderings, and an earthquake,
and great hail.   What kind of temple will the people in
Jerusalem build without the ark of the covenant? Contrary
to what Indiana Jones may think the last true report of the
ark's location is in heaven.

CHAPTER 12

Revelation 12:1-6 And there appeared a great
wonder in heaven; a woman clothed with the sun,
and the moon under her feet, and upon her head a
crown of twelve stars: And she being with child
cried, travailing in birth, and pained to be delivered.
And there appeared another wonder in heaven; and

behold a great red dragon, having seven heads and ten horns, and seven crowns upon his heads. And his tail drew the third part of the stars of heaven, and did cast them to the earth: and the dragon stood before the woman which was ready to be delivered, for to devour her child as soon as it was born. And she brought forth a man child, who was to rule all nations with a rod of iron: and her child was caught up unto God, and [to] his throne. And the woman fled into the wilderness, where she hath a place prepared of God, that they should feed her there a thousand two hundred [and] threescore days.

Up in heaven John is not bound by time and space and it may be easier to perhaps think of someone showing him a video tape which makes him wonder. There are wide varieties of possible interpretation here. Consider the following possibility. Israel is the leading lady in this video. She is seen clothed with the brightness of the sun and having a 12 star crown representing the 12 tribes of Israel. Jesus is the great manchild of Israel, far greater than Moses or any of the patriarchs. He will rule all nations with a rod of iron. Then Satan is seen as the great red dragon who seeks to destroy Israel. His last chance to make any word of God be found untrue is to destroy the nation if Israel. Israel is being protected by God and to some extent God has been using the United States with its 5.5 million Jews (almost half of the total) to frustrate his destruction of Israel. God gives Satan unrestrained control of the earth under the Antichrist symbolized by the 7 (meaning = complete or full) heads and crowns. Antichrist may divide the earth into 10 regions but he will have full power and control.   Satan tried to destroy the Great Manchild of Israel when he had Herod kill all male babies less than 2 years old.

Revelation 12:7-10 And there was war in heaven: Michael and his angels fought against the dragon; and the dragon fought and his angels, And prevailed not; neither was their place found any more in heaven. And the great dragon was cast out, that old serpent, called the Devil, and Satan, which deceiveth the whole world: he was cast out into the earth, and his angels were cast out with him. And I heard a loud voice saying in heaven, Now is come salvation, and strength, and the kingdom of our God, and the power of his Christ: for the accuser of our brethren is cast down, which accused them before our God day and night.

Satan is finally kicked out of heaven for good. Lucifer and all of his demons are cast out of heaven and down to earth.

Revelation 12:13-17 And when the dragon saw that he was cast unto the earth, he persecuted the woman which brought forth the man [child]. And to the woman were given two wings of a great eagle, that she might fly into the wilderness, into her place, where she is nourished for a time, and times, and half a time, from the face of the serpent. And the serpent cast out of his mouth water as a flood after the woman, that he might cause her to be carried away of the flood.

And the earth helped the woman, and the earth

opened her mouth, and swallowed up the flood
which the dragon cast out of his mouth.
And the dragon was wroth with the woman, and went
to make war with the remnant of her seed, which
keep the commandments of God, and have the
testimony of Jesus Christ.
If the world thought they saw anti Semitism under Hitler
the persecution of the Jews under Antichrist will be no
comparison. This is some of the best pre tribulation rapture
text that there is. Here all the action centers around Israel
and the church is conspicuously absent from this heavenly
video. The main message is still that anyone who does not
love the Jews is anti Christ and anti God. We should be
cautioned about being over dogmatic about the
interpretation of such a heavenly video.

CHAPTER 13

SOME THINGS IN THIS CHAPTER WILL BE
DOGMATIC.
   Revelation 13:3 And I saw one of his heads as it
were wounded to death; and his deadly wound was
healed: and all the world wondered after the beast.
The beast is the Antichrist. He will recover from a wound
that appears to be deadly. He thus counterfeits the
resurrection of Christ and the world is captivated by him.

   Revelation 13:4 And they worshipped the dragon
which gave power unto the beast: and they
worshipped the beast, saying, Who [is] like unto the

beast? who is able to make war with him?   Those at
the highest echelons of the New Age Movement, and New
World Order are openly worshipping Lucifer but the
majority are just caught up in the Antichrist web with its
many tentacles and facets.

Revelation 13:5 - 6 And there was given unto him
a mouth speaking great things and blasphemies; and
power was given unto him to continue forty [and] two
months. And he opened his mouth in blasphemy
against God, to blaspheme his name, and his
tabernacle, and them that dwell in heaven. Antichrist
will have absolute power for 3 and 1/2 years. The great
tribulation will start so gradually it will take him 3 and 1/2
years to come to full power. This juggernaut of Antichrist
may be building momentum now. The U.S. attorney general
has said that anyone who believes that the bible is literally
true is a cultist. We only have to look to Waco to see how
cultists may expect to see justice.

Expect to hear much more outrageous blasphemies
than the new cultist definition in the days to come. The
coming world order will be a world of Antichrist lovers and
God haters.

Revelation 13:7 And it was given unto him to
make war with the saints, and to overcome them: and
power was given him over all kindreds, and tongues,
and nations. This is a strong verse relating to the timing
of the rapture. Who can explain how Antichrist could wage
war on a raptured saint? It would be illogical and God's
word may be beyond our logic but it is never illogical. The
only possibility is that the rapture occurs at the end of the

tribulation.

Revelation 13:8-9 And all that dwell upon the earth shall worship him, whose names are not written in the book of life of the Lamb slain from the foundation of the world. If any man have an ear, let him hear. If God has given us ears, we are to hear this. The purpose of the tribulation is a shakedown for marginal believers. We will make a final decision to either serve God or the Antichrist. The tribulation will shake everyone off the fence for or against Christ.

Revelation 13:10 He that leadeth into captivity shall go into captivity: he that killeth with the sword must be killed with the sword. Here is the patience and the faith of the saints. The weapons of our warfare are not carnal but mighty to the pulling down of strongholds. The tribulation will require us to live by faith. Now it is rather optional. Many can sort of fake it with their faith for their good standing in the local congregation. The tribulation will eliminate wavering one way or another. Revelation 13:11-15 And I beheld another beast coming up out of the earth; and he had two horns like a lamb, and he spake as a dragon.
 And he exerciseth all the power of the first beast before him, and causeth the earth and them which dwell therein to worship the first beast, whose deadly wound was healed. And he doeth great wonders, so that he maketh fire come down from heaven on the earth in the sight of men, And deceiveth them that dwell on the earth by [the means of] those miracles which he had power to do in the

sight of the beast; saying to them that dwell on the earth, that they should make an image to the beast, which had the wound by a sword, and did live. And he had power to give life unto the image of the beast, that the image of the beast should both speak, and cause that as many as would not worship the image of the beast should be killed.

The Antichrist will have his false prophet.

Revelation 13:16 -18 And he causeth all, both small and great, rich and poor, free and bond, to receive a mark in their right hand, or in their foreheads: And that no man might buy or sell, save he that had the mark, or the name of the beast, or the number of his name.

Here is wisdom. Let him that hath understanding count the number of the beast: for it is the number of a man; and his number [is] Six hundred threescore [and] six. It is time to be dogmatic. Everybody must wise up that WE WILL BE FORCED BY THE GOVERNMENT OF ANTICHRIST TO TAKE THAT LITTLE 666 SCANNER MARK THAT IS ALREADY ON ALMOST EVERYTHING WE BUY OR SELL, EITHER IN THE RIGHT WRIST OR FOREHEAD. BOTH THE *UPC* AND *SKU* SYMBOLS ARE BASED ON 666. Even if it means starving to death DON'T DO IT. No matter what - DON'T DO IT. Call it blaspheming the Holy Spirit, whatever - JUST DON'T DO IT.

CHAPTER 14

Revelation 14:7-13 Saying with a loud voice, Fear God, and give glory to him; for the hour of his judgment is come: and worship him that made heaven, and earth, and the sea, and the fountains of waters. And there followed another angel, saying, Babylon is fallen, is fallen, that great city, because she made all nations drink of the wine of the wrath of her fornication. And the third angel followed them, saying with a loud voice, If any man worship the beast and his image, and receive [his] mark in his forehead, or in his hand, The same shall drink of the wine of the wrath of God, which is poured out without mixture into the cup of his indignation; and he shall be tormented with fire and brimstone in the presence of the holy angels, and in the presence of the Lamb: And the smoke of their torment ascendeth up for ever and ever: and they have no rest day nor night, who worship the beast and his image, and whosoever receiveth the mark of his name. Here is the patience of the saints: here [are] they that keep the commandments of God, and the faith of Jesus. And I heard a voice from heaven saying unto me, Write, Blessed [are] the dead which die in the Lord from henceforth: Yea, saith the Spirit, that they may rest from their labours; and their works do follow them.

THIS IS WHY IT IS SO VITAL NOT TO TAKE THE LITTLE 666 SCANNER MARK OF THE BEAST IN THE

RIGHT WRIST OR FOREHEAD. The sins and
destruction of Babylon are introduced, but much more
detail is given later. THE MAIN THING TO KNOW
HERE IS WHAT IT MEANS FOR OUR ETERNAL
DESTINY IF WE TAKE THE MARK.

CHAPTER 15

Revelation 15:1-4 And I saw another sign in
heaven, great and marvelous, seven angels having
the seven last plagues; for in them is filled up the
wrath of God. And I saw as it were a sea of glass
mingled with fire: and them that had gotten the
victory over the beast, and over his image, and over
his mark, [and] over the number of his name, stand
on the sea of glass, having the harps of God. And
they sing the song of Moses the servant of God, and
the song of the Lamb, saying, Great and marvelous
[are] thy works, Lord God Almighty; just and true
[are] thy ways, thou King of saints. Who shall not
fear thee, O Lord, and glorify thy name? for [thou]
only [art] holy: for all nations shall come and worship
before thee; for thy judgments are made manifest.
We know the bad news if we take the mark of the beast.
This is the good news for those who resist the mark.

Revelation 15:8 And the temple was filled with smoke
from the glory of God, and from his power; and no
man was able to enter into the temple, till the seven
plagues of the seven angels were fulfilled.

CHAPTER 16

Revelation 16:1-7 And I heard a great voice out of the temple saying to the seven angels, Go your ways, and pour out the vials of the wrath of God upon the earth. And the first went, and poured out his vial upon the earth; and there fell a noisome and grievous sore upon the men which had the mark of the beast, and [upon] them which worshipped his image. And the second angel poured out his vial upon the sea; and it became as the blood of a dead [man]; and every living soul died in the sea. And the third angel poured out his vial upon the rivers and fountains of waters; and they became blood.
And I heard the angel of the waters say, Thou art righteous, O Lord, which art, and wast, and shalt be, because thou hast judged thus.
For they have shed the blood of saints and prophets, and thou hast given them blood to drink; for they are worthy. And I heard another out of the altar say, Even so, Lord God Almighty, true and righteous [are] thy judgments.

When the first angel poured out his vial that there fell a noisome and grievous sore upon them that worshipped the beast and his image. If all of the saints had been raptured John likely would have said the first angel poured out his vial on all men and all men received a noisome and grievous sore. Since all men who were not written in the lamb's book of life will be caused to receive the mark, we have another indication the rapture occurs at the end. Things are really getting bloody. Antichrist's war on the saints who refuse to receive the mark must be very bloody. It is likely antichrist will entertain his followers with the bloodshed of the saints much like Rome's gladiators, and Waco's cultists. Never forget that vengeance is God's business. God's judgments, and only God's judgments, are always true and righteous.

Revelation 16:8-9 The fourth angel poured out his vial upon the sun; and power was given unto him to scorch men with fire. And men were scorched with great heat, and blasphemed the name of God, which hath power over these plagues: and they repented not to give him glory.

They would not repent. Could it be that they still could be forgiven if they would repent?

Revelation 16:10 -11 And the fifth angel poured out his vial upon the seat of the beast; and his kingdom was full of darkness; and they gnawed their tongues for pain, And blasphemed the God of heaven because of their pains and their sores, and repented not of their deeds.

The only possible true hope they have is repentance and they blaspheme God. That is what happens when we think we are a god. This will be what happens to the gods of the new age and new world order.

Revelation 16:12 And the sixth angel poured out his vial upon the great river Euphrates; and the water thereof was dried up, that the way of the kings of the east might be prepared.

We have seen this before how the kings of the east will be able to march across a dry Euphrates on their way to the battle of Armageddon. The book of revelation has different perspectives and further details of the total judgement of the rebellion of men who follow Lucifer in disobedience to God. That is why the timing sequence of some things gets confusing as there are apparent shifts forward and backward to give a more detailed picture.

Revelation 16:13-16 And I saw three unclean spirits like frogs [come] out of the mouth of the dragon, and out of the mouth of the beast, and out of the mouth of the false prophet. For they are the spirits of devils, working miracles, [which] go forth unto the kings of the earth and of the whole world, to gather them to the battle of that great day of God Almighty. Behold, I come as a thief. Blessed [is] he that watcheth, and keepeth his garments, lest he walk naked, and they see his shame. And he gathered them together into a place called in the Hebrew tongue Armageddon.

Lucifer and his Antichrist and false prophet are leading rebellious men in rebellion against God. It would seem obvious that when one attempts to lead a world of rebels in rebellion sooner or later they would rebel against you. This is why we need to respect and be under God's authority structures.

Revelation 16:17-21 show different views of things that we have seen before in revelation or will soon see again in a much more detailed way. We hear again of the great earthquake, Babylon, and it will seem like the stars of heaven are falling when the 100 pound hail stones are falling. The only chance is repentance and instead they blaspheme.

CHAPTERS 17

Let's just look at the verses in which the angel gives explanation about Babylon. The information about Antichrist will be grouped together in Chapter 18. **BABYLON THE GREAT, THE MOTHER OF HARLOTS AND ABOMINATIONS OF THE EARTH. The woman was drunken with the blood of the saints, and with the blood of the martyrs of Jesus. I will tell thee the mystery of the woman, and of the beast that carrieth her, which hath the seven heads and ten horns.** Antichrist will bring MYSTERY BABYLON to power. Antichrist himself will have come to power by his counterfeit resurrection.

And here [is] the mind which hath wisdom. The seven heads are seven mountains, on which the woman sitteth. (Some may have heard of the 7 hills of Rome.)

Where the whore sitteth, are peoples, and multitudes, and nations, and tongues. And the ten horns which thou sawest upon the beast, these shall hate the whore, and shall make her desolate and naked, and shall eat her flesh, and burn her with fire. For God hath put in their hearts to fulfil his will, and to agree, and give their kingdom unto the beast, until

the words of God shall be fulfilled.

Mystery Babylon, the woman which thou sawest, is that great city, which reigneth over the kings of the earth. Babylon means tyranny and confusion. Since the scriptures themselves say this whore is MYSTERY Babylon we should be careful not to be too dogmatic. Whoredom or adultery is to depart from the true God and worship Lucifer or any other false god. What is the great city that rules over the kings of the earth?

And I heard another voice from heaven, saying, Come out of her, my people, that ye be not partakers of her sins, and that ye receive not of her plagues. For her sins have reached unto heaven, and God hath remembered her iniquities.

If there is apostasy preached, shout it down; and, if not corrected, shake the dust off your feet. Get out of any church that denies essential doctrines of Christ. In this first section MYSTERY BABYLON sounds like an apostate religion. In the destruction section it sounds more like a nation. Israel and America are the only 2 nations founded for the glory of God. When Israel played the whore and as a nation turned to false gods, then God had other nations destroy them. This following section could very well be referring to how America has turned to follow Lucifer and antichrist. Does this describe how America will be judged as Russia launches a first strike nuclear destruction of America?

The great angel cried mightily with a strong voice, saying, Babylon the great is fallen, is fallen, and is become the habitation of devils, and the hold of every foul spirit, and a cage of every unclean and hateful bird. For all nations have drunk of the wine of the wrath of her fornication, and the kings of the earth have committed fornication with her, and the merchants of the earth are waxed rich through the abundance of her delicacies.

Reward her even as she rewarded you, and double unto her double according to her works: in the cup which she hath filled fill to her double. How much she hath glorified herself, and lived deliciously, so much torment and sorrow give her: for she saith in her heart, I sit a queen, and am no widow, and shall see no sorrow.

Therefore shall her plagues come in one day, death, and mourning, and famine; and she shall be utterly burned with fire: for strong [is] the Lord God who judgeth her. And the kings of the earth, who have committed fornication and lived deliciously with her, shall bewail her, and lament for her, when they shall see the smoke of her burning, Standing afar off for the fear of her torment, saying, Alas, alas that great city Babylon, that mighty city! for in one hour is thy judgment come. And the merchants of the earth shall weep and mourn over her; for no man buyeth their merchandise any more:

The merchandise of gold, and silver, and precious stones, and of pearls, and fine linen, and purple, and silk, and scarlet, and all thyine wood, and all manner vessels of ivory, and all manner vessels of most precious wood, and of brass, and iron, and marble,

And cinnamon, and odours, and ointments, and frankincense, and wine, and oil, and fine flour, and wheat, and beasts, and sheep, and horses, and chariots, and slaves, and souls of men.

And the fruits that thy soul lusted after are departed from thee, and all things which were dainty and goodly are departed from thee, and thou shalt find them no more at all. The merchants of these things, which were made rich by her, shall stand afar off for the fear of her torment, weeping and wailing, And saying, Alas, alas, that great city, that was clothed in fine linen, and purple, and scarlet, and decked with gold, and precious stones, and pearls! For in one hour so great riches is come to nought. And every shipmaster, and all the company in ships, and sailors, and as many as trade by sea, stood afar off, And cried when they saw the smoke of her burning, saying, What [city is] like unto this great city! And they cast dust on their heads, and cried, weeping and wailing, saying, Alas, alas, that great city, wherein were made rich all that had ships in the sea by reason of her costliness! for in one hour is she made desolate.

Rejoice over her, [thou] heaven, and [ye] holy apostles and prophets; for God hath avenged you on her. And a mighty angel took up a stone like a great millstone, and cast [it] into the sea, saying, Thus with violence shall that great city Babylon be thrown down, and shall be found no more at all. And the voice of harpers, and musicians, and of pipers, and

trumpeters, shall be heard no more at all in thee; and
no craftsman, of whatsoever craft [he be], shall be
found any more in thee; and the sound of a millstone
shall be heard no more at all in thee; And the light of
a candle shall shine no more at all in thee; and the
voice of the bridegroom and of the bride shall be
heard no more at all in thee: for thy merchants were
the great men of the earth; for by thy sorceries were
all nations deceived.

And in her was found the blood of prophets, and
of saints, and of all that were slain upon the earth.
For true and righteous [are] his judgments: for he
hath judged the great whore, which did corrupt the
earth with her fornication, and hath avenged the
blood of his servants at her hand. And again they
said, Alleluia. And her smoke rose up for ever and
ever.

CHAPTER 18

Antichrist will come to full power by his counterfeit
resurrection. The beast that thou sawest was, and is
not; and shall ascend out of the bottomless pit, and
go into perdition: and they that dwell on the earth
shall wonder, whose names were not written in the
book of life from the foundation of the world, when
they behold the beast that was, and is not, and yet is.

The Antichrist counterfeits Christ's resurrection. The
frozen body of Lenin is a great tourist attraction in Moscow.
Think of frozen Lenin. People could possibly be led to

follow a demon possessed lookalike if the necessary physical records were replaced and the frozen corpse cremated. The same could be done with a Hitler lookalike. There will be a counterfeit resurrection of some sort. This is just a suggestion of the type of Luciferian delusion and deception that could possibly be used. It will get the masses, who do not know the Scriptures relating to the counterfeit resurrection of antichrist, in lockstep following antichrist. **And the beast that was, and is not, even he is the eighth, and is of the seven, and goeth into perdition.**

It sounds like the antichrist may divide his new world order into ten regions since **the ten horns which thou sawest are ten kings, which have received no kingdom as yet; but receive power as kings one hour with the beast. These have one mind, and shall give their power and strength unto the beast. These shall make war with the Lamb, and the Lamb shall overcome them: for he is Lord of lords, and King of kings: and they that are with him [are] called, and chosen, and faithful.**

CHAPTER 19

Revelation 19:4-9 And the four and twenty elders and the four beasts fell down and worshipped God that sat on the throne, saying, Amen; Alleluia. And a voice came out of the throne, saying, Praise our God, all ye his servants, and ye that fear him, both small and great. And I heard as it were the voice of a great

multitude, and as the voice of many waters, and as the voice of mighty thunderings, saying, Alleluia: for the Lord God omnipotent reigneth. Let us be glad and rejoice, and give honour to him: for the marriage of the Lamb is come, and his wife hath made herself ready. And to her was granted that she should be arrayed in fine linen, clean and white: for the fine linen is the righteousness of saints. And he saith unto me, Write, Blessed [are] they which are called unto the marriage supper of the Lamb. And he saith unto me, These are the true sayings of God.

This is a celebration that we should not miss.

Revelation 19:10 And I fell at his feet to worship him. And he said unto me, See [thou do it] not: I am thy fellowservant, and of thy brethren that have the testimony of Jesus: worship God: for the testimony of Jesus is the spirit of prophecy.

The testimony of Jesus is the spirit of prophecy.

Revelation 19:11- 21 And I saw heaven opened, and behold a white horse; and he that sat upon him [was] called Faithful and True, and in righteousness he doth judge and make war. His eyes [were] as a flame of fire, and on his head [were] many crowns; and he had a name written, that no man knew, but he himself.   And he [was] clothed with a vesture dipped in blood: and his name is called The Word of God. And the armies [which were] in heaven followed him upon white horses, clothed in fine linen, white and clean. And out of his mouth goeth a sharp sword, that with it he should smite the nations: and he shall rule them with a rod of iron: and he treadeth the winepress of the fierceness and wrath of Almighty God. And he hath on [his] vesture and on his thigh a name written, KING OF KINGS, AND LORD OF LORDS. And I saw an angel standing in the sun; and he cried with a loud voice, saying to all the fowls that fly in the midst of heaven, Come and gather yourselves together unto the supper of the great God; That ye may eat the flesh of kings, and the flesh of captains, and the flesh of mighty men, and the flesh of horses, and of them that sit on them, and the flesh of all [men, both] free and bond, both small and great. And I saw the beast, and the kings of the earth, and their armies, gathered together to make war against him that sat on the horse, and against his army. And the beast was taken, and with him the false prophet that wrought miracles before him, with which he deceived them that had received the mark of the beast, and them that worshipped his image. These both were cast alive into a lake of fire burning with brimstone. And the remnant were slain with the sword of him that sat upon the horse, which [sword] proceeded out of his mouth: and all the fowls were filled with their flesh.

Many have thought that because the description of the Marriage supper of the Lamb occurs in chapter 19 before the description of the Lord on His white horse returning in great power and glory is a proof that the rapture occurs before the tribulation. By now we have seen how by God's design and plan there are many shifts back and forth in time within a given chapter. This is not a very strong proof of the rapture occurring before the Lord's return. Even in the above passage we see the Lord's glorious return before the assembling of the armies of antichrist. We need to prepare to be overcommers in tribulation by strengthening our faith now and praise God if we are raptured out first. The good news is that we may have eternal abundant life here and now in Jesus. Most importantly, He will be with us in the presence of the Holy Spirit.

CHAPTER 20

Revelation 20:1-3 And I saw an angel come down from heaven, having the key of the bottomless pit and a great chain in his hand.
And he laid hold on the dragon, that old serpent, which is the Devil, and Satan, and bound him a thousand years, And cast him into the bottomless pit, and shut him up, and set a seal upon him, that he should deceive the nations no more, till the thousand years should be fulfilled: and after that he must be loosed a little season. If we stay strong with Jesus we win with Him. The ultimate final victory in Jesus is as certain as the integrity of God's word. As we have seen, Satan and his Antichrist will wage a bloody war on the saints; but there remains certain victory in Jesus.
Revelation 20:4-7 And I saw thrones, and they sat upon them, and judgment was given unto them:

and [I saw] the souls of them that were beheaded for the witness of Jesus, and for the word of God, and which had not worshipped the beast, neither his image, neither had received [his] mark upon their foreheads, or in their hands; and they lived and reigned with Christ a thousand years. But the rest of the dead lived not again until the thousand years were finished. This [is] the first resurrection. Blessed and holy [is] he that hath part in the first resurrection: on such the second death hath no power, but they shall be priests of God and of Christ, and shall reign with him a thousand years. It is not at all pleasant to think that we may well have our head chopped off if we refuse to follow the Antichrist and deny the Lord Jesus Christ. Remember what Jesus told Martha just before He raised Lazarus - John 11:25-26 Jesus said unto her, I am the resurrection, and the life: he that believeth in me, though he were dead, yet shall he live: And whosoever liveth and believeth in me shall never die. Believest thou this?

 DO YOU BELIEVE? If we do believe this we probably won't even feel the blade of the ax or guillotine and it will be instantly with the Lord. No matter what - DON'T TAKE THE MARK & DON'T DENY JESUS.

Revelation 20:7-10 And when the thousand years are expired, Satan shall be loosed out of his prison, And they went up on the breadth of the earth, and compassed the camp of the saints about, and the beloved city: and fire came down from God out of

heaven, and devoured them. And the devil that
deceived them was cast into the lake of fire and
brimstone, where the beast and the false prophet
[are], and shall be tormented day and night for ever
and ever. Perhaps there will be those either born during
the Millennium or coming through the tribulation who have
not been thoroughly tested. Whatever may be God's reason,
at the end of the Millennium, Satan will again be allowed to
lead a rebellion against God. It will not get very far and
Satan will be cast into the lake of fire.

Revelation 20:11-12 & 15 And I saw a great white
throne, and him that sat on it, from whose face the
earth and the heaven fled away; and there was found
no place for them. And I saw the dead, small and
great, stand before God; and the books were opened:
and another book was opened, which is [the book] of
life: and the dead were judged out of those things
which were written in the books, according to their
works.
And whosoever was not found written in the book of
life was cast into the lake of fire. IS OUR NAME
WRITTEN IN THE LAMB'S BOOK OF LIFE?

CHAPTER 21

Revelation 21:1-2 And I saw a new heaven and a
new earth: for the first heaven and the first earth
were passed away; and there was no more sea.
And I John saw the holy city, new Jerusalem, coming

down from God out of heaven, prepared as a bride adorned for her husband.

If some of the details of the horrible judgments coming upon the earth are getting you down READ CHAPTERS 21 & 22. We probably should read chapters 21 & 22 every day to keep a right perspective on where our eternal dwelling is. We are strangers and sojourners in this world. This world will hate us and persecute us and even kill us if we are totally committed to following Jesus. We need to keep in the front of our mind that Jesus is leading us to heaven and the world and antichrist is leading people to the lake of fire. It may be difficult but it would probably be very worthwhile to memorize sections of Revelation 21 & 22.

Revelation 21:3-6 And I heard a great voice out of heaven saying, Behold, the tabernacle of God [is] with men, and he will dwell with them, and they shall be his people, and God himself shall be with them, [and be] their God. And God shall wipe away all tears from their eyes; and there shall be no more death, neither sorrow, nor crying, neither shall there be any more pain: for the former things are passed away. And he that sat upon the throne said, Behold, I make all things new. And he said unto me, Write: for these words are true and faithful. And he said unto me, It is done. I am Alpha and Omega, the beginning and the end. I will give unto him that is athirst of the fountain of the water of life freely.

God Himself will dwell with us. God shall wipe away all tears. There shall be no more death. There will be no sorrow. God will make all things new. If this world is beautiful, just wait until we see the new heaven and new earth that God has for us. Jesus is the Alpha and Omega, and He will give us freely of the water of eternal life, full of joy, with no sorrow.

Revelation 21:7-8 He that overcometh shall inherit all things; and I will be his God, and he shall be my son. But the fearful, and unbelieving, and the abominable, and murderers, and whoremongers, and sorcerers, and idolaters, and all liars, shall have their part in the lake which burneth with fire and brimstone: which is the second death.
It may not be easy or pleasant but BE AN OVERCOMMER! Do not be fearful or unbelieving and don't be tempted to tell lies. Do you know how to be an overcommer? They overcame him (the antichrist and his followers) by the blood of the lamb and the word of their testimony and they loved not their lives unto the death. Would you rather die than to deny Jesus?

Revelation 21:12 & 14 And had a wall great and high, [and] had twelve gates, and at the gates twelve angels, and names written thereon, which are [the names] of the twelve tribes of the children of Israel: And the wall of the city had twelve foundations, and in them the names of the twelve apostles of the Lamb.

There are those who would say that God deals with Israel and the Church differently. Some would even say that Israel and the Church have different eternal purposes and destinies. Some would say that it is Israel that will go through the tribulation and not the Church. However, we see clearly here that Israel and the Church have the same destiny and eternal purpose. Israel becomes part of the Church. Whenever any Jew recognizes and trusts Messiah Jesus Christ for his salvation, that Jew becomes part of the Church. Antichrist will wage war on the saints whether those saints are Jews or Gentiles will make no difference to him.

Revelation 21: 16 And the city lieth foursquare, and the length is as large as the breadth: and he measured the city with the reed, twelve thousand furlongs. The length and the breadth and the height of it are equal.

There is plenty of room in New Jerusalem. This is so big that it will be hard to imagine. Only God could build something like this. It is 1500 miles long, wide, and HIGH. If its rooms have 10 foot high ceilings it would contain the entire dry land surface area of planet Earth.

Revelation 21:22-27 And I saw no temple therein: for the Lord God Almighty and the Lamb are the temple of it. And the city had no need of the sun, neither of the moon, to shine in it: for the glory of God did lighten it, and the Lamb [is] the light thereof. And the nations of them which are saved shall walk

in the light of it: and the kings of the earth do bring their glory and honour into it. And the gates of it shall not be shut at all by day: for there shall be no night there. And they shall bring the glory and honour of the nations into it. And there shall in no wise enter into it any thing that defileth, neither [whatsoever] worketh abomination, or [maketh] a lie: but they which are written in the Lamb's book of life. This present world is not our home. Think about this place God will make for us. Everyone in this place will be people that we will love. All of them will never defile, never work any abominable thing, or ever lie. IS OUR NAME WRITTEN IN THE LAMB'S BOOK OF LIFE? This is going to be our home. Our citizenship needs to be of this place and not of this world in which we now live as strangers.

CHAPTER 22

Revelation 22:1 And he shewed me a pure river of water of life, clear as crystal, proceeding out of the throne of God and of the Lamb.

Revelation 22:2 In the midst of the street of it, and on either side of the river, [was there] the tree of life, which bare twelve [manner of] fruits, [and] yielded her fruit every month: and the leaves of the tree [were] for the healing of the nations.

Revelation 22:3 And there shall be no more curse:

but the throne of God and of the Lamb shall be in it; and his servants shall serve him:

Revelation 22:4 And they shall see his face; and his name [shall be] in their foreheads.

Revelation 22:5 And there shall be no night there; and they need no candle, neither light of the sun; for the Lord God giveth them light: and they shall reign for ever and ever.

Revelation 22:6 And he said unto me, These sayings [are] faithful and true: and the Lord God of the holy prophets sent his angel to shew unto his servants the things which must shortly be done.

Revelation 22:7 Behold, I come quickly: blessed [is] he that keepeth the sayings of the prophecy of this book.

Revelation 22:8 And I John saw these things, and heard [them]. And when I had heard and seen, I fell down to worship before the feet of the angel which shewed me these things.

Revelation 22:9 Then saith he unto me, See [thou do it] not: for I am thy fellowservant, and of thy brethren the prophets, and of them which keep the sayings of this book: worship God.

Revelation 22:10 And he saith unto me, Seal not the sayings of the prophecy of this book: for the time is at hand.

Revelation 22:11 He that is unjust, let him be unjust still: and he which is filthy, let him be filthy still: and he that is righteous, let him be righteous still: and he that is holy, let him be holy still.

Revelation 22:12 And, behold, I come quickly; and my reward [is] with me, to give every man according as his work shall be.

Revelation 22:13 I am Alpha and Omega, the beginning and the end, the first and the last.

Revelation 22:14 Blessed [are] they that do his commandments, that they may have right to the tree of life, and may enter in through the gates into the city.

Revelation 22:15 For without [are] dogs, and sorcerers, and whoremongers, and murderers, and idolaters, and whosoever loveth and maketh a lie.

Revelation 22:16 I Jesus have sent mine angel to testify unto you these things in the churches. I am the root and the offspring of David, [and] the bright and morning star.

Revelation 22:17 And the Spirit and the bride say, Come. And let him that heareth say, Come. And let him that is athirst come. And whosoever will, let him take the water of life freely.

Revelation 22:18 For I testify unto every man that heareth the words of the prophecy of this book, If any man shall add unto these things, God shall add unto him the plagues that are written in this book:

Revelation 22:19 And if any man shall take away from the words of the book of this prophecy, God shall take away his part out of the book of life, and out of the holy city, and [from] the things which are written in this book.

Revelation 22:20 He which testifieth these things saith, Surely I come quickly. Amen. Even so, come, Lord Jesus.

Revelation 22:21 The grace of our Lord Jesus Christ [be] with you all. Amen.

DANIEL

Daniel was taken captive to Babylon as a boy. He was
selected for duty in the king's service. This was a high
honor requiring physical and mental excellence. The
prophecies in Daniel are so detailed and accurate that it
probably has been attacked more than any other book. The
amazing and very detailed accuracy of the prophecies which
have already been fulfilled should cause us to study it very
carefully. Daniel has many keys to other prophecies. God
made many of the end time prophecies in Daniel impossible
to understand until the time of the end. When God lifts
the seal from Daniel's end time prophecies it will be
understandable for anyone who would seek to know. There
is every reason to believe the seal has been removed. It will
also help understand many other difficult end time
prophecies. Try to memorize Daniel 11:32 and do exploits.

**Daniel 1:1-2 In the third year of the reign of
Jehoiakim king of Judah came Nebuchadnezzar
king of Babylon unto Jerusalem, and besieged it.
And the Lord gave Jehoiakim king of Judah into his
hand, with part of the vessels of the house of God:
which he carried into the land of Shinar to the house
of his god; and he brought the vessels into the
treasure house of his god.**
Comparing these verses with Jeremiah 36:1-3 we see that it
was a year after Nebuchadnezzar had defeated Jehoiakim

and taken captives and treasures back to Babylon that God
told Jeremiah to write the scroll with all of the prophecies.
God was giving the remaining people of Judah and King
Jehoiakim a last chance to repent. In his absolutely hopeless
situation Jehoiakim insults God and burns the scroll
personally page by page.

**Daniel 1:4   Children in whom [was] no blemish, but
well favoured, and skilful in all wisdom, and cunning
in knowledge, and understanding science, and such
as [had] ability in them to stand in the king's palace,
and whom they might teach the learning and the
tongue of the Chaldeans.**
The Babylonians were ruthless. Yet they were wise empire
builders. The king sought out the brightest and strongest of
the children who were taken captive and sought to prepare
them to be vassal rulers of the captives. This is a time
proven means of quelling possible insurrection.

**Daniel 1:6-7   Now among these were of the children
of Judah, Daniel, Hananiah, Mishael, and Azariah:
Unto whom the prince of the eunuchs gave names:
for he gave unto Daniel [the name] of Belteshazzar;
and to Hananiah, of Shadrach; and to Mishael, of
Meshach; and to Azariah, of Abed-nego.**
Among these outstanding young captives were Daniel and
his three friends Shadrach, Meshach, and Abednego of fiery
furnace fame.

Daniel 1:9-10   Now God had brought Daniel into

favour and tender love with the prince of the
eunuchs. And the prince of the eunuchs said unto
Daniel, I fear my lord the king, who hath appointed
your meat and your drink: for why should he see your
faces worse liking than the children which [are] of
your sort? then shall ye make [me] endanger my head
to the king.

Daniel and his friends knew the word of God. They did not
want to drink the king's wine or eat the pork and other non
kosher foods. The prince of the eunuchs was going to loose
his life if he did not follow orders to see that these chosen
children be properly indoctrinated into the Babylonian
culture including drunkenness and rich foods expressly
forbidden and held to be abominable by the Jews.

Daniel 1:12   Prove thy servants, I beseech thee, ten
days; and let them give us pulse to eat, and water to
drink.

Daniel proposes a diplomatic solution. Just check us out
after 10 days and see if we have not gained more weight and
are in better physical condition than the other privileged
children who were in competition with them.

Daniel 1:15-17 & 19-21
And at the end of ten days their countenances
appeared fairer and fatter in flesh than all the children
which did eat the portion of the king's meat.
Thus Melzar took away the portion of their meat, and
the wine that they should drink; and gave them pulse.
As for these four children, God gave them knowledge

and skill in all learning and wisdom: and Daniel had understanding in all visions and dreams. And the king communed with them; and among them all was found none like Daniel, Hananiah, Mishael, and Azariah: therefore stood they before the king.
And in all matters of wisdom [and] understanding, that the king inquired of them, he found them ten times better than all the magicians [and] astrologers that [were] in all his realm.
And Daniel continued [even] unto the first year of king Cyrus.

God honored the obedience of Daniel and his friends. They excelled in every aspect beyond their peers. Whenever we are forced to choose between obeying God or obeying men we should choose to obey God. We should also notice how Daniel gave a diplomatic and creative alternative choice to the authority placed over him. His way was not that of defiant rebellion. He offered a creative alternative and avoided rebellion. Rebellion is as the sin of witchcraft and must be avoided.

Daniel 2:4-5 Then spake the Chaldeans to the king in Syriack, O king, live for ever: tell thy servants the dream, and we will shew the interpretation.
The king answered and said to the Chaldeans, The thing is gone from me: if ye will not make known unto me the dream, with the interpretation thereof, ye shall be cut in pieces, and your houses shall be made a dunghill.

Nebuchadnezzar knew the Chaldean wizards would come

up with some sort of answer to interpret his dream. He knew the dream was important. The dream made a tremendous impression on him. The image was probably made in his likeness. He told the magicians that they must both tell him the dream and the interpretation. He wanted a sure answer from God regarding the interpretation of this dream. He also knew that if the dream was from God that God would reveal the dream to someone to give him the interpretation. If someone knew the dream then and only then could he trust the interpretation.

Daniel 2:9-12 But if ye will not make known unto me the dream, [there is but] one decree for you: for ye have prepared lying and corrupt words to speak before me, till the time be changed: therefore tell me the dream, and I shall know that ye can shew me the interpretation thereof. The Chaldeans answered before the king, and said, There is not a man upon the earth that can shew the king's matter: therefore [there is] no king, lord, nor ruler, [that] asked such things at any magician, or astrologer, or Chaldean. And [it is] a rare thing that the king requireth, and there is none other that can shew it before the king, except the gods, whose dwelling is not with flesh. For this cause the king was angry and very furious, and commanded to destroy all the wise [men] of Babylon.

The king, in his wisdom, really got to the Chaldean wizards. He knew that supernatural power would be involved in interpreting the dream correctly. The wizards could easily fake any kind of interpretation. There was no way they could fake telling the king the dream itself. The king knew the only way to verify the accuracy of the interpretation.

Daniel 2:16-20

Then Daniel went in, and desired of the king that he would give him time, and that he would shew the king the interpretation. Then Daniel went to his house, and made the thing known to Hananiah, Mishael, and Azariah, his companions: That they would desire mercies of the God of heaven concerning this secret; that Daniel and his fellows should not perish with the rest of the wise [men] of Babylon. Then was the secret revealed unto Daniel in a night vision. Then Daniel blessed the God of heaven. Daniel answered and said, Blessed be the name of God for ever and ever: for wisdom and might are his:

Notice how Daniel sought his friends to pray with him. We should seek faithful people to go to God and be in prayer agreement. Notice how careful Daniel is to give God the glory. Wisdom and power are attributes of God. No wisdom can compare with God's wisdom. No power is comparable to God's power.

Daniel 2:25-30 Then Arioch brought in Daniel before the king in haste, and said thus unto him, I have found a man of the captives of Judah, that will make known unto the king the interpretation. The king answered and said to Daniel, whose name [was]

Belteshazzar, Art thou able to make known unto me
the dream which I have seen, and the interpretation
thereof? Daniel answered in the presence of the
king, and said, The secret which the king hath
demanded cannot the wise [men], the astrologers,
the magicians, the soothsayers, shew unto the king;
But there is a God in heaven that revealeth secrets,
and maketh known to the king Nebuchadnezzar what
shall be in the latter days. Thy dream, and the visions
of thy head upon thy bed, are these; As for thee, O
king, thy thoughts came [into thy mind] upon thy bed,
what should come to pass hereafter: and he that
revealeth secrets maketh known to thee what shall
come to pass. But as for me, this secret is not
revealed to me for [any] wisdom that I have more
than any living, but for [their] sakes that shall make
known the interpretation to the king, and that thou
mightest know the thoughts of thy heart.

The king gives Daniel a great chance to promote himself -
are you able to tell me the dream? Daniel says that only
God can do it and it is God who has given him the dream.
Daniel is so very careful to give all glory to God.

Daniel 2:31-33 Thou, O king, sawest, and behold a
great image. This great image, whose brightness
[was] excellent, stood before thee; and the form
thereof [was] terrible. This image's head [was] of fine
gold, his breast and his arms of silver, his belly and
his thighs of brass, His legs of iron, his feet part of
iron and part of clay.

At this point the king is certain of an accurate interpretation of the dream because of the accuracy of the description of the dream itself which God has given Daniel. H ow much more certain can we be of the accuracy of Daniel's interpretation having almost 2600 years of history proving the absolute accuracy of Daniel's prophetic interpretation. Pay very close attention to this and all of Daniel's prophecies because it is indeed likely that it is our generation which will witness the culmination of Daniel's prophecies. No generation whose feet have ever walked this planet are witnessing prophesy being fulfilled more than ours. Daniel's prophecies here and in the rest of Daniel's book must get our attention.

WAKE UP!! GET READY!! MOST IMPORTANTLY - STAY READY!!!!

Daniel 2:34-35 Thou sawest till that a stone was cut out without hands, which smote the image upon his feet [that were] of iron and clay, and brake them to pieces. Then was the iron, the clay, the brass, the silver, and the gold, broken to pieces together, and became like the chaff of the summer threshingfloors; and the wind carried them away, that no place was found for them: and the stone that smote the image became a great mountain, and filled the whole earth.

Let's take a quick look at what else the bible says about this stone.

Psalms 118:22 The stone [which] the builders refused is become the head [stone] of the corner.

Isaiah 8:14 And he shall be for a sanctuary; but for a

stone of stumbling and for a rock of offence to both
the houses of Israel, for a gin and for a snare to the
inhabitants of Jerusalem.

Isaiah 28:16 Therefore thus saith the Lord GOD,
Behold, I lay in Zion for a foundation a stone, a
tried stone, a precious corner [stone], a sure
foundation: he that believeth shall not make haste.

Zechariah 3:9 For behold the stone that I have laid
before Joshua; upon one stone [shall be] seven eyes:
behold, I will engrave the graving thereof, saith the
LORD of hosts, and I will remove the iniquity of that
land in one day.

Matthew 21:44 And whosoever shall fall on this stone
shall be broken: but on whomsoever it shall fall, it will
grind him to powder.

Mark 12:10 And have ye not read this scripture; The
stone which the builders rejected is become the head
of the corner:

Luke 20:17-18 And he beheld them, and said, What is
this then that is written, The stone which the builders
rejected, the same is become the head of the corner?
Whosoever shall fall upon that stone shall be broken;
but on whomsoever it shall fall, it will grind him to
powder.

Ephesians 2:20 And are built upon the foundation of
the apostles and prophets, Jesus Christ himself
being the chief corner [stone];

I Peter 2:4 To whom coming, [as unto] a living stone,
disallowed indeed of men, but chosen of God, [and]
precious,

I Peter 2:6 -8 Wherefore also it is contained in the scripture, Behold, I lay in Sion a chief corner stone, elect, precious: and he that believeth on him shall not be confounded. Unto you therefore which believe[he is] precious: but unto them which be disobedient, the stone which the builders disallowed, the same is made the head of the corner, And a stone of stumbling, and a rock of offence, [even to them] which stumble at the word, being disobedient: whereunto also they were appointed.

We may be confident this Stone of which Daniel speaks, is Jesus Christ. Jesus is coming soon to put down and destroy forever the world government of antichrist.

Jesus will rule and reign over the whole earth for 1000 years after He destroys all other world government.

Daniel 2:36-38   This [is] the dream; and we will tell the interpretation thereof before the king. Thou, O king, [art] a king of kings: for the God of heaven hath given thee a kingdom, power, and strength, and glory. And wheresoever the children of men dwell, the beasts of the field and the fowls of the heaven hath he given into thine hand, and hath made thee ruler over them all. Thou [art] this head of gold.

Nebuchadnezzar was the king who brought Babylon to be the first great world empire. Thus it was N ebuchadnezzar's Babylon which was the head of gold.

Daniel 2:39-40 And after thee shall arise another kingdom inferior to thee, and another third kingdom

of brass, which shall bear rule over all the earth.
And the fourth kingdom shall be strong as iron:
forasmuch as iron breaketh in pieces and subdueth
all [things]: and as iron that breaketh all these, shall
it break in pieces and bruise.

The subsequent world empires were the silver empire of the
Medo-Persians. This would be followed by the brass empire
of the Greeks under Alexander the Great. This would be
followed by the mighty iron rule of the Roman empire. Its
division into the eastern and western empires being
simulated by the two legs of the image.

Daniel 2:41-44 And whereas thou sawest the feet and
toes, part of potters' clay, and part of iron, the
kingdom shall be divided; but there shall be in it of
the strength of the iron, forasmuch as thou sawest
the iron mixed with miry clay. And [as] the toes of the
feet [were] part of iron, and part of clay, [so] the
kingdom shall be partly strong, and partly broken.
And whereas thou sawest iron mixed with miry clay,
they shall mingle themselves with the seed of men:
but they shall not cleave one to another, even as iron
is not mixed with clay. And in the days of these kings
shall the God of heaven set up a kingdom, which
shall never be destroyed: and the kingdom shall not
be left to other people, [but] it shall break in pieces
and consume all these kingdoms, and it shall stand
for ever.

The feet and toes likely refer to the world empire to control
our generation. The revived Roman empire of a 10 nation

confederacy will form the new world order under antichrist.
Demonic unions and a tremendous revival of dark age
occultism will mark this final world empire which
immediately precedes the return of Messiah King J esus.
God will finally kick Satan and the one third of all fallen
angels out of heaven down to earth. These demons are
spirit beings who will indwell the leaders of this New World
Order and suck in all New Age movement followers who
will be getting their instructions from their spirit guides
and/or ascended masters. These people will be kept
ignorant of the fact that these spirit entities are actually
demon fallen angels. This system will prosper and wage
war on the saints who are indwelt by the Holy Spirit. B ut
God Himself in the person of Jesus Christ will descend
from heaven and totally crush this new world order of
antichrist. Jesus Christ will then establish an everlasting
kingdom of righteousness and peace.

**Daniel 2:45 Forasmuch as thou sawest that the
stone was cut out of the mountain without hands,
and that it brake in pieces the iron, the brass, the
clay, the silver, and the gold; the great God hath
made known to the king what shall come to pass
hereafter: and the dream [is] certain, and the
interpretation thereof sure.**
If the king could be convinced of the certainty of the
interpretation, how much more certain should we be. We
have seen the exact fulfillment over the span of history of
the first four world empires. We are seeing this mixture of
men and demons working to establish a new world order or

world empire in our time.

Daniel 2:46-49 Then the king Nebuchadnezzar fell upon his face, and worshipped Daniel, and commanded that they should offer an oblation and sweet odours unto him. The king answered unto Daniel, and said, Of a truth [it is], that your God [is] a God of gods, and a Lord of kings, and a revealer of secrets, seeing thou couldest reveal this secret. Then the king made Daniel a great man, and gave him many great gifts, and made him ruler over the whole province of Babylon, and chief of the governors over all the wise [men] of Babylon. Then Daniel requested of the king, and he set Shadrach, Meshach, and Abed-nego, over the affairs of the province of Babylon: but Daniel [sat] in the gate of the king.

Daniel was made a great man. He did not forget his friends and prayer partners. King Nebuchadnezzar knew the truth of Daniel's prophecies. He fell on his face. We should be on our face in repentance for our sins as we see this final new world order which immediately precedes the return of Jesus Christ being formed. Christians must be in the word daily in order to avoid being sucked into the demonic new world order and new age movement of antichrist. If we are ignorant of the bible we will likely be sucked into this system of tyranny, confusion, and ultimate destruction.

Daniel 3:1 Nebuchadnezzar the king made an image of gold, whose height [was] threescore cubits, [and] the breadth thereof six cubits: he set it up in the plain of Dura, in the province of Babylon.

Recall the dream God gave to Nebuchadnezzar that only Daniel was able to interpret. King Nebuchadnezzar was the head of gold which represented the first and greatest world empire. The breastplate of silver represented the empire of the Medo-Persians. King Nebuchadnezzar made the whole image of gold. He did not want any of the other empires of the image to succeed his empire. He wanted his golden Babylonian empire to last forever. By now Daniel held the highest position in the empire and his friends Shadrach, Meshech, and Abed-nego had high positions as well. No doubt many Babylonian nobles were jealous of the high positions which these Jews had in the empire. Worshipping the golden image of Nebuchadnezzar was a loyalty oath. The Babylonian nobles knew the Jews could not go along with this type of loyalty oath and it was a slick way for them to get rid of these Jews who were holding coveted positions in the empire. It was easy for them to get Nebuchadnezzar to impose the death penalty for not going along with the loyalty oath because Nebuchadnezzar saw it as a way to help keep the peace in the empire and perhaps be a way to quell possible insurrection and rebellion.

Daniel 3:2-3 Then Nebuchadnezzar the king sent to gather together the princes, the governors, and the captains, the judges, the treasurers, the counselors, the sheriffs, and all the rulers of the provinces, to come to the dedication of the image which Nebuchadnezzar the king had set up. Then the

princes, the governors, and captains, the judges,
the treasurers, the counselors, the sheriffs, and all
the rulers of the provinces, were gathered together
unto the dedication of the image that
Nebuchadnezzar the king had set up; and they stood
before the image that Nebuchadnezzar had set up.
All of the rulers from all over the empire were brought in
for the dedication of the image and to worship it and to
pledge their loyalty to the king.

Daniel 3:4-6   Then an herald cried aloud, To you it is
commanded, O people, nations, and languages,
[That] at what time ye hear the sound of the cornet,
flute, harp, sackbut, psaltery, dulcimer, and all kinds
of music, ye fall down and worship the golden image
that Nebuchadnezzar the king hath set up: And
whoso falleth not down and worshippeth shall the
same hour be cast into the midst of a burning fiery
furnace.
The death penalty was on anyone who would not prove their
loyalty to the world government of King Nebuchadnezzar.
Look for this same sort of worship of the image of the
antichrist to have a death penalty tied to it. Jews and
Christians will be the target then as it was when Babylon
ruled the world.

Daniel 3:12   There are certain Jews whom thou hast
set over the affairs of the province of Babylon,
Shadrach, Meshach, and Abed-nego; these men, O
king, have not regarded thee: they serve not thy gods,

nor worship the golden image which thou hast set up.

The Babylonian astrologers were quick to seize the opportunity to get rid of the Jews who were holding coveted positions in the empire. If we are Christians we need to expect this same type of treatment at the hands of our peers in the workplace.

Daniel 3:14-15 Nebuchadnezzar spake and said unto them, [Is it] true, O Shadrach, Meshach, and Abed-nego, do not ye serve my gods, nor worship the golden image which I have set up? Now if ye be ready that at what time ye hear the sound of the cornet, flute, harp, sackbut, psaltery, and dulcimer, and all kinds of music, ye fall down and worship the image which I have made; [well]: but if ye worship not, ye shall be cast the same hour into the midst of a burning fiery furnace; and who [is] that God that shall deliver you out of my hands?

How would we answer the most powerful king in the world? We need to meditate on exactly how these men answered the king.

Daniel 3:16 Shadrach, Meshach, and Abed-nego, answered and said to the king, O Nebuchadnezzar, we [are] not careful to answer thee in this matter.

First of all they did not have to think about it. Their answer was immediate. Would we be able to answer such a question of life or death so readily without having to think about it at all? Meditate on their perfect answer.

Daniel 3:17-18 If it be [so], our God whom we serve is able to deliver us from the burning fiery furnace, and he will deliver [us] out of thine hand, O king.
But if not, be it known unto thee, O king, that we will not serve thy gods, nor worship the golden image which thou hast set up.

There is absolutely no doubt that our God is able to deliver us out of this situation. My God is more than able to deliver us from any difficulty. And he will deliver. Now we see the great faith of these men. Our God will deliver us. They did not only know that God was able but their faith told them that God would deliver them. How many blessings do we miss because we fail to believe that God will deliver us? But if God doesn't save us we still want you to know that we certainly would rather die than to disobey our God. They still were letting God be God. They were not demanding or commanding God to deliver them. They had total confidence that God would deliver them but they were totally committed to God's sovereignty. They were totally willing to die rather than to disobey God. They would obey God rather than to try to save their lives by obeying the king. Would we be this brave when our life is on the line?

Daniel 3:19-22 Then was Nebuchadnezzar full of fury, and the form of his visage was changed against Shadrach, Meshach, and Abed-nego: [therefore] he spake, and commanded that they should heat the furnace one seven times more than it was wont to be heated. And he commanded the most mighty men that [were] in his army to bind Shadrach, Meshach, and Abed-nego, [and] to cast [them] into the burning fiery furnace. Then these men were bound in their coats, their hosen, and their hats, and their [other] garments, and were cast into the midst of the burning fiery furnace. Therefore because the king's commandment was urgent, and the furnace exceeding hot, the flame of the fire slew those men that took up Shadrach, Meshach, and Abed-nego. The king was furious. He commanded the furnace to be made seven times hotter than it was designed to be. The king's men were so nervous over his fury that the men who were stoking the furnace were killed by the flames.

Daniel 3:23-25 And these three men, Shadrach, Meshach, and Abed-nego, fell down bound into the midst of the burning fiery furnace. Then Nebuchadnezzar the king was astonied, and rose up in haste, [and] spake, and said unto his counsellors, Did not we cast three men bound into the midst of the fire? They answered and said unto the king, True, O king. He answered and said, Lo, I see four men loose, walking in the midst of the fire, and they have no hurt; and the form of the fourth is like the Son of God.

The furious king knew who was in the middle of the furnace with Shadrack, Meshach, and A bed-nego. The king said that he was like the Son of God. He was right. That is exactly who it was. Jesus Himself was right there in the middle of the fire with Shadrack, Meshach, and A bed-nego.

What tremendous encouragement there is here for us. When we are in tribulation, Jesus, in the presence of His Holy Spirit, promises to be right in the middle of our tribulation. If God is with us, what should we fear? If the government of the antichrist threatens to kill us if we will not worship his image, will we be like these men? Will we be strong, courageous, and faithful in tribulation?

Daniel 3:26-29 Then Nebuchadnezzar came near to the mouth of the burning fiery furnace, [and] spake, and said, Shadrach, Meshach, and Abed-nego, ye servants of the most high God, come forth, and come [hither]. Then Shadrach, Meshach, and Abed-nego, came forth of the midst of the fire. And the princes, governors, and captains, and the king's counsellors, being gathered together, saw these men, upon whose bodies the fire had no power, nor was an hair of their head singed, neither were their coats changed, nor the smell of fire had passed on them. [Then] Nebuchadnezzar spake, and said, Blessed [be] the God of Shadrach, Meshach, and Abed-nego, who hath sent his angel, and delivered his servants that trusted in him, and have changed the king's word, and yielded their bodies, that they might not serve nor worship any god, except their own God. Therefore I make a decree, That every people, nation, and language, which speak any thing amiss against the God of Shadrach, Meshach, and Abed-nego, shall be cut in pieces, and their houses shall be made a dunghill: because there is no other God that can

deliver after this sort.

See how God was protecting His people. The Jews had been taken captive and were dispersed throughout the world. They were no doubt being persecuted for their peculiar culture, Sabbath worship, and diet. The king's decree gave them protection and total freedom to be obedient and openly worship the one true God. The reprisals were ended for them.

Daniel 3:30 Then the king promoted Shadrach, Meshach, and Abed-nego, in the province of Babylon. What a great sense of humor the Lord has. How did the Babylonian astrologers like it when the fiery furnace men got promoted?

Daniel 4:1-9 Nebuchadnezzar the king, unto all people, nations, and languages, that dwell in all the earth; Peace be multiplied unto you. I thought it good to shew the signs and wonders that the high God hath wrought toward me. How great [are] his signs! and how mighty [are] his wonders! his kingdom [is] an everlasting kingdom, and his dominion [is] from generation to generation. I saw a dream which made me afraid, and the thoughts upon my bed and the visions of my head troubled me. Therefore made I a decree to bring in all the wise [men] of Babylon before me, that they might make known unto me the interpretation of the dream. Then came in the magicians, the astrologers, the Chaldeans, and the soothsayers: and I told the dream before them; but

they did not make known unto me the interpretation thereof. But at the last Daniel came in before me, whose name [was] Belteshazzar, according to the name of my god, and in whom [is] the spirit of the holy gods: and before him I told the dream, [saying], O Belteshazzar, master of the magicians, because I know that the spirit of the holy gods [is] in thee, and no secret troubleth thee, tell me the visions of my dream that I have seen, and the interpretation thereof. Nebuchadnezzar is doing the talking Daniel is just doing the writing. The king has indeed come to know the true God and he is telling the world about Him.

Daniel 4:13-37

I saw in the visions of my head upon my bed, and, behold, a watcher and an holy one came down from heaven; He cried aloud, and said thus, Hew down the tree, and cut off his branches, shake off his leaves, and scatter his fruit: let the beasts get away from under it, and the fowls from his branches: Nevertheless leave the stump of his roots in the earth, even with a band of iron and brass, in the tender grass of the field; and let it be wet with the dew of heaven, and [let] his portion [be] with the beasts in the grass of the earth: Let his heart be changed from man's, and let a beast's heart be given unto him; and let seven times pass over him. This matter [is] by the decree of the watchers, and the demand by the word of the holy ones: to the intent that the living may know that the most High ruleth in the kingdom of men, and giveth it to whomsoever he will, and setteth up over it the basest of men. Then Daniel, whose name [was] Belteshazzar, was astonied for one hour, and his thoughts troubled him. The king spake, and said, Belteshazzar, let not the dream, or the interpretation thereof, trouble thee. Belteshazzar answered and said, My lord, the dream [be] to them that hate thee, and the interpretation thereof to thine enemies. The tree that thou sawest, which grew, and was strong, whose height reached unto the heaven, and the sight thereof to all the earth; Whose leaves [were] fair, and the fruit thereof much, and in it [was] meat for all; under which the beasts of the field dwelt, and upon whose branches the fowls of the heaven had their habitation: It [is] thou, O king, that art grown and become strong: for thy greatness is grown, and reacheth unto heaven, and thy dominion to the end of the earth. And whereas the king saw a watcher and an holy one coming down from heaven, and saying, Hew the tree down, and destroy it; yet leave the stump of the roots thereof in the earth, even with a band of iron and brass, in the tender grass of the field; and let it be wet with the dew of heaven, and [let] his portion [be] with the beasts of the field, till seven times pass over him; This [is] the interpretation, O king, and this [is] the decree of the most High, which is come upon my lord the king: That they shall drive thee from men, and thy dwelling shall be with the beasts of the field, and they shall make thee to eat grass as oxen, and they shall wet thee with the dew of heaven, and seven times shall pass over thee, till thou know that the most High ruleth in the kingdom of men, and giveth it to whomsoever he will. And whereas they commanded to leave the stump of the tree roots; thy kingdom shall be sure unto thee, after that thou shalt have known that the heavens do rule. Wherefore, O king, let my counsel be acceptable unto thee, and break off thy sins by righteousness, and thine iniquities by shewing mercy to the poor; if it may be a lengthening of thy tranquillity. At the end of twelve months he walked in the palace of the kingdom of Babylon. The king spake, and said, Is not this great Babylon, that I have built for the house of the kingdom by the might of my power, and for the honour of my majesty?

While the word [was] in the king's mouth, there fell a voice from heaven, [saying], O king Nebuchadnezzar, to thee it is spoken; The kingdom is departed from thee. And they shall drive thee from men, and thy dwelling [shall be] with the beasts of the field: they shall make thee to eat grass as oxen, and seven times shall pass over thee, until thou know that the most High ruleth in the kingdom of men, and giveth it to whomsoever he will. The same hour was the thing fulfilled upon Nebuchadnezzar: and he was driven from men, and did eat grass as oxen, and his body was wet with the dew of heaven, till his hairs were grown like eagles' [feathers], and his nails like birds' [claws].

And at the end of the days I Nebuchadnezzar lifted up mine eyes unto heaven, and mine understanding returned unto me, and I blessed the most High, and I praised and honoured him that liveth for ever, whose dominion [is] an everlasting dominion, and his kingdom [is] from generation to generation: And all the inhabitants of the earth [are] reputed as nothing: and he doeth according to his will in the army of heaven, and [among] the inhabitants of the earth: and none can stay his hand, or say unto him, What doest thou? At the same time my reason returned unto me; and for the glory of my kingdom, mine honour and brightness returned unto me; and my counsellors and my lords sought unto me; and I was established in my kingdom, and excellent majesty was added unto me. Now I Nebuchadnezzar praise and extol and honour the King of heaven, all whose works [are] truth, and his ways judgment: and those that walk in pride he is able to abase.

Does king Nebuchadnezzar humble himself and give glory to God, or what? Remember this king of the world is doing the talking and Daniel is just doing the writing. Fantastic!

Daniel 5:1-6

Belshazzar the king made a great feast to a thousand of his lords, and drank wine before the thousand. Belshazzar, whiles he tasted the wine, commanded to bring the golden and silver vessels which his father Nebuchadnezzar had taken out of the temple which [was] in Jerusalem; that the king, and his princes, his

wives, and his concubines, might drink therein.
Then they brought the golden vessels that were taken
out of the temple of the house of God which [was] at
Jerusalem; and the king, and his princes, his wives,
and his concubines, drank in them. They drank wine,
and praised the gods of gold, and of silver, of brass,
of iron, of wood, and of stone.
In the same hour came forth fingers of a man's hand,
and wrote over against the candlestick upon the
plaster of the wall of the king's palace: and the king
saw the part of the hand that wrote. Then the king's
countenance was changed, and his thoughts
troubled him, so that the joints of his loins were
loosed, and his knees smote one against another.

King Belshazzar had gone too far when he decided to use
the vessels which were taken from the temple of the Lord in
Jerusalem to use in his drunken party. A hand appeared
(just a hand) and wrote on the wall. This frightened the
king to the point that his legs gave way as he fainted in fear.
Is it time for American Christians to see the handwriting on
the wall?

Daniel 5:23-31
But hast lifted up thyself against the Lord of heaven;
and they have brought the vessels of his house
before thee, and thou, and thy lords, thy wives, and
thy concubines, have drunk wine in them; and thou
hast praised the gods of silver, and gold, of brass,
iron, wood, and stone, which see not, nor hear, nor
know: and the God in whose hand thy breath [is], and

whose [are] all thy ways, hast thou not glorified:
Then was the part of the hand sent from him; and this
writing was written. And this [is] the writing that was
written, MENE, MENE, TEKEL, UPHARSIN.
This [is] the interpretation of the thing: MENE; God
hath numbered thy kingdom, and finished it. TEKEL;
Thou art weighed in the balances, and art found
wanting. PERES; Thy kingdom is divided, and given
to the Medes and Persians.
Then commanded Belshazzar, and they clothed
Daniel with scarlet, and [put] a chain of gold about
his neck, and made a proclamation concerning him,
that he should be the third ruler in the kingdom.
In that night was Belshazzar the king of the
Chaldeans slain. And Darius the Median took the
kingdom, [being] about threescore and two years old.
Have not the rulers of America done as Belshazzar with
their Antichrist political correctness? How arrogant are
America's rulers who set themselves against the word of
God? God had numbered their days of preeminence and
they were finished. God's judgment was upon them. That
same night Belshazzar was killed and the Medo-Persian
empire began.

Daniel 6:3   Then this Daniel was preferred above the
presidents and princes, because an excellent spirit
[was] in him; and the king thought to set him over the
whole realm.
Daniel's righteousness and wisdom were legendary.
Proverbs 11:30 - The fruit of the righteous [is] a tree

of life; and he that winneth souls [is] wise.
He served under at least 4 kings who literally ruled the
world of his day. He became the top man in their
administrations. He shared the knowledge of his God with
all of them. There is no doubt that Nebuchadnezzar and
Darius came to accept Daniel's God as the true God. The
captain of the imperial guard who was sent to seek out and
care for Jeremiah among the captives of Judah had come to
believe in Daniel's God. <u>This is an important key to
understanding how the book of Daniel applies to Christians
as well as Jews in the last days.</u> Dr. Franklin D. Watts says
that all humanity can be placed in the 3 categories of Jew,
Gentile, and Christian. Anyone who accepts Jesus Christ as
Savior and Lord becomes a saint, a child of God, a part of
the body of Christ, a Christian. The Jew or gentile who
accepts Jesus Christ as Savior and Lord becomes a saint. If
Daniel were asked if Nebuchadnezzar, the captain of the
imperial guard, or Darius was one of his people, a child of
God, or a saint, he would most definitely have said yes.
Understanding this will help us understand that Daniel's
end time prophesies have much broader application than
just the Jews and nation of Israel. There is information
which we must understand. It is important to know that
not all Jews were Daniel's people. <u>Daniel's people were the
people of his God. The angel who told Daniel what would
happen to "thy" people was telling what will be for us if our
God is Daniel's God. One should not limit the application
of Daniel's or any other end time prophesies to Israel.</u> We
should keep our mind open and seek the guidance of the
Holy Spirit in the interpretation of Daniel's end time

prophesies.

Daniel 6:5   Then said these men, We shall not find any occasion against this Daniel, except we find [it] against him concerning the law of his God.
Everyone was jealous of Daniel's position. All of the king's other leaders conspired to get rid of him. The only possible way that they could entrap him would be in regard to his great loyalty and faithfulness to his God.

Daniel 6:7   All the presidents of the kingdom, the governors, and the princes, the counsellors, and the captains, have consulted together to establish a royal statute, and to make a firm decree, that whosoever shall ask a petition of any God or man for thirty days, save of thee, O king, he shall be cast into the den of lions.
Daniel's enemies entrapped the king to harm Daniel by a very devious plot playing upon the king's pride and even his confidence in them.

Daniel 6:11   Then these men assembled, and found Daniel praying and making supplication before his God.
It did not take long for the conspirators to bring the death penalty charge against Daniel.

Daniel 6:13-14   Then answered they and said before the king, That Daniel, which [is] of the children of the captivity of Judah, regardeth not thee, O king, nor the

decree that thou hast signed, but maketh his petition
three times a day.
Then the king, when he heard [these] words, was
sore displeased with himself, and set [his] heart on
Daniel to deliver him: and he laboured till the going
down of the sun to deliver him.

The king realized that he had been entrapped by the
conspirators. He was displeased with himself for falling into
the trap these conspirators had set just to kill his most
trustworthy friend and servant.

Daniel 6:16-20 Then the king commanded, and they
brought Daniel, and cast [him] into the den of lions.
[Now] the king spake and said unto Daniel, Thy God
whom thou servest continually, he will deliver thee.
And a stone was brought, and laid upon the mouth of
the den; and the king sealed it with his own signet,
and with the signet of his lords; that the purpose
might not be changed concerning Daniel.
Then the king went to his palace, and passed the
night fasting: neither were instruments of music
brought before him: and his sleep went from him.
Then the king arose very early in the morning, and
went in haste unto the den of lions. And when he
came to the den, he cried with a lamentable voice
unto Daniel: [and] the king spake and said to Daniel,
O Daniel, servant of the living God, is thy God,
whom thou servest continually, able to deliver thee
from the lions?

Think about what the king said when Daniel was put in with

the lions. "Thy God, whom thou servest continually, He will deliver thee." This king has great faith in Daniel's God. Do we even have this measure of faith in God as the king expresses here. This king was a saint. This king had come to know the true God from his friend Daniel. He was one of "thy people" though he was not a Jew. The king sealed the lion's den with his signet to be sure the conspirators would not disturb the lions or kill Daniel to help the lions. Early in the morning, after a sleepless night of concern and possibly prayer for Daniel, the king comes to the lion's den. "Daniel, oh Daniel, servant of the living God, is thy God, whom thou servest continually, able to deliver thee from the lions?"

Daniel 6:22-24 My God hath sent his angel, and hath shut the lions' mouths, that they have not hurt me: forasmuch as before him innocency was found in me; and also before thee, O king, have I done no hurt. Then was the king exceeding glad for him, and commanded that they should take Daniel up out of the den. So Daniel was taken up out of the den, and no manner of hurt was found upon him, because he believed in his God. And the king commanded, and they brought those men which had accused Daniel, and they cast [them] into the den of lions, them, their children, and their wives; and the lions had the mastery of them, and brake all their bones in pieces or ever they came at the bottom of the den.

Always careful to give glory to God, Daniel reports that God has delivered him. The king was exceeding glad. In

verse 23 we find why Daniel was not hurt by the lions -
because he believed in his God. We can be sure that D aniel
knew the promise God gave to Noah and how that promise
would apply to his present circumstance with the lions.
Recall what God promised Noah after the flood in **Genesis
9:2 - And the fear of you and the dread of you shall be
upon every beast of the earth, and upon every fowl of
the air, upon all that moveth [upon] the earth, and
upon all the fishes of the sea; into your hand are they
delivered.** Daniel knew that God had put the fear of men
in the hearts of all animals. Daniel was not afraid of the
lions because of his great faith in the integrity of God's
word. If Daniel had had any fear the lions would have
sensed his fear immediately. The angel was probably sent
so that Daniel could get a good nights sleep. I f we know
this promise of God and do not have fear, we can back
down even a lion. The problem is whether or not we have
any fear because most animals seem to be able to sense fear.
If we have fear, we either don't know or believe the
promise of God and we will be in trouble. This could be
very important during the great tribulation when animals
may even be possessed by demons.

**Daniel 6:26-28 I make a decree, That in every
dominion of my kingdom men tremble and fear before
the God of Daniel: for he [is] the living God, and
stedfast for ever, and his kingdom [that] which shall
not be destroyed, and his dominion [shall be even]
unto the end. He delivereth and rescueth, and he
worketh signs and wonders in heaven and in earth,**

who hath delivered Daniel from the power of the
lions. So this Daniel prospered in the reign of
Darius, and in the reign of Cyrus the Persian.

Is king Darius a believer, a child of God, one of Daniel's
people? He was not a Jew but he was one of "thy people"
more than the people who were born Jews and had rejected
the God of their fathers. Those who had obedient faith in
Daniel's God were Daniel's people. Daniel's end time
prophesies apply to the saints. There is emphasis on Israel
but it is unwise to say they only apply to Israel to assuage
fear of great tribulation. We need to cause our faith to
grow to assuage our fear of tribulation.

Romans 10:17 - So then faith [cometh] by hearing,
and hearing by the word of God.

The period of great tribulation promises to be the most
exciting time in which any believer has ever had
opportunity to live. The people living during the great
tribulation will see the blessed hope of the Lord's triumphal
return in great power and glory. We will live
supernaturally by God's miraculous provision. It will
require great faith. That is why we must all make study of
God's word our highest priority. This is the way to great
faith that assuages fear of great tribulation.

Daniel 7:1-3 In the first year of Belshazzar king of
Babylon Daniel had a dream and visions of his head
upon his bed: then he wrote the dream, [and] told the
sum of the matters. Daniel spake and said, I saw in
my vision by night, and, behold, the four winds of the
heaven strove upon the great sea. And four great

beasts came up from the sea, diverse one from another.

Daniel's prophetic dreams are so absolutely accurate that men have had to try to resort to saying they were written after the fact. Various archaeological finds and because of the way in which Jewish scriptures gave so many names of various contemporary rulers firmly fix the accuracy of the date of these prophecies at 552 BC. It is our generation which is most likely to see the last pieces of Daniel's prophecy fulfilled. Remember that Jesus H imself told us to pay particularly close attention to Daniel's prophecies as they relate to His return. See M atthew 24:15 and Mark 13:14 where Jesus solemnly warns and encourages us to get understanding of Daniel's prophecy. As we shall see, some parts were to be sealed up for a generation such as ours at the time of the return of the King of Kings. N o generation in history has ever had greater incentive to carefully study the following scriptures. Read them over and over with prayer. Memorizing them would be worthwhile. Get understanding of these scriptures. There is no longer reason for them to be sealed.

Daniel 7:4-28 The first [was] like a lion, and had eagle's wings: I beheld till the wings thereof were plucked, and it was lifted up from the earth, and made stand upon the feet as a man, and a man's heart was given to it. And behold another beast, a second, like to a bear, and it raised up itself on one side, and [it had] three ribs in the mouth of it between the teeth of it: and they said thus unto it, Arise, devour much flesh. After this I beheld, and lo another, like a leopard, which had upon the back of it four wings of a fowl; the beast had also four heads; and dominion was given to it. After this I saw in the night visions, and behold a fourth beast, dreadful and terrible, and strong exceedingly; and it had great iron teeth: it devoured and brake in pieces, and stamped the residue with the feet of it: and it [was] diverse from all the beasts that [were] before it; and it had ten horns. I considered the horns, and, behold, there came up among them another little horn, before whom there were three of the first horns plucked up by the roots: and, behold, in this horn [were] eyes like the eyes of man, and a mouth speaking great things.

I beheld till the thrones were cast down, and the Ancient of days did sit, whose garment [was] white as snow, and the hair of his head like the pure wool: his throne [was like] the fiery flame, [and] his wheels [as] burning fire. A fiery stream issued and came forth from before him: thousand thousands ministered unto him, and ten thousand times ten thousand stood before him: the judgment was set, and the books were opened.

I beheld then because of the voice of the great words which the horn spake: I beheld [even] till the beast was slain, and his body destroyed, and given to the burning flame. As concerning the rest of the beasts, they had their dominion taken away: yet their lives were prolonged for a season and time.

I saw in the night visions, and, behold, [one] like the Son of man came with the clouds of heaven, and came to the Ancient of days, and they brought him near before him. And there was given him dominion, and glory, and a kingdom, that all people, nations, and languages, should serve him: his dominion [is] an everlasting dominion, which shall not pass away, and his kingdom [that] which shall not be destroyed. I Daniel was grieved in my spirit in the midst of [my] body, and the visions of my head troubled me.

I came near unto one of them that stood by, and asked him the truth of all this. So he told me, and made me know the interpretation of the things.

These great beasts, which are four, [are] four kings, [which] shall arise out of the earth. But the saints of the most High shall take the kingdom, and possess the kingdom for ever, even for ever and ever.

Then I would know the truth of the fourth beast, which was diverse from all the others, exceeding dreadful, whose teeth [were of] iron, and his nails [of] brass; [which] devoured, brake in pieces, and stamped the residue with his feet; And of the ten horns that [were] in his head, and [of] the other which came up, and before whom three fell; even [of] that horn that had eyes, and a mouth that spake very great things, whose look [was] more stout than his fellows. I beheld, and the same horn made war with the saints, and prevailed against them; Until the

Ancient of days came, and judgment was given to the saints of the most High; and the time came that the saints possessed the kingdom.

Thus he said, The fourth beast shall be the fourth kingdom upon earth, which shall be diverse from all kingdoms, and shall devour the whole earth, and shall tread it down, and break it in pieces.

And the ten horns out of this kingdom [are] ten kings [that] shall arise: and another shall rise after them; and he shall be diverse from the first, and he shall subdue three kings. And he shall speak [great] words against the most High, and shall wear out the saints of the most High, and think to change times and laws: and they shall be given into his hand until a time and times and the dividing of time. But the judgment shall sit, and they shall take away his dominion, to consume and to destroy [it] unto the end.

And the kingdom and dominion, and the greatness of the kingdom under the whole heaven, shall be given to the people of the saints of the most High, whose kingdom [is] an everlasting kingdom, and all dominions shall serve and obey him.

Hitherto [is] the end of the matter. As for me Daniel, my cogitations much troubled me, and my countenance changed in me: but I kept the matter in my heart.

Daniel saw how Babylon would be succeeded by the Medo-Persian empire. They would be succeeded by Alexander the Great establishing the Greek empire which

was divided by his four generals. They were succeeded by
Rome. In the last days there would finally be another world
empire of the short reign of the antichrist, who would make
war on the saints. Praise God! The King of Kings returns
to set up His everlasting kingdom in righteousness and His
saints shall be part of this glorious wonderful everlasting
kingdom. Please get understanding of this. It is quite likely
for our generation to see the conclusion. It is so important
and so open to deception that we must seek the answers for
ourself. Pray and ask the Holy Spirit to let you see these
fantastic truths for yourself. Discussing and sharing the
revelations contained in these scriptures is a source of
tremendous joy and encouragement. Look for the world to
see the rise of 10 great nations or to be divided into 10
regions. Look for someone to overcome three great nations
or world regions. Most of all look to see how near is the
return of the Lord Jesus Christ to put down the world
ruler who makes war with His saints. Look up for our
redemption draws neigh.

Daniel 8:1-27 In the third year of the reign of king
Belshazzar a vision appeared unto me, [even unto]
me Daniel, after that which appeared unto me at the
first. And I saw in a vision; and it came to pass, when
I saw, that I [was] at Shushan [in] the palace, which
[is] in the province of Elam; and I saw in a vision, and
I was by the river of Ulai. Then I lifted up mine eyes,
and saw, and, behold, there stood before the river a
ram which had [two] horns: and the [two] horns
[were] high; but one [was] higher than the other, and

the higher came up last. I saw the ram pushing westward, and northward, and southward; so that no beasts might stand before him, neither [was there any] that could deliver out of his hand; but he did according to his will, and became great.

And as I was considering, behold, an he goat came from the west on the face of the whole earth, and touched not the ground: and the goat [had] a notable horn between his eyes. And he came to the ram that had [two] horns, which I had seen standing before the river, and ran unto him in the fury of his power. And I saw him come close unto the ram, and he was moved with choler against him, and smote the ram, and brake his two horns: and there was no power in the ram to stand before him, but he cast him down to the ground, and stamped upon him: and there was none that could deliver the ram out of his hand. Therefore the he goat waxed very great: and when he was strong, the great horn was broken; and for it came up four notable ones toward the four winds of heaven. And out of one of them came forth a little horn, which waxed exceeding great, toward the south, and toward the east, and toward the pleasant [land]. And it waxed great, [even] to the host of heaven; and it cast down [some] of the host and of the stars to the ground, and stamped upon them. Yea, he magnified [himself] even to the prince of the host, and by him the daily [sacrifice] was taken away, and the place of his sanctuary was cast down. And an host was given [him] against the daily [sacrifice] by reason of transgression, and it cast down the truth to the ground; and it practised, and prospered.

Then I heard one saint speaking, and another saint said unto that certain [saint] which spake, How long [shall be] the vision [concerning] the daily [sacrifice], and the transgression of desolation, to give both the sanctuary and the host to be trodden under foot? And he said unto me, Unto two thousand and three hundred days; then shall the sanctuary be cleansed. And it came to pass, when I, [even] I Daniel, had seen the vision, and sought for the meaning, then, behold, there stood before me as the appearance of a man. And I heard a man's voice between [the banks of] Ulai, which called, and said, Gabriel, make this [man] to understand the vision.

So he came near where I stood: and when he came, I was afraid, and fell upon my face: but he said unto me, Understand, O son of man: for at the time of the end [shall be] the vision. Now as he was speaking with me, I was in a deep sleep on my face toward the ground: but he touched me, and set me upright. And he said, Behold, I will make thee know what shall be in the last end of the indignation: for at the time appointed the end [shall be]. The ram which thou sawest having [two] horns [are] the kings of Media and Persia. And the rough goat [is] the king of Grecia: and the great horn that [is] between his eyes [is] the first king. Now that being broken, whereas four stood up for it, four kingdoms shall stand up out of the nation, but not in his power.

And in the latter time of their kingdom, when the transgressors are come to the full, a king of fierce countenance, and understanding dark sentences, shall stand up. And his power shall be mighty, but not by his own power: and he shall destroy wonderfully, and shall prosper, and practise, and shall destroy the mighty and the holy people. And through his policy also he shall cause craft to prosper in his hand; and he shall magnify [himself] in his heart, and by peace shall destroy many: he shall also stand up against the Prince of princes; but he shall be broken without hand.

And the vision of the evening and the morning which was told [is] true: wherefore shut thou up the vision; for it [shall be] for many days.

And I Daniel fainted, and was sick [certain] days; afterward I rose up, and did the king's business; and I was astonished at the vision, but none understood [it].

Daniel was given more detail to reveal the same prophecy most of which is now history. There would be world empires of Babylon, Medo-Persia, Greece, Rome and finally the New World Order of antichrist. When we realize we are in the middle of this total war of antichrist on the saints we should know in that in less than 2300 days Jesus will be

back to put an end to all unrighteousness. It brings to mind the Rush Limbaugh daily countdown of the days remaining in the Clinton presidency. Understand this, if Jesus is your Lord, you win. There will be those who will ridicule and persecute you for knowing the truth. The apostle John gives more light to the short reign of antichrist in the book of Revelation. Remember what Jesus says in **Revelation 16:15 Behold, I come as a thief. Blessed [is] he that watcheth, and keepeth his garments, lest he walk naked, and they see his shame. Revelation 22:7 Behold, I come quickly: blessed [is] he that keepeth the sayings of the prophecy of this book.**
Revelation 22:12 And, behold, I come quickly; and my reward [is] with me, to give every man according as his work shall be.

Daniel 9:20-23
And whiles I [was] speaking, and praying, and confessing my sin and the sin of my people Israel, and presenting my supplication before the LORD my God for the holy mountain of my God;
Yea, whiles I [was] speaking in prayer, even the man Gabriel, whom I had seen in the vision at the beginning, being caused to fly swiftly, touched me about the time of the evening oblation.
And he informed [me], and talked with me, and said, O Daniel, I am now come forth to give thee skill and understanding. At the beginning of thy supplications the commandment came forth, and I am come to shew [thee]; for thou [art] greatly beloved: therefore

understand the matter, and consider the vision.

When we read Daniel's prayer in verses 4-19 is easy to see why Daniel was addressed by the angel Gabriel as greatly beloved. God sent the angel Gabriel to give Daniel understanding. Daniel had asked God to glorify Himself by restoring Israel because the city and the people were the city and people of Jehovah. Daniel was not asking anything for himself. He was jealous for God's glory. He never left the land of captivity where he was the highest ruler under the king whether the king be Babylonian or Mede. Pay special attention to this fantastic prophecy which God sent to Daniel by the angel Gabriel.

Daniel 9:24-27 Seventy weeks are determined upon thy people and upon thy holy city, to finish the transgression, and to make an end of sins, and to make reconciliation for iniquity, and to bring in everlasting righteousness, and to seal up the vision and prophecy, and to anoint the most Holy. Know therefore and understand, [that] from the going forth of the commandment to restore and to build Jerusalem unto the Messiah the Prince [shall be] seven weeks, and threescore and two weeks: the street shall be built again, and the wall, even in troublous times. And after threescore and two weeks shall Messiah be cut off, but not for himself: and the people of the prince that shall come shall destroy the city and the sanctuary; and the end thereof [shall be] with a flood, and unto the end of the war desolations

are determined. And he shall confirm the covenant
with many for one week: and in the midst of the week
he shall cause the sacrifice and the oblation to cease,
and for the overspreading of abominations he shall
make [it] desolate, even until the consummation, and
that determined shall be poured upon the desolate.
70 weeks are determined to wrap up everything (Hebrew =
seventy 7's = 490 years). From the going fourth of the
command to rebuild Jerusalem until Messiah would be 7 and
62 weeks (7's) or in exactly 483 years. What was to happen
483 years from the going forth of the command to rebuild
Jerusalem? Messiah the Prince would come! This prophecy
predicted, almost to the day, when Jesus would enter
Jerusalem on the first Palm Sunday. That is why Jesus told
the Pharisees even the very rocks would cry out if the people
were to remain silent. What was Messiah going to do?
Messiah would make an end of sins! Messiah would make
reconciliation for iniquity! Messiah would bring everlasting
righteousness! Can you see it? Had the princes of this
world known, they would not have crucified the Lord of
glory. They didn't see it but we can. He who knew no sin,
was made to be sin for us. Can you see it? We are free from
sin - alleluia! Jesus made an end of sins. There is no penalty
for us because Messiah made the reconciliation for iniquity
which none of us could ever make no matter how hard we
tried! All we have to do is agree with God and accept His
forgiveness and that sin is thrown into the sea of
forgetfulness and we are justified. "Just as if I'd" never
sinned." We need a tight hold on the understanding that
Gabriel gave to Daniel? Messiah was killed 483 years after

the command was issued but not for Himself. H e did it for us. That is the big understanding that we must get.

There is another understanding which we also must get. We are possible members of that generation which will join the prince (little p prince signifying antichrist) in making war on the saints. If we don't become knowledgeable of the word of God we will be sucked into the antichrist's global New World Order and New Age Movement. W e will be guided and controlled by a demonic spirit guide, ascended master, master of wisdom, or whatever else your higher consciousness leader demon directs. The tribulation precedes the rapture and only Jesus and the knowledge of His word can keep us and make us an overcommer in tribulation. We need to get serious about making our faith grow strong. How do we get more faith? Faith cometh by hearing, and hearing by the word of God. Clinton brought Yasser Arifat to Washington to make a peace treaty with Israel. Watch out if the treaty is broken near the end of Clinton's first term.

Daniel 10:5-6

Then I lifted up mine eyes, and looked, and behold a certain man clothed in linen, whose loins [were] girded with fine gold of Uphaz: His body also [was] like the beryl, and his face as the appearance of lightning, and his eyes as lamps of fire, and his arms and his feet like in colour to polished brass, and the voice of his words like the voice of a multitude.

Who was this that Daniel saw? W as it Jesus? Compare this description with John's description of Jesus on the isle of

Patmos. Revelation 1:13-15 And in the midst of the
seven candlesticks [one] like unto the Son of man,
clothed with a garment down to the foot, and girt
about the paps with a golden girdle. His head and
[his] hairs [were] white like wool, as white as snow;
and his eyes [were] as a flame of fire; And his feet
like unto fine brass, as if they burned in a furnace;
and his voice as the sound of many waters. Could it
be that Daniel was so beloved of God that Jesus Himself
would come to give him the answers to his prayers?

Daniel 10:10-14
And, behold, an hand touched me, which set me upon
my knees and [upon] the palms of my hands.
And he said unto me, O Daniel, a man greatly beloved,
understand the words that I speak unto thee, and
stand upright: for unto thee am I now sent. And when
he had spoken this word unto me, I stood trembling.
Then said he unto me, Fear not, Daniel: for from the
first day that thou didst set thine heart to understand,
and to chasten thyself before thy God, thy words
were heard, and I am come for thy words.
But the prince of the kingdom of Persia withstood me
one and twenty days: but, lo, Michael, one of the chief
princes, came to help me; and I remained there with
the kings of Persia. Now I am come to make thee
understand what shall befall thy people in the latter
days: for yet the vision [is] for [many] days.
Could it be that Jesus Himself had personally been working
to soften the heart of Cyrus for 21 days since Daniel began

his earnest prayer. It seems logical that Daniel had shown Cyrus the scriptures of Isaiah. Perhaps Cyrus' initial rejection of those scriptures is what caused Daniel to begin his mourning and earnest prayer. Perhaps Cyrus was resisting and Jesus Himself was reasoning with Cyrus during those 21 days? What do you think?

Daniel 10:18-21

Then there came again and touched me [one] like the appearance of a man, and he strengthened me, And said, O man greatly beloved, fear not: peace [be] unto thee, be strong, yea, be strong. And when he had spoken unto me, I was strengthened, and said, Let my lord speak; for thou hast strengthened me. Then said he, Knowest thou wherefore I come unto thee? and now will I return to fight with the prince of Persia: and when I am gone forth, lo, the prince of Grecia shall come. But I will shew thee that which is noted in the scripture of truth: and [there is] none that holdeth with me in these things, but Michael your prince.

Fear not, peace be unto thee, be strong, yea be strong. God does not want us to fear. He wants us to be strong.

Daniel 11:2-4 And now will I shew thee the truth. Behold, there shall stand up yet three kings in Persia; and the fourth shall be far richer than [they] all: and by his strength through his riches he shall stir up all against the realm of Grecia. And a mighty king shall stand up, that shall rule with great dominion, and do according to his will. And when he shall stand up, his kingdom shall be broken, and shall be divided toward the four winds of heaven; and not to his posterity, nor according to his dominion which he ruled: for his kingdom shall be plucked up, even for others beside those.

The Lord tells Daniel of the rise and fall of the Persian empire which will be overthrown by Alexander the Great who will fall at the height of his conquests and have his kingdom divided in four parts. Alexander was reported to have only about 35,000 soldiers and about $75,000 to start the war with Persia while the Persian king had an annual income of about $11,000,000 and hundreds of thousands of soldiers. All of Alexander's 3 wives, 2 sons, his brother and his mother were murdered. Ptolemy, Alexander's general, king of the south, became strong by adding Cypress, Phonecia, Caria and Corinth to his kingdom of Egypt. The wars between the north (Syria) and south (Egypt) ended by the marriage of Berenice, who was Ptolemy II's daughter, to Antiochus II, king of Syria. The marriage required Antiochus to divorce his wife Laodice. After the marriage Antiochus brought back Laodice. Laodice then poisoned both Antiochus and Berenice and put her son Seleucus II on the throne. The Egyptian women who had come with Berenice tried to defend Berenice when she was killed, and many of them were killed. Then Berneice's brother Ptolemy III invaded Syria. He killed Seleucus who was also known as Antiochus. This whole section in Daniel 11:5-30 while rather confusing is absolutely accurate in every historical detail.

Daniel 11:21

And in his estate shall stand up a vile person, to whom they shall not give the honour of the kingdom: but he shall come in peaceably, and obtain the kingdom by flatteries.

Many believe that this verse strongly indicates that the antichrist will be a Syrian. The historical person in this verse was Antiochus Epiphanes. When Rome made him stop short of conquering Egypt Antiochus Epiphanes attacked Jerusalem. He killed 40,000 Jews and sold many as slaves. He boiled pigs and sprinkled this pig soup in the temple and on the alter. He broke into the Holy of Holies and looted the golden vessels. He stopped the Jewish worship and dedicated the temple to Jupiter. His contemptible and abominable deeds caused the Maccabeean revolt of the Jews.

Daniel 11:32-39

And such as do wickedly against the covenant shall he corrupt by flatteries: but the people that do know their God shall be strong, and do [exploits].
And they that understand among the people shall instruct many: yet they shall fall by the sword, and by flame, by captivity, and by spoil, [many] days. Now when they shall fall, they shall be holpen with a little help: but many shall cleave to them with flatteries. And [some] of them of understanding shall fall, to try them, and to purge, and to make [them] white, [even] to the time of the end: because [it is] yet for a time appointed. And the king shall do

according to his will; and he shall exalt himself, and magnify himself above every god, and shall speak marvellous things against the God of gods, and shall prosper till the indignation be accomplished: for that that is determined shall be done. Neither shall he regard the God of his fathers, nor the desire of women, nor regard any god: for he shall magnify himself above all. But in his estate shall he honour the God of forces: and a god whom his fathers knew not shall he honour with gold, and silver, and with precious stones, and pleasant things. Thus shall he do in the most strong holds with a strange god, whom he shall acknowledge [and] increase with glory: and he shall cause them to rule over many, and shall divide the land for gain.

Here is where the transition is made to end time last days prophecy which has not had historical fulfillment. We need to be carefully watching to see the details of these prophecies unfolding. <u>The people who know their God will be strong and do exploits.</u> Can we be corrupted by flatteries? Does what people think of us make much difference to us? Do we seek the praise of people or the approval of God? Will we be corrupted by flatteries and be sucked into the global new age government and religious system? Will we get serious about winning souls for the Lord Jesus Christ? They that have true understanding and wisdom will try with all their might to instruct many in the way of salvation. It will cost them their families and possessions. It will cost them their freedom. It will cost many of these saints their life. Those who have true wisdom

and understanding will be tried and tested in great
tribulation. All the saints, not just Israel, will experience
great tribulation unless perhaps they are nuked. Fear not,
be strong, and do exploits in the power of the Holy Spirit.
Do not fear it, get hold of God's purpose and power to do
exploits for His glory. Antichrist will exalt himself and
magnify himself above every god. He will say unheard-of
things against Almighty God.

Daniel 11:44-45

But tidings out of the east and out of the north shall
trouble him: therefore he shall go forth with great
fury to destroy, and utterly to make away many. And
he shall plant the tabernacles of his palace between
the seas in the glorious holy mountain; yet he shall
come to his end, and none shall help him.

For a time antichrist will appear to be invincible. But he
will be troubled by reports from the north and east. The
kings of the east, Red China, today boasts of an army
of 200,000,000 soldiers. This is the exact size of the eastern
army John tells us about to come against antichrist. The
time is definitely at hand. Antichrist will set up his palace
in Jerusalem. Our blessed hope, the Lord Jesus Christ will
destroy him and his armies with the brightness of His
glorious powerful return.

Daniel 12:1

And at that time shall Michael stand up, the great
prince which standeth for the children of thy people:
and there shall be a time of trouble, such as never

was since there was a nation [even] to that same
time: and at that time thy people shall be delivered,
every one that shall be found written in the book.
Who are Daniel's people at the time of the end? They are
Jews who know Messiah Jesus as Lord and Savior. What
about Nebuchadnezzar, Cyrus, Darius, and Nebuzaradan are
they not also Daniel's people? These people were not Jews
but Daniel won them to his God by his witness. They too are
Daniel's people. Everyone who shall be found written in
the book shall be delivered. What book is this?
Philippians 4:3 ......and [with] other my
fellowlabourers, whose names [are] in the book of
life.
Revelation 3:5 He that overcometh, the same shall be
clothed in white raiment; and I will not blot out his
name out of the book of life, but I will confess his
name before my Father, and before his angels.
Revelation 13:8 And all that dwell upon the earth
shall worship him, whose names are not written in
the book of life of the Lamb slain from the foundation
of the world.
Revelation 20:15 And whosoever was not found
written in the book of life was cast into the lake of
fire.
Revelation 21:27 And there shall in no wise enter into
it any thing that defileth, neither [whatsoever] worketh
abomination, or [maketh] a lie: but they which are
written in the Lamb's book of life.
Much more than Israel is referred to in these verses. What
he is talking about in reality is the body of Christ. Jesus

said He would always be with us till the end and even the gates of hell could not prevail against His church. When any Jew accepts Jesus Christ as Savior and Lord he becomes part of the body of Christ and his name is then entered into the Lambs book of life. Christians, must be made aware of the possibility and probability that we will experience the great tribulation. Is our name written in the Lamb's book of life? Will the great tribulation cause it to be blotted out? How will antichrist wage war on the saints? You can't very well wage war on someone who has been raptured out. The rapture will occur at the end of the great tribulation coincidentally with the glorious powerful return of the Lord Jesus Christ. Is our faith greater than our fear of tribulation? Is our faith growing or shrinking? Will we be strong, courageous, and do exploits for the glory of God by the power of His Holy Spirit? Will we be sucked into the global New Age government and religious system of antichrist?

Daniel 12:2-4

And many of them that sleep in the dust of the earth shall awake, some to everlasting life, and some to shame [and] everlasting contempt. And they that be wise shall shine as the brightness of the firmament; and they that turn many to righteousness as the stars for ever and ever. But thou, O Daniel, shut up the words, and seal the book, [even] to the time of the end: many shall run to and fro, and knowledge shall be increased.

The apostle Paul told about this mystery when the dead in

Christ would rise. It happens at the time of the end just
before the rapture coincident with our blessed hope the
powerful glorious return of the Lord Jesus Christ. It is high
time to get serious about winning souls. We may be the first
people who could ever fully understand the entire book of
Daniel. Daniel was told to seal up the book until the time of
the end. Don't put too much confidence in old commentaries
on Daniel. Parts of D aniel's book were sealed to all but
those reading it when it was the time of the end. Read it
frequently asking God by His H oly Spirit to open it. It will
be open and beautifully simple if it is the time of the end. At
the time of the end many shall run to and fro and knowledge
shall be increased. That is more true today than it has ever
been.

Daniel 12:8-12

And I heard, but I understood not: then said I, O my
Lord, what [shall be] the end of these [things]?
And he said, Go thy way, Daniel: for the words [are]
closed up and sealed till the time of the end. Many
shall be purified, and made white, and tried; but the
wicked shall do wickedly: and none of the wicked
shall understand; but the wise shall understand.
And from the time [that] the daily [sacrifice] shall be
taken away, and the abomination that maketh
desolate set up, [there shall be] a thousand two
hundred and ninety days. Blessed [is] he that
waiteth, and cometh to the thousand three hundred
and five and thirty days.

The words are closed and sealed up till the time of the end.

We are to be tried and perhaps give our life to try to bring people to understand the way of salvation. When antichrist sets up the abomination in the temple there will be a maximum of 1290 days left. God would have us not fear and be strong and patient in tribulation.

MOSES

Moses wrote the first 5 books of the bible. The law was given through Moses. All of the blood sacrifices pointed to the truth that without the shedding of blood there is no remission of sins. Messiah Jesus Christ is the perfect Lamb of God who took away the sins of the whole world. All Christians must love the Jews. It is sad how many Jews continue to fail to see Jesus in the writings of Moses. The Exodus record of how God plagued Egypt while protecting His people in Goshen is very important as we near and enter great tribulation. It illustrates how God will protect and provide for us as Jews and Gentile Christians stand together in the war Antichrist wages on the saints.

Genesis 3:5 - ...ye shall be as gods.
This is the lie. It forms fundamental thesis of Hinduism, Buddhism, Mormonism, New A ge Movement, globalism, reincarnation, the occult and almost every other ism other than Orthodox Judaism and Christianity. Learn to recognize this lie regardless of which of the thousands of new sugar coatings that Satan puts over this basic fundamental lie designed to take us to hell.

Genesis 5:24
And Enoch walked with God: and he <was> not; for God took him.
Enoch walked with God. Are we walking with God or away from Him? Enoch did not die. God took him.

Hebrews 9:27 - And as it is appointed unto men [once to die], but after this the judgment:
Elijah is the only other man who did not die. Perhaps Enoch and Elijah are god's 2 special witnesses in the tribulation who stand powerfully against antichrist.

Genesis 8:21 ... and the LORD said in his heart, I will not again curse the ground any more for man's sake; for the imagination of man's heart <is> evil from his youth; neither will I again smite any more every thing living, as I have done.
The earth will never again be destroyed. Man now has nuclear capability of destroying all life on earth; however, God will not allow it. We can forget about all of the scientists who predict doom. Ozone depletion, global warming, etc., is all a bunch of horsefeathers. We should not trash the environment but God will not allow the destruction of the planet. Environmental extremism illustrates the height of human vanity and plays right into the hands of antichrist. God will intervene at the Lord's second coming to prevent the destruction of all flesh by antichrist.

The imagination of man's heart is evil from his youth. This is why we must be born again by the Spirit of God. Otherwise we cannot help but think and do evil. Man's greatest problem is that he tries to hide or excuse his sin, just like the alcoholic denies that he has a drinking problem. We need the Holy Spirit to convince us of our sins and lead us to confess them and help us repent from our sins. Jesus

paid the full price for all of our sins but we still have
to confess and repent. This we cannot do without the Holy
Spirit.

Genesis 10:8-10

And Cush begat Nimrod: he began to be a mighty one
in the earth. He was a mighty hunter before the
LORD: wherefore it is said, Even as Nimrod the
mighty hunter before the LORD. And the beginning
of his kingdom was Babel, and Erech, and Accad,
and Calneh, in the land of Shinar.

Noah cursed Ham's son. The curse would make the
descendants of Cannan to be slaves, as a result of Ham's sin
against Noah. Ham also begat Cush. Cush did not want
this curse to have effect on his descendants. Cush begat
Nimrod whose name in Hebrew means "we will rebel".
This points to violent and open rebellion against God. No
doubt Ham told Cush about the curse. Cush didn't like it to
the point he named his son "we will rebel." We begin to see
the seeds of antichrist right here. Nimrod became a mighty
one in the earth by bold and daring deeds. His deeds were
to hunt men by tyranny, force and confusion. He built
Babel and hence, in scripture, Babylon means more than
the capital city of Chaldea. Babylon means tyranny and
confusion and open rebellion against God. Nimrod was
obsessed with rage against the curse and prophesy of Noah
regarding the generations of Ham being slaves. He would
not be a slave. He would hunt slaves. He lorded it over
others, hunting and destroying all who opposed him in his
tyranny. He persuaded men, not to ascribe their trust to

God, but to him. He taught men to centralize and federalize government. He directly opposed God's command to N oah to replenish the earth (Gen. 9:1), concentrating people in a single large city as opposed to dispersing them. He openly defied God to send another flood. He established the first kingdom and established the first great universal religion opposing God since the flood. This was done openly "before the lord" in open defiance to God.

His wife, Semiramis, became pregnant after his death and was the unwed mother of Tammuz. The roots of almost all ancient religions and many modern ones including the New Age movement can be traced to these three people N imrod, Semiramis, and Tammuz. Just a few are the ancient Babylonian sun god, and his wife Ishtar, or Aphrodite, or Venus; Osiris and I sis of the Egyptians, as well as the Hindu gods, all reincarnation religions, Buddhists, and all of the occult religions including Mother Earth can trace their roots to Nimrod.

God had a real problem with what was going on in Nimrod's crown jewel city of Babel. The way N imrod was going, the righteous God fearing children of Shem and J aphet did not stand a chance unless God somehow directly intervened on their behalf. We see here a picture of how God will directly intervene with the return of the Lord Jesus Christ to deliver His saints from the war which antichrist wages on them.

Genesis 11:5-9 And the LORD came down to see the city and the tower, which the children of men builded.

And the LORD said, Behold, the people <is> one, and they have all one language; and this they begin to do: and now nothing will be restrained from them, which they have imagined to do. Go to, let us go down, and there confound their language, that they may not understand one another's speech. So the LORD scattered them abroad from thence upon the face of all the earth: and they left off to build the city. Therefore is the name of it called Babel; because the LORD did there confound the language of all the earth: and from thence did the LORD scatter them abroad upon the face of all the earth.

Can we see the mercy of God protecting His people? Can we see what Nimrod started being carried on today? Are political leaders calling for centralized government? Do political leaders seem to be calling for a global or one world government?

<u>Christians, and all people, need to know that any world government prior to the millennial reign of Jesus Christ will be headed by antichrist.</u>

Genesis 28:4 And give thee the blessing of Abraham, to thee, and to thy seed with thee; that thou mayest inherit the land wherein thou art a stranger, which God gave unto Abraham.

The Arab Israeli conflict over Palestine cannot be resolved. If it is ever appears to be resolved at the peace table, it will be antichrist who is in control of the negotiating process. God gave the land to Israel. Satan is stirring up the Arabs to fight Israel for this land given to Israel by God. Beware

of the person behind any Arab/Israeli peace treaties. He
may be antichrist.

**Exodus 9:23-26 And Moses stretched forth his rod
toward heaven: and the LORD sent thunder and hail,
and the fire ran along upon the ground; and the
LORD rained hail upon the land of Egypt. So there
was hail, and fire mingled with the hail, very
grievous, such as there was none like it in all the
land of Egypt since it became a nation. And the hail
smote throughout all the land of Egypt all that [was]
in the field, both man and beast; and the hail smote
every herb of the field, and brake every tree of the
field. Only in the land of Goshen, where the children
of Israel [were], was there no hail.**

Notice how God protected His people in the middle of all of
these plagues. During the tribulation God will provide
supernatural protection for His people. Don't worry about
the rapture occurring at the end of the tribulation. Get
right with God. When we are under the great umbrella of
God's protection we do not have to be hurt by the plagues
of the great tribulation. The teaching of a pretribulation
rapture may be a part of the end time strong delusion
designed to lead away even the elect if it were possible. We
all must get right with God and stay in a right relationship
with Him. The plagues soon coming again upon all the
earth will destroy everyone who is not protected by God.

**Exodus 9:29-30 And Moses said unto him, As soon
as I am gone out of the city, I will spread abroad my**

hands unto the LORD; [and] the thunder shall cease, neither shall there be any more hail; that thou mayest know how that the earth [is] the LORD'S.
But as for thee and thy servants, I know that ye will not yet fear the LORD God.

We know that during the great tribulation the plagues come as waves growing more and more severe. Most people will have their hearts hardened against God instead of repenting.

Dr. Dan Juster has written a wonderful book titled *Revelation: The Passover Key*. This small book is perhaps the best book available for a clear understanding of Revelation. The book relates how God's protection of His people in Goshen during the plagues in Egypt is central to understanding end time prophecy and especially Revelation. The book is available from Tikkun-MBI Books, PO Box 7538, Gaithersburg, MD 20898.

ISAIAH

Isaiah was a great prophet. He was probably the greatest prophet regarding the coming of Messiah. To share the gospel with the Jews take them to the book of Isaiah especially chapter 53. Most of Isaiah's prophecies about Messiah concerned His first coming to earth. The following scriptures will focus on his prophecies concerning Messiah's second coming as the Lion of the tribe of Judah. No Lamb is Messiah when He comes this time. It will be no secret. Every eye shall see the glorious powerful King of Kings when He will give total victory to His saints and concludes their war with Antichrist. The time frame of Isaiah's writing is approximately 760-698 BC. His mission was to get the people to wake up and repent. He was warning of God's coming judgment. Isaiah was bold, and courageous. He was killed for his work of warning the people of God by being placed in a hollow log and having the log sawed while he was inside. America needs a prophet like Isaiah today.

Isaiah 1:18-20 Come now, and let us reason together, saith the LORD: though your sins be as scarlet, they shall be as white as snow; though they be red like crimson, they shall be as wool. If ye be willing and obedient, ye shall eat the good of the land: But if ye refuse and rebel, ye shall be devoured with the sword: for the mouth of the LORD hath spoken [it]. Hear the word of the Lord. Will we see His love and desire to bless us? He says come now - let us reason together.

Let's talk about it. God says let Me help you figure out
what is really important. No matter how bad and bloody
our sins may be, God wants to make us as though we had
never sinned. God can do that. We can't do that. It is only
Jesus who has ever lived a life without sin. We have all
sinned. None of us can ever make up for any sin. It makes
no difference how great our sin may be. In fact, Jesus
pointed out that the one who has been forgiven much,
generally loves God more than someone who has not been
forgiven much. Though your sins be as scarlet they shall be
as white as snow; though they be red like crimson, they shall
be as wool. God forgives and forgets just as if I'd never
sinned. Come now to Jesus. Be forgiven. Be justified by
God. Self justification is the main road to hell.

Isaiah 2:2-5 And it shall come to pass in the last
days, [that] the mountain of the LORD'S house shall
be established in the top of the mountains, and shall
be exalted above the hills; and all nations shall flow
unto it. And many people shall go and say, Come ye,
and let us go up to the mountain of the LORD, to the
house of the God of Jacob; and he will teach us of
his ways, and we will walk in his paths: for out of
Zion shall go forth the law, and the word of the LORD
from Jerusalem. And he shall judge among the
nations, and shall rebuke many people: and they shall
beat their swords into plowshares, and their spears
into pruninghooks: nation shall not lift up sword
against nation, neither shall they learn war any more.
O house of Jacob, come ye, and let us walk in the

light of the LORD.

In the last days when the Lord returns at the end of the 7 years of the great tribulation, Jesus will annihilate the armies of antichrist and all of the unrighteous and lead the saints in heaven back to earth to set up His millennial kingdom. Jesus will set up His kingdom in Jerusalem. He will rule the world with a rod of iron. There will be no more wars. There will be no more violence. Everyone will know and follow the ways of the Lord. It will be fantastic joyful peace and prosperity for everyone.

Isaiah 2:10-12 Enter into the rock, and hide thee in the dust, for fear of the LORD, and for the glory of his majesty. The lofty looks of man shall be humbled, and the haughtiness of men shall be bowed down, and the LORD alone shall be exalted in that day. For the day of the LORD of hosts [shall be] upon every [one that is] proud and lofty, and upon every [one that is] lifted up; and he shall be brought low:

At the time of the day of the Lord the proud and the mighty will be brought down. They will seek to hide in the rocks and even seek to die but they will not be able. We need to humble ourselves and submit to God before His return otherwise it will be too late. His coming may be very soon. We need to be ready. Are we ready?

Isaiah 3:9-10 The shew of their countenance doth witness against them; and they declare their sin as Sodom, they hide [it] not. Woe unto their soul! for they have rewarded evil unto themselves.

Say ye to the righteous, that [it shall be] well [with him]: for they shall eat the fruit of their doings.
We have this here today too. They declare their sin as Sodom. The homosexuals blatantly and openly demonstrate their sin and are demanding special privileges. There never has been a society in history that was not suddenly destroyed when homosexuals in that society openly and blatantly paraded their sin.

Isaiah 5:8   Woe unto them that join house to house, [that] lay field to field, till [there be] no place, that they may be placed alone in the midst of the earth!
Greed is a cruel master and its slave does not ever find joy. One of the richest men in the world was asked how much money was enough. He responded "a little more than what I have got." What a trap he is in. We need to be content with what we have. Everything we own takes our time. We end up becoming slaves to our possessions.

Isaiah 5:15-16 And the mean man shall be brought down, and the mighty man shall be humbled, and the eyes of the lofty shall be humbled: But the LORD of hosts shall be exalted in judgment, and God that is holy shall be sanctified in righteousness.
In the day of the Lord - God will be exulted. There will be no place for the pride of anyone.

Isaiah 5:20-22 Woe unto them that call evil good, and good evil; that put darkness for light, and light for darkness; that put bitter for sweet, and sweet for

bitter! Woe unto [them that are] wise in their own
eyes, and prudent in their own sight! Woe unto [them
that are] mighty to drink wine, and men of strength to
mingle strong drink:

Woe - grief, regret, distress, lamentably bad, deep suffering,
affliction. This is what is coming to those who call evil good
and good evil. Sodomy is sin, not an alternate lifestyle.
What God says is right no matter what anybody else thinks.
Ultimately it is woe for those who do not agree with God.
We can apparently get away with it for a time but ultimately
it is woe. Are we wise in our own eyes or do we get our
wisdom from God? Is what God said important to us?

Isaiah 5:24-25 Therefore as the fire devoureth the
stubble, and the flame consumeth the chaff, [so] their
root shall be as rottenness, and their blossom shall
go up as dust: because they have cast away the law
of the LORD of hosts, and despised the word of the
Holy One of Israel. Therefore is the anger of the
LORD kindled against his people, and he hath
stretched forth his hand against them, and hath
smitten them: and the hills did tremble, and their
carcases [were] torn in the midst of the streets.
For all this his anger is not turned away, but his
hand [is] stretched out still.

God's judgment will be severe. Judah has pushed God's
patience to the limit. God's anger is the most fearsome and
awesome thing in the universe. Intelligence without wisdom
is not worth much. Knowledge without wisdom is not worth
much. Here is a form of wisdom - learn and do those things

which please and glorify God; learn and avoid those things which make God angry. The source of Judah's problem is the same as the intelligent and knowledgeable people everywhere who lack true wisdom. They have cast away the law of the Lord and despised the word of the Holy One of Israel. Will we seek wisdom? Will we study God's word? God wants to bless us. We tie His hands when we reject His word. Our human wisdom is not true wisdom. We need God's wisdom more than anything else. It is only available in the bible or the school of hard knocks.

Isaiah 6:1-10 In the year that king Uzziah died I saw also the Lord sitting upon a throne, high and lifted up, and his train filled the temple. Above it stood the seraphims: each one had six wings; with twain he covered his face, and with twain he covered his feet, and with twain he did fly. And one cried unto another, and said, Holy, holy, holy, [is] the LORD of hosts: the whole earth [is] full of his glory. And the posts of the door moved at the voice of him that cried, and the house was filled with smoke. Then said I, Woe [is] me! for I am undone; because I [am] a man of unclean lips, and I dwell in the midst of a people of unclean lips: for mine eyes have seen the King, the LORD of hosts. Then flew one of the seraphims unto me, having a live coal in his hand, [which] he had taken with the tongs from off the altar: And he laid [it] upon my mouth, and said, Lo, this hath touched thy lips; and thine iniquity is taken away, and thy sin purged. Also I heard the voice of

the Lord, saying, Whom shall I send, and who will go for us? Then said I, Here [am] I; send me. And he said, Go, and tell this people, Hear ye indeed, but understand not; and see ye indeed, but perceive not. Make the heart of this people fat, and make their ears heavy, and shut their eyes; lest they see with their eyes, and hear with their ears, and understand with their heart, and convert, and be healed.

In the year king Uzziah died Isaiah has the vision of the Lord in His temple which gives him his mission of preaching repentance to the people of Judah. Isaiah could not adequately describe the beauty and majesty of the Lord on His throne. The Lord is surrounded by mighty seraphim angels who proclaim - holy, holy, holy is the Lord, the whole earth is full of His glory. Isaiah was filled with awe, fear, and awareness of his own corruption at the sights and sounds as his spirit witnessed the vision of the Lord on His throne. Here is true conviction. Isaiah is overwhelmed by concern over what he is. His concern is not so much what he has done or what he has not done. What a person is, is more important that what he has done. God is much more interested in His servants, than in what they do for Him. Holiness of life is much more important than holiness of doctrine. Doing right is infinitely more important than talk about it. The angel flies with a hot coal in tongs from the fire before the Lord's alter and touches Isaiah's lips to assure him that his uncleanness was going to be cleansed by God. This is the only way any sins can be cleansed. God has to do it for us. We cannot cleanse ourselves. When he hears God say, "Whom shall I send, and who will go for

Us?", Isaiah immediately says - here I am, send me. Isaiah got his marching orders from God. N o wonder he had such boldness before the kings and priests where he delivered the hard messages that they did not want to hear.

Isaiah 8:19-20 And when they shall say unto you, Seek unto them that have familiar spirits, and unto wizards that peep, and that mutter: should not a people seek unto their God? for the living to the dead? To the law and to the testimony: if they speak not according to this word, [it is] because [there is] no light in them.

As it was for Judah just before they were to experience God's fiery judgment so it is for us today. Seek them that have familiar spirits - wizards that peep and mutter. Does Hillary Clinton boast of her conversations with the spirit of Eleanor Roosevelt? How far from judgment are we? When we see such things here is the answer - to the law and to the testimony. If they speak not according to the bible they are in darkness.

Isaiah 11:6-10 The wolf also shall dwell with the lamb, and the leopard shall lie down with the kid; and the calf and the young lion and the fatling together; and a little child shall lead them. And the cow and the bear shall feed; their young ones shall lie down together: and the lion shall eat straw like the ox. And the sucking child shall play on the hole of the asp, and the weaned child shall put his hand on the cockatrice' den. They shall not hurt nor destroy in all

my holy mountain: for the earth shall be full of the
knowledge of the LORD, as the waters cover the sea.
And in that day there shall be a root of Jesse, which
shall stand for an ensign of the people; to it shall the
Gentiles seek: and his rest shall be glorious.

Will you have a place in the reign of King Jesus? Think
about this glorious kingdom which Jesus will establish. All
animals will be gentle. All people will be kind and
gentle. Everyone will try to find ways to be a blessing to
others. There will be no violence, no sickness, no death.
"His rest shall be glorious." Will you be there?

Isaiah 11:11-12 And it shall come to pass in that day,
[that] the Lord shall set his hand again the second
time to recover the remnant of his people, which
shall be left, from Assyria, and from Egypt, and from
Pathros, and from Cush, and from Elam, and from
Shinar, and from Hamath, and from the islands of the
sea. And he shall set up an ensign for the nations,
and shall assemble the outcasts of Israel, and
gather together the dispersed of Judah from the
four corners of the earth.

This is fantastic! We are the generation to see this thing
come to pass before our eyes which was spoken by Isaiah
2700 years ago. The second regathering is occurring
right now. The first dispersion had not happened when
Isaiah gave this prophecy. The second dispersion happened
in 70AD. The second regathering is happening in the
1990's. Jesus said when you see these things come to pass
know that I am near, even at the door. We are living in the

most exciting time of all human history. Jesus has come the first time as the spotless perfect Lamb Who was slain for all of our sins. He was resurrected and ascended into heaven. He is coming back again. His 2nd coming is near. He does not make any secret of His 2nd coming. He will come again in great power and glory. We are seeing the prophesy which tells us when to expect his return being fulfilled before our eyes right now in the 1990's. Israel, the down trodden Jews who have been dispersed and scattered throughout the world, are being gathered back to their homeland. It is happening now. There is no secret 2nd coming. A secret 2nd coming is not scriptural. It is a myth designed for the end times to lead away even the elect if it were possible. When Jesus comes again it will not be in secret. It can only be the powerful and glorious 2nd coming. Every eye shall see Him at His 2nd coming. Are we ready? If we are not ready it is high time to get ready.

Isaiah 12:1-6 And in that day thou shalt say, O LORD, I will praise thee: though thou wast angry with me, thine anger is turned away, and thou comfortedst me. Behold, God [is] my salvation; I will trust, and not be afraid: for the LORD JEHOVAH [is] my strength and [my] song; he also is become my salvation. Therefore with joy shall ye draw water out of the wells of salvation. And in that day shall ye say, Praise the LORD, call upon his name, declare his doings among the people, make mention that his name is exalted. Sing unto the LORD; for he hath done excellent things: this [is] known in all the earth.

Cry out and shout, thou inhabitant of Zion: for great [is] the Holy One of Israel in the midst of thee.
Some day soon the Jews in Israel will finally begin to see that Jesus is their Savior and Lord. To some extent it is already happening in the Messianic Jewish congregations in Israel. The number of Jews placing their faith in Messiah Jesus is growing exponentially. Salvation can only be found in Jesus, for there is no other name given under heaven by which men can be saved.

Acts 4:10-12 Be it known unto you all, and to all the people of Israel, that by the name of Jesus Christ of Nazareth, whom ye crucified, whom God raised from the dead, [even] by him doth this man stand here before you whole. This is the stone which was set at nought of you builders, which is become the head of the corner. Neither is there salvation in any other: for there is none other name under heaven given among men, whereby we must be saved.

No one knows the day or the hour that the Lord will return. There are things which we will recognize as we are in the final 7 years of great tribulation. Since the great tribulation will start so gradually that no one will know when the great tribulation began, then even in the middle of the great tribulation we will not know the day or the hour of the Lord's 2nd coming. What we will know when we realize we are in the final 7 years is that in less than 7 years our King Jesus is coming. That is our blessed hope. The pre-tribulation rapture is not our blessed hope. In fact, it is not scriptural and possibly is part of the end time strong delusion. Keep attention focused on what the bible actually

says and not what people tell us it says. Also keep attention
focused on what is happening in Israel. When we see the
people of Israel finally recognizing Jesus, their Messiah,
then we may know His return is very near indeed. At his
2nd coming everyone will recognize Him. Every eye shall
see him.

**Isaiah 19:1 The burden of Egypt. Behold, the LORD
rideth upon a swift cloud, and shall come into Egypt:
and the idols of Egypt shall be moved at his
presence, and the heart of Egypt shall melt in the
midst of it.**
The 19th chapter of Isaiah finds much of its fulfillment in
the tribulation and millennium.

**Isaiah 19:2 And I will set the Egyptians against the
Egyptians: and they shall fight every one against his
brother, and every one against his neighbour; city
against city, [and] kingdom against kingdom.**
It is not clear when this Egyptian civil war will occur. Most
of Egypt today is Muslim. Some Muslims may not go along
with the anti-christ world religion. This may be what
precipitates the Egyptian civil war. It will most likely have
a tribulation fulfillment.

**Isaiah 19:4 And the Egyptians will I give over into the
hand of a cruel lord; and a fierce king shall rule over
them, saith the Lord, the LORD of hosts.**
This fierce king is the anti-christ.

Isaiah 19:8 The fishers also shall mourn, and all they that cast angle into the brooks shall lament, and they that spread nets upon the waters shall languish.

We have seen fulfillment of this prophesy. It came with the construction of the Aswan dam. Prior to the construction of this dam the waters of the Nile were always muddy and turbid which made them easy to fish commercially with nets. Now they have become relatively clear and there are over 30,000 egyptian commercial fishermen who lost their livelihood.

Isaiah 19:17 And the land of Judah shall be a terror unto Egypt, every one that maketh mention thereof shall be afraid in himself, because of the counsel of the LORD of hosts, which he hath determined against it.

We have also seen at least a partial fulfillment of this prophesy. Israel has soundly defeated Egyptian forces in all battles since the 6 day war of 1963. Israel took vast land areas of Egypt all the way to the Suez Canal in this war. This is what brought about the Carter peace treaty between Sadat and Begin when Israel returned much of this territory back to Egypt.

Isaiah 19:20 And it shall be for a sign and for a witness unto the LORD of hosts in the land of Egypt: for they shall cry unto the LORD because of the oppressors, and he shall send them a saviour, and a great one, and he shall deliver them.

Egypt's Savior is none other then the Savior of all mankind.

It is Jesus Christ and this prophesy likely will be fulfilled in the millennium.

Isaiah 46:8-10 Remember this, and shew yourselves men: bring [it] again to mind, O ye transgressors. Remember the former things of old: for I [am] God, and [there is] none else; [I am] God, and [there is] none like me, Declaring the end from the beginning, and from ancient times [the things] that are not [yet] done, saying, My counsel shall stand, and I will do all my pleasure:

God is God. Believe it or go to hell. It is just that simple. We are all sinners. Jesus paid the price for our ransom. We can never pay that price ourselves. Only God declares the end from the beginning. All of God's prophecies have and will come to pass with 100% accuracy. Will we live for God or will we live for ourselves? Will we do it God's way or will we do it our own way? These are important questions which all will soon answer in the great tribulation. God's word will stand. God will do what ever He says He will and no one can prevent Him. We are either our own boss or we let Jesus be Lord of our life. Everyone will make a final choice during the great tribulation. Are we ready? Have we made the right choice? There is still time to change our mind if we have not made the right choice. It is important to have read the entire word of God from Genesis to Revelation. Do not depend on any preacher. We need to read it for ourselves and have the Holy Spirit give us the necessary understanding of God's word.

Isaiah 65:1-2 I am sought of [them that] asked not [for me]; I am found of [them that] sought me not: I said, Behold me, behold me, unto a nation [that] was not called by my name. I have spread out my hands all the day unto a rebellious people, which walketh in a way [that was] not good, after their own thoughts; God explains why Israel and Judah are going to be judged and go into the captivity in Babylon. If he did judge Israel with great affliction, what makes Americans think we are not on a collision course with God's judgment. Are we not a rebellious people? Rebellion is as the sin of witchcraft. The young people brag of their rebellion as though it is a virtue. This nation walks in a way not good. Political correctness in this corrupt nation is antichrist and diametrically opposed to God's principles. Everyone walks after their own thoughts which have no place for God and His principles. Get ready for judgment.

Isaiah 65:5 Which say, Stand by thyself, come not near to me; for I am holier than thou. These [are] a smoke in my nose, a fire that burneth all the day. This may be the most offensive and obnoxious of sins. "Stay away from me - I am holier than you are." Wow, how repulsive this must be to God. We are all sinners. All of our righteousness is filthy rags to God. The true mark of holiness is the realization of the desperate wickedness which everyone hides deeply in their innermost being. God loves the unlovable. Will we reach out to the poor, the oppressed, and the outcast? Holy people, who think they are holy, stink to high heaven.

Isaiah 65:11-12 But ye [are] they that forsake the LORD, that forget my holy mountain, that prepare a table for that troop, and that furnish the drink offering unto that number. Therefore will I number you to the sword, and ye shall all bow down to the slaughter: because when I called, ye did not answer; when I spake, ye did not hear; but did evil before mine eyes, and did choose [that] wherein I delighted not.

God is calling America. Will America hear? Will America repent? Will this nation which was founded for the glory of God and the advancement of the Christian religion continue its collision course with God's judgment? God is calling. The greatest slaughter of all time is imminent. God is calling. Will we Answer? Will we continue going our own way? Will we ignore the call of God?

JEREMIAH

Jeremiah ministered from about 630BC to about 595BC. He is known as the weeping prophet. He continued warning about the approach of God's judgment. He was the weeping prophet because he had to tell the bad news that it was too late for repentance. He saw the fulfillment of many of his and Isaiah's prophecies of judgment as he witnessed his nation go into captivity. He was one of the minority of bold prophets who was not killed for his ministry.

Jeremiah 10:6-7   Forasmuch as [there is] none like unto thee, O LORD; thou [art] great, and thy name [is] great in might. Who would not fear thee, O King of nations? for to thee doth it appertain: forasmuch as among all the wise [men] of the nations, and in all their kingdoms, [there is] none like unto thee.
Who would not fear God? Only a classic fool would not fear God. The fool says in his heart there is no God. It is hard to understand the fear of the Lord when we have seen just a tiny glimpse of His love. Fear of the Lord is the only healthy fear. God is so great, so powerful, so majestic that it is really impossible not to fear Him. Perhaps to think of the fear of the Lord as reverence would be helpful. Fear of God is a motive of obedience. Love of God is a better motive. However, if we don't have enough love of God to overcome a big trial or temptation, fear of the Lord could be quite helpful.

Jeremiah 10:8 But they are altogether brutish and foolish: the stock [is] a doctrine of vanities.

They are all senseless and foolish who do not fear the Lord. One will either choose to fear God or He will waste away in vanity. We are born in vanity. The whole creation was subjected to vanity in God's hope that with this self conscious vanity man would choose to love God from his own free will. **Romans 8:20-21 For the creature was made subject to vanity, not willingly, but by reason of him who hath subjected [the same] in hope, Because the creature itself also shall be delivered from the bondage of corruption into the glorious liberty of the children of God.**

Jeremiah 10:10 But the LORD [is] the true God, he [is] the living God, and an everlasting king: at his wrath the earth shall tremble, and the nations shall not be able to abide his indignation.

All those who worship Lucifer directly or indirectly will end up facing the wrath of God. Nothing can be more fearful than to face the wrath of God. Referring to indirect worship of Lucifer speaks of those who are unwittingly sucked into contact with spirit guides, ascended masters, familiar spirits, the occult, astrology, the new age movement, the new world order, and various other orders which will all fall in line under antichrist. It is all quickly boiling down to following Jesus Christ or antichrist.

Jeremiah 10:15 They [are] vanity, [and] the work of errors: in the time of their visitation they shall perish.

All beliefs except orthodox Christianity and Judaism will fall in line under antichrist's regime. It is all vanity under Lucifer, the father of lies. It is pride and vanity which causes people to buy the lie, "Ye shall be as god." When Jesus Christ returns they shall all perish while the faithful believers in Jesus Christ are being raptured to meet the Lord in the air as He proceeds to destroy all others with the brightness of His coming and the power of His word.

Jeremiah 10:23-24 O LORD, I know that the way of man [is] not in himself: [it is] not in man that walketh to direct his steps. O LORD, correct me, but with judgment; not in thine anger, lest thou bring me to nothing.

Our life is a gift from God. No matter how corrupt or bad our situation may be thank God for our life. Find abundant, powerful, eternal life in Jesus Christ right here and now. Jesus Christ is coming back soon to set this whole world the way it should be. Do not think our government or any world government can do what only Jesus Christ can do. He is going to make everything right and it may be coming to pass sooner than we think. There may be as many as 7 years of great tribulation but hang in there - Jesus, our blessed hope is coming soon.

Jeremiah 11:1 The word that came to Jeremiah from the LORD, saying,

Jeremiah is not just making idle chatter. The Lord is telling him exactly what to say.

Jeremiah 11:3 And say thou unto them, Thus saith the LORD God of Israel; Cursed [be] the man that obeyeth not the words of this covenant,

Think about this. It is very serious to be cursed by God. Those who do not obey the words of the covenant are going to be cursed. The covenant is the 10 commandments. In America the law forbids a copy of the covenant to be displayed in any public school in the land. Could we already be in the 7 last years and not even know it?

Jeremiah 11:14 Therefore pray not thou for this people, neither lift up a cry or prayer for them: for I will not hear [them] in the time that they cry unto me for their trouble.

There comes a time when it is too late to pray? Let's hope that we have never come to that point in God's timetable and longsuffering patience.

Jeremiah 12:1-3 Righteous [art] thou, O LORD, when I plead with thee: yet let me talk with thee of [thy] judgments: Wherefore doth the way of the wicked prosper? [wherefore] are all they happy that deal very treacherously? Thou hast planted them, yea, they have taken root: they grow, yea, they bring forth fruit: thou [art] near in their mouth, and far from their reins. But thou, O LORD, knowest me: thou hast seen me, and tried mine heart toward thee: pull them out like sheep for the slaughter, and prepare them for the day of slaughter.

It is good to ask God why? We must not let our why's

become a whine. Jeremiah asks why do the wicked prosper.
The wicked will prosper for a short time. Antichrist will
be given power to wage war on the saints. But what is
seven years of the prospering of wickedness compared to
eternity? If judgment begins with the house of God, how
shall the wicked stand? None shall be able to stand the
wrath of the Lamb.

**Jeremiah 12:7 I have forsaken mine house, I have
left mine heritage; I have given the dearly beloved of
my soul into the hand of her enemies.**
This is God talking. God is greatly grieved when He is
forced to punish His rebellious children. It hurts like it
hurts any parent to discipline a rebellious child. God's
perfect will is to shower us with the blessings of obedience.
We force Him to give us the judgment of rebellion and it
grieves Him.

**Jeremiah 12:10-11 Many pastors have destroyed my
vineyard, they have trodden my portion under foot,
they have made my pleasant portion a desolate
wilderness. They have made it desolate, [and being]
desolate it mourneth unto me; the whole land is
made desolate, because no man layeth [it] to heart.**
How many pastors today excuse if not outright encourage
their people to continue living in their sins. There are even
"Christian" pastors who see nothing wrong with global
government or the new world order. Some even think that
getting in touch with a spirit guide or ascended master is ok.
Some would say abortion is a woman's right. Hell, fire, and

brimstone preachers are few and far between and unpopular to say the least. This land can be made utterly desolate very quickly.

Jeremiah 13:15-16   Hear ye, and give ear; be not proud: for the LORD hath spoken. Give glory to the LORD your God, before he cause darkness, and before your feet stumble upon the dark mountains, and, while ye look for light, he turn it into the shadow of death, [and] make [it] gross darkness.

What is it that prevents us hearing God? It is vanity and our pride? We cannot help having vanity and pride. We are born with this affliction. But it is only by hearing God that we can break free of our vanity and pride. We receive righteousness as a gift of God by faith. How do we get faith? Romans 10:17 So then faith [cometh] by hearing, and hearing by the word of God. Faith comes by hearing, and hearing by the word of God. This is not a catch 22 situation. It is the fundamental choice which every human being will make. Will we choose to humble ourself and listen to God or will we persist in our vanity and die in ours sins. Give glory to God before the darkness of death overtakes us. We don't know the day or the hour when death will overtake us. Will we let the true God be God or will we persist in the futile vain attempt to be our own god?

Jeremiah 13:23   Can the Ethiopian change his skin, or the leopard his spots? [then] may ye also do good, that are accustomed to do evil.

Can the leopard change his spots? Of course he can not. It

is the same with man and his vanity. It is just as impossible
for a man to overcome his vanity. He can put on a good
show but God knows the vanity condition of the heart. The
more a man tries to do enough good works to cover his sins
the more the vanity grows in his heart. It will grow into self
righteousness and hypocrisy which stinks to high heaven.
What can be done about this?????   **Romans 7:24-8:2**
**O wretched man that I am! who shall deliver me from
the body of this death? I thank God through Jesus
Christ our Lord. So then with the mind I myself serve
the law of God; but with the flesh the law of sin.
[There is] therefore now no condemnation to them
which are in Christ Jesus, who walk not after the
flesh, but after the Spirit. For the law of the Spirit of
life in Christ Jesus hath made me free from the law
of sin and death.**
The leopard cannot change his spots. But God can change
the leopard's spots for him. We cannot cover or make up to
God for any of our sins. But God can cover our sins for us.

**Jeremiah 14:7   O LORD, though our iniquities testify
against us, do thou [it] for thy name's sake: for our
backslidings are many; we have sinned against thee.**
This is powerful prayer. Do it for your name's sake. God
identified Himself to the world as the God of Israel.
Jeremiah asks God to save Israel for the sake of God's
name, the God of Israel.

**Jeremiah 14:11-12 Then said the LORD unto me, Pray
not for this people for [their] good. When they fast, I**

will not hear their cry; and when they offer burnt offering and an oblation, I will not accept them: but I will consume them by the sword, and by the famine, and by the pestilence.

God tells Jeremiah that it is too late. This nation is so bad. They have been so bad for so long God, the Holy God, cannot stand any longer to be identified with them. What about America - that other nation founded for the glory of God whose money even says "In God we trust"? Is it too late? Which God is the God of America? Is it the one whose covenant has been banned from all public schools of the land? The godly culture peculiar to America's founding fathers is systematically being destroyed. Is it too late for America? Christian, what will we do about it?

Jeremiah 14:13-14 Then said I, Ah, Lord GOD! behold, the prophets say unto them, Ye shall not see the sword, neither shall ye have famine; but I will give you assured peace in this place. Then the LORD said unto me, The prophets prophesy lies in my name: I sent them not, neither have I commanded them, neither spake unto them: they prophesy unto you a false vision and divination, and a thing of nought, and the deceit of their heart.

Peace, peace they say. The Soviet Union is no longer a threat, they say. The prophets prophesy lies. Are the people who are telling us these things getting their information from the true God? Ephesians 2:2 Wherein in time past ye walked according to the course of this world, according to the prince of the power of the air, the

spirit that now worketh in the children of disobedience: The truth is that their information comes from the prince of the power of the air, Lucifer. Our media prophets are telling us things out of the deceit of their heart. Their information comes from Lucifer and his antichrist - the gods of the new age.

Jeremiah 15:16 Thy words were found, and I did eat them; and thy word was unto me the joy and rejoicing of mine heart: for I am called by thy name, O LORD God of hosts.

Are we delighted to read God's word every day? When we love God we love to read His word. It is a delight to feed our spirit and it will make our heart rejoice. The Christian who expects to be fed by his pastor is a baby Christian. Some Christians die as babies. They never grow enough to feed themselves so that they may grow strong enough to even participate in the spiritual warfare. In the last days the spiritual warfare becomes total war. Babies are not capable of fighting the good fight. We all need to grow and grow quickly. Our spiritual growth is not our pastor's job. It is our job.

Jeremiah 15:19-21 Therefore thus saith the LORD, If thou return, then will I bring thee again, [and] thou shalt stand before me: and if thou take forth the precious from the vile, thou shalt be as my mouth: let them return unto thee; but return not thou unto them. And I will make thee unto this people a fenced brasen wall: and they shall fight against thee, but they shall

not prevail against thee: for I [am] with thee to save
thee and to deliver thee, saith the LORD. And I will
deliver thee out of the hand of the wicked, and
I will redeem thee out of the hand of the terrible.

Jeremiah has been having a pity party before the Lord. His
people will not listen to him give them God's warnings. God
says grit up your gut. Do not even try to reach out to your
people any more. Make them come to you if they want any
more truth. There comes a time no matter how much you
may love someone, that you must let them go and experience
the pains that their rebellion will bring them. God will take
care of His people just as He promised and did take care of
Jeremiah during the period of Judah's judgment.

Jeremiah 16:19-21 O LORD, my strength, and my
fortress, and my refuge in the day of affliction, the
Gentiles shall come unto thee from the ends of the
earth, and shall say, Surely our fathers have inherited
lies, vanity, and [things] wherein [there is] no profit.
Shall a man make gods unto himself, and they [are]
no gods? Therefore, behold, I will this once cause
them to know, I will cause them to know mine hand
and my might; and they shall know that my name [is]
The LORD.

Is God our strength and fortress for the days of affliction
which are coming? This new age movement and new world
order of antichrist coming upon the world is being brought
in through lies and vanity. People are ignorant of God's
word and therefore will be sucked into this coming system
of destruction.

Jeremiah 18:8-10 If that nation, against whom I have pronounced, turn from their evil, I will repent of the evil that I thought to do unto them. And [at what] instant I shall speak concerning a nation, and concerning a kingdom, to build and to plant [it]; If it do evil in my sight, that it obey not my voice, then I will repent of the good, wherewith I said I would benefit them.

God responds to the free will choices we make. There is little doubt that America has been blessed greatly by God. No other nation has been so blessed. The founders of this nation sought to found the nation for God's glory. This nation has turned its back on the true God and seeks the gods of Lucifer and antichrist. Without repentance we may be sure of judgment on this great land so blessed by God.

Jeremiah 18:12 And they said, There is no hope: but we will walk after our own devices, and we will every one do the imagination of his evil heart.

We all have evil hearts. Only God can fix them. When everyone keeps doing their own thing - there is no hope.

Jeremiah 25:11-12 And this whole land shall be a desolation, [and] an astonishment; and these nations shall serve the king of Babylon seventy years. And it shall come to pass, when seventy years are accomplished, [that] I will punish the king of Babylon, and that nation, saith the LORD, for their iniquity, and the land of the Chaldeans, and will make it perpetual desolations.

The children going into captivity would be able to tell their children and grandchildren that their freedom and return to their homeland was something to look forward to with certainty. God has also let our generation know a similar thing to give us a blessed hope. We do not know when the 7 years of great tribulation begins because it will begin so gradually. Whenever we do however, realize that we are in the middle of it, we will know that in less than 7 years our blessed hope will be realized. Jesus is coming, not in secret, but in great power and glory. Every eye shall see Him. Those who have remained faithful in tribulation and have not received the mark of the beast antichrist, will be raptured when their eyes see Him returning. Those who have not remained faithful and have taken the mark of the beast will want to die and not be able to die.

Jeremiah 25:4 And the LORD hath sent unto you all his servants the prophets, rising early and sending [them]; but ye have not hearkened, nor inclined your ear to hear.
It never seems to change. We could be saved from so much grief and hardship if we would listen to God and diligently study the bible.

Jeremiah 25:29-31 For, lo, I begin to bring evil on the city which is called by my name, and should ye be utterly unpunished? Ye shall not be unpunished: for I will call for a sword upon all the inhabitants of the earth, saith the LORD of hosts. Therefore prophesy thou against them all these words, and say unto them,

The LORD shall roar from on high, and utter his voice from his holy habitation; he shall mightily roar upon his habitation; he shall give a shout, as they that tread [the grapes], against all the inhabitants of the earth. A noise shall come [even] to the ends of the earth; for the LORD hath a controversy with the nations, he will plead with all flesh; he will give them [that are] wicked to the sword, saith the LORD.

There have been 2 world wars. Yet even in the second world war there were places on earth where bullets were not fired and bombs were not dropped. When God calls for a sword upon all the inhabitants of the earth, must refer to the 2nd coming of the Lord Jesus Christ. The Lord shall roar from on high against all the inhabitants of the earth. He will have a controversy with the nations who have all fallen under the reign of antichrist and his new world order. He will destroy all the wicked with the sword of the power of His word at His powerful and glorious return to earth.

Jeremiah 35:18-19 And Jeremiah said unto the house of the Rechabites, Thus saith the LORD of hosts, the God of Israel; Because ye have obeyed the commandment of Jonadab your father, and kept all his precepts, and done according unto all that he hath commanded you: Therefore thus saith the LORD of hosts, the God of Israel; Jonadab the son of Rechab shall not want a man to stand before me for ever.

Over and over we see how God blesses and rewards

obedience and how rebellion is punished. Few realize that
rebellion is as the sin of witchcraft and that obedience is
better than sacrifice. The Rechabites did not go into
captivity with the rest of Judah. They simply picked up
and moved again out of the path of the armies of
Nebuchadnezzar.

EZEKIEL

Ezekiel ministered from captivity in Babylon between 592 - 570BC. Judah did not fall until 586BC. He was predicting the fall of Jerusalem while his older contemporary Jeremiah was witnessing the fall in Judah. Ezekiel was a faithful watchman who preached the warning of judgment to a rebellious and idolatrous people. After the fall of Jerusalem he brought a message of salvation and hope of restoration. Ezekiel tells of the direct intervention of God to destroy Russia when Russia invades Israel. Our generation will likely be the generation to witness God destroy the armies of Russia which will soon be invading Israel. Even though this prophecy was given 2500 years ago, much of its fulfillment is for our generation.

Ezekiel 1:1   Now it came to pass in the thirtieth year, in the fourth [month], in the fifth [day] of the month, as I [was] among the captives by the river of Chebar, [that] the heavens were opened, and I saw visions of God.
Ezekiel saw visions of God. The glory of God defies human description. Ezekiel gives it his best effort. The description of God's glory is incomprehensible.

Ezekiel 2:2-7 And the spirit entered into me when he spake unto me, and set me upon my feet, that I heard him that spake unto me. And he said unto me, Son of man, I send thee to the children of Israel, to a

rebellious nation that hath rebelled against me: they
and their fathers have transgressed against me,
[even] unto this very day. For [they are] impudent
children and stiffhearted. I do send thee unto them;
and thou shalt say unto them, Thus saith the Lord
GOD. And they, whether they will hear, or whether
they will forbear, (for they [are] a rebellious house,)
yet shall know that there hath been a prophet among
them. And thou, son of man, be not afraid of them,
neither be afraid of their words, though briers and
thorns [be] with thee, and thou dost dwell among
scorpions: be not afraid of their words, nor be
dismayed at their looks, though they [be] a rebellious
house. And thou shalt speak my words unto them,
whether they will hear, or whether they will forbear:
for they [are] most rebellious.

It was impossible for Ezekiel to describe what he had seen
of God's glory. He did the best he could, but God's glory is
overwhelming. He fainted at the vision of God. Ezekiel of
course had no difficulty in hearing or remembering or
recording God's words because as God spoke to him the
Holy Spirit came into him. God commissioned him to
deliver His word to the rebellious children of Israel. Every
father has such a commission. Even if our children are
rebellious. That does not relieve us of the responsibility that
every father has been given by God. Just as Ezekiel was
commissioned, every father is commissioned to give his best
effort to deliver the word of God to his children. Every
father is a God commissioned prophet to his children. The
primary job of the prophet has little or nothing to do with

predicting future events. The primary job of the prophet is
to preach righteousness. Whether the children want to hear
it or not, the father is obligated by God to preach it. The
father ought to live what he preaches as well. I confess
failure to live out what I would preach to my children. God
can and will forgive this failure even if my children can not
or will not.

**Ezekiel 3:2-3 So I opened my mouth, and he caused
me to eat that roll. And he said unto me, Son of man,
cause thy belly to eat, and fill thy bowels with this
roll that I give thee. Then did I eat [it]; and it was in
my mouth as honey for sweetness.**
Here is a most graphic example that our spiritual food is the
word of God. Jesus is the living word of God. That was the
meaning Jesus intended when He said **John 6:47-51
Verily, verily, I say unto you, He that believeth on me
hath everlasting life. I am that bread of life. Your
fathers did eat manna in the wilderness, and are
dead. This is the bread which cometh down from
heaven, that a man may eat thereof, and not die. I
am the living bread which came down from heaven:
if any man eat of this bread, he shall live for ever:
and the bread that I will give is my flesh, which I will
give for the life of the world.** We are spirit beings
contained in a physical body. We are spiritually dead until
we are born again by the Spirit of God by receiving Jesus
Christ as Lord and Savior. We are born again as spiritual
babies. We will stay babies and even die as spiritual babies
if we do not eat spiritual food. The spiritual food we must

eat to sustain our spiritual life and spiritual growth is the word of God.

Ezekiel 3:7-9 But the house of Israel will not hearken unto thee; for they will not hearken unto me: for all the house of Israel [are] impudent and hardhearted. Behold, I have made thy face strong against their faces, and thy forehead strong against their foreheads. As an adamant harder than flint have I made thy forehead: fear them not, neither be dismayed at their looks, though they [be] a rebellious house.

Just as God strengthened and gave courage to Ezekiel, we too should be strong and courageous regarding the truth of the word of God. We need to be fearless, bold and unwavering regarding the truth. It is the Holy Spirit who gives this unwavering courage. You can afford to be narrow minded when you are right. When you take your stand on the absolute truth of the word of God you are right. Be strong, courageous, bold, and narrow minded. Being wrong and broadminded or pluralistic is foolish. Be right, know you are right, and take your stand with God.

Ezekiel 3:17-21 Son of man, I have made thee a watchman unto the house of Israel: therefore hear the word at my mouth, and give them warning from me. When I say unto the wicked, Thou shalt surely die; and thou givest him not warning, nor speakest to warn the wicked from his wicked way, to save his life; the same wicked [man] shall die in his iniquity; but his

blood will I require at thine hand.

Yet if thou warn the wicked, and he turn not from his wickedness, nor from his wicked way, he shall die in his iniquity; but thou hast delivered thy soul. Again, When a righteous [man] doth turn from his righteousness, and commit iniquity, and I lay a stumblingblock before him, he shall die: because thou hast not given him warning, he shall die in his sin, and his righteousness which he hath done shall not be remembered; but his blood will I require at thine hand. Nevertheless if thou warn the righteous [man], that the righteous sin not, and he doth not sin, he shall surely live, because he is warned; also thou hast delivered thy soul.

Every father is a God ordained watchman to his children. Most fathers are keenly aware of their God given responsibility to provide for their families. Most of the problems in America today may be traced to the fact that fathers have failed to realize that God has called them to be prophet and watchmen to their children. The spiritual leadership and training of the children is the responsibility of the father. The father is pastor and shepherd of his family. Pastoral responsibility and accountability does not end at the church. The family is also the church. M any women are forced to try to take up the slack from the father who does not realize or accept his responsibility as spiritual watchman for the children. However, woe to the woman who usurps that responsibility from the father.

Ezekiel 8:17-18 Then he said unto me, Hast thou

seen [this], O son of man? Is it a light thing to the house of Judah that they commit the abominations which they commit here? for they have filled the land with violence, and have returned to provoke me to anger: and, lo, they put the branch to their nose. Therefore will I also deal in fury: mine eye shall not spare, neither will I have pity: and though they cry in mine ears with a loud voice, [yet] will I not hear them.

Whenever the moral standards of God are forsaken it is inevitable that the land will be filled with violence. We are seeing this coming to pass in America today. The moral absolutes of the 10 commandments have been removed from all the public classrooms of America. It is against the law to pray. Violence filling the land will be the result. The politically correct socialist engineers who reject God will bring in tyranny, confusion, and violence. How long will it be before God brings judgment on America? Christian it is up to us. We make all the difference if we will humble ourselves, pray, study God's word, (that is how you seek His face), God will hear and heal our land. If we continue rejecting God we will face His judgment.

Ezekiel 9:4 And the LORD said unto him, Go through the midst of the city, through the midst of Jerusalem, and set a mark upon the foreheads of the men that sigh and that cry for all the abominations that be done in the midst thereof.

Are we groaning and sighing over the 1,500,000 babies per year being killed by abortions in America? Does it make us feel like crying that the children of America are systematically being indoctrinated to be atheists, socialists, and to mock the faith of our fathers? Even in judgment God would care for His people. We are called to be an overcomer in tribulation. The rapture ride is scheduled to occur at the end of the great tribulation. We must know and understand the worst case scenario. Prepare for the worst, and praise God if we find that we have been given a better scenario. Do not be unprepared for the tribulation. Know what it means to take the mark of the beast in the right hand or forehead. We must not take that scanner mark symbol no matter what. God will provide for us supernaturally. We must have faith to survive. How do we get faith? It comes by hearing and hearing by the word of God. We must read our bibles daily.

Ezekiel 9:7-9 And he said unto them, Defile the house, and fill the courts with the slain: go ye forth. And they went forth, and slew in the city. And it came to pass, while they were slaying them, and I was left, that I fell upon my face, and cried, and said, Ah Lord GOD! wilt thou destroy all the residue of Israel in thy pouring out of thy fury upon Jerusalem? Then said he unto me, The iniquity of the house of Israel and Judah [is] exceeding great, and the land is full of blood, and the city full of perverseness: for they say, The LORD hath forsaken the earth, and the LORD seeth not.

How much greater are the national sins of America? Was ancient Israel killing 1,500,000 babies per year? Were the homosexuals openly demonstrating for special privileges

and openly recruiting young people into their perversion?
"Ah Lord God!" Will you destroy the righteous in America
with the wicked as you pour out the fury of your judgment
on America? Christians it is high time that we get serious
about the spiritual war that is raging about us in this land.
We need to put on the full armour and stand.

**Ezekiel 10:18-19 Then the glory of the LORD
departed from off the threshold of the house, and
stood over the cherubims. And the cherubims lifted
up their wings, and mounted up from the earth in my
sight: when they went out, the wheels also [were]
beside them, and [every one] stood at the door of the
east gate of the LORD'S house; and the glory of the
God of Israel [was] over them above.**
The glory of the Lord departed from the temple in Israel
and it will not return again until the return of Jesus Christ
at the end of the tribulation when He will return for His
saints and to put down the armies of the antichrist who will
have been waging war on His saints during the tribulation.
There are many good reasons to believe that we will be the
generation to see the return of the Lord in great power and
glory.

**Ezekiel 16:14-15 And thy renown went forth among
the heathen for thy beauty: for it [was] perfect
through my comeliness, which I had put upon thee,
saith the Lord GOD. But thou didst trust in thine own
beauty, and playedst the harlot because of thy
renown, and pouredst out thy fornications on every**

one that passed by; his it was.

Consider the parallel between Israel and the United States of America. Israel was established for the glory of God. When we read the Mayflower Compact we find that America was established for the glory of God and the advancement of the Christian religion. America was founded as a Christian country and developed a uniquely Christian culture. It was made a great land by its hard working, risk taking, God fearing people. God's blessing was upon the land of America just as surely as it was upon Israel. Only these 2 nations were founded for the glory of the true God. America has played the harlot. Today America leads the world in the rush to the global new world order which will be headed by the antichrist. The national agenda of America is spiritual harlotry from God's perspective. Without national repentance and a great revival, God's judgment of America is certain.

Ezekiel 16:20-21 Moreover thou hast taken thy sons and thy daughters, whom thou hast borne unto me, and these hast thou sacrificed unto them to be devoured. [Is this] of thy whoredoms a small matter, That thou hast slain my children, and delivered them to cause them to pass through [the fire] for them?
America is guilty of sacrificing 1,500,000 of their babies every year. Abortion is exactly the same thing as sacrificing children to Molech. No way could Israel, the other nation founded for the glory of the true God, which was being warned of God's impending judgment, have been sacrificing even 1% of the children America is sacrificing every year?

America - wake up! Judgment is inevitable if the national course of antichrist and anti God continues in America.

Ezekiel 16:48-49 [As] I live, saith the Lord GOD, Sodom thy sister hath not done, she nor her daughters, as thou hast done, thou and thy daughters. Behold, this was the iniquity of thy sister Sodom, pride, fulness of bread, and abundance of idleness was in her and in her daughters, neither did she strengthen the hand of the poor and needy.
What a description of America. America is leading the way to the new world order of the global government of antichrist. Consider how this applies to us.

Ezekiel 16:60   Nevertheless I will remember my covenant with thee in the days of thy youth, and I will establish unto thee an everlasting covenant.
Here is where the announcement of impending judgment to Israel and the probable judgment of America are different. America has no such promise of limited destruction and the saving of even remnants or anything short of total annihilation by strategic nuclear war. America's national sins are on a much greater scale. God has not given His word so clearly that America will even exist in the last days when He will have regathered Israel and will defend them from the Russian invasion.

Ezekiel 16:62-63 And I will establish my covenant with thee; and thou shalt know that I [am] the LORD: That thou mayest remember, and be confounded,

and never open thy mouth any more because of thy
shame, when I am pacified toward thee for all that
thou hast done, saith the Lord GOD.

Israel has such glorious promises of God to see them
surviving in the last days. Are we aware of any such
promises which would guarantee that America will even
exist in the last days?

**Ezekiel 18:20-23 The soul that sinneth, it shall die.
The son shall not bear the iniquity of the father,
neither shall the father bear the iniquity of the son:
the righteousness of the righteous shall be upon
him, and the wickedness of the wicked shall be
upon him.
But if the wicked will turn from all his sins that he
hath committed, and keep all my statutes, and do
that which is lawful and right, he shall surely live, he
shall not die. All his transgressions that he hath
committed, they shall not be mentioned unto him: in
his righteousness that he hath done he shall live.
Have I any pleasure at all that the wicked should die?
saith the Lord GOD: [and] not that he should return
from his ways, and live?**

Many denominational debates could possibly be started and
ended with these verses. Once saved always saved?
Backsliding? Perhaps he was never really saved in the first
place? These verses have some strong meat answers to some
questions that have caused denominational differences.
There should be truth here to unify the body of Christ. The
soul that sinneth it shall die. We are not responsible for the

sins of our fathers or our children. We are each responsible and accountable for our own sins. Jesus Christ has paid the full price for all the sins of all mankind. However, we can either confess our sins and accept and receive forgiveness for our sins or else we will die in them. God provides no other way for man to be passed over in judgment unless their sins have been covered by the blood. The wicked must turn away from his sins and the righteous must continue in righteousness. The walk always has a direction. We cannot stand still in the walk with God. We either walk with and toward Him or we walk away and apart from Him. It is the direction that we are walking when we die that sets our direction for eternity. God has no pleasure in the second death of anyone. However, God does allow all mankind to make a freewill choice to accept Him and His love and His grace or to reject Him and have the eternal torment that comes from hopeless eternal separation from God. It is not God's will that any should perish but that all should come to repentance. The key word is repentance. We must repent. Oh dearly beloved of God! - will you repent? Any of us could die at any second. Do we know with absolute certainty where we will spend eternity?

Ezekiel 18:25-28 Yet ye say, The way of the Lord is not equal. Hear now, O house of Israel; Is not my way equal? are not your ways unequal? When a righteous [man] turneth away from his righteousness, and committeth iniquity, and dieth in them; for his iniquity that he hath done shall he die. Again, when the wicked [man] turneth away from his wickedness that

he hath committed, and doeth that which is lawful and right, he shall save his soul alive.

Because he considereth, and turneth away from all his transgressions that he hath committed, he shall surely live, he shall not die.

Does it seem that God is not fair to make the acceptance of Jesus Christ as Lord and Savior the only criteria for eternal life or death? The fact is that every human being is a born sinner. Sinning is as natural as breathing. Whether we sin big or we sin little none of us can ever make up to God for any sin. God must pay the price of sin for us. We are much too puny and our self righteousness stinks. God has paid the required price of our sins for us in the shed blood of the spotless perfect Lamb of God. God could not possibly be more fair or more gracious. Will we believe it and live accordingly or will we die in our sins? God is God. His provision is the only provision that can save us.

Ezekiel 18:30b-32 Repent, and turn [yourselves] from all your transgressions; so iniquity shall not be your ruin. Cast away from you all your transgressions, whereby ye have transgressed; and make you a new heart and a new spirit: for why will ye die, O house of Israel? For I have no pleasure in the death of him that dieth, saith the Lord GOD: wherefore turn [yourselves], and live ye.

This is worth memorizing. Turn away from all our offenses; then sin will not be our downfall. Rid ourselves of all the offenses we have committed, and get a new heart and a new spirit. Why will you die? For I take no pleasure in the death of anyone, declares the sovereign Lord. Repent and live! The truth is that we need a new heart and new spirit. How do we get a new heart and a new spirit? Repent. Agree with God when the H oly Spirit makes us aware of sins.

Ezekiel 21:25-27   And thou, profane wicked prince of Israel, whose day is come, when iniquity [shall have] an end, Thus saith the Lord GOD; Remove the diadem, and take off the crown: this [shall] not [be] the same: exalt [him that is] low, and abase [him that is] high. I will overturn, overturn, overturn, it: and it shall be no [more], until he come whose right it is; and I will give it [him].

Zedekiah was the last king of Judah. Israel has had some puppet kings like Herod set up by Rome but Z edekiah was the last king on the throne of David. The genealogies in Matthew 1 and Luke 3 prove Jesus' birthright to the throne of David. Pilate insisted the inscription "Jesus of Nazareth king of the Jews" be on the cross at Calvary. God said that Zedekiah would be overthrown and that <u>the throne would remain empty until He comes to Whom it rightfully belongs(Eze. 21:27).</u> Jesus is coming again soon and He will take his rightful position on this throne which has been vacant and in ruins since Zedekiah. Jesus Christ will rule the world from Jerusalem as King of K ings and Lord of Lords for 1000 years. Will we have a place in this soon coming wonderful kingdom?

Ezekiel 24:1-2 Again in the ninth year, in the tenth

month, in the tenth [day] of the month, the word of
the LORD came unto me, saying, Son of man, write
thee the name of the day, [even] of this same day: the
king of Babylon set himself against Jerusalem this
same day.

How very amazing it is that on the very day of the siege,
while up to 700 miles from Jerusalem, Ezekiel gets word of
the siege. No messenger in Ezekiel's day could travel
400-700 miles. Only God could have given Ezekiel the
message on the day which he recorded it. All the more
reason for us to pay close attention to Ezekiel's prophecies
as they relate to us.

Ezekiel 24:16-24   Son of man, behold, I take away
from thee the desire of thine eyes with a stroke: yet
neither shalt thou mourn nor weep, neither shall thy
tears run down. Forbear to cry, make no mourning
for the dead, bind the tire of thine head upon thee,
and put on thy shoes upon thy feet, and cover not
[thy] lips, and eat not the bread of men. So I spake
unto the people in the morning: and at even my
wife died; and I did in the morning as I was
commanded. And the people said unto me, Wilt
thou not tell us what these [things are] to us, that
thou doest [so]? Then I answered them, The word
of the LORD came unto me, saying, Speak unto the
house of Israel, Thus saith the Lord GOD; Behold, I
will profane my sanctuary, the excellency of your
strength, the desire of your eyes, and that which
your soul pitieth; and your sons and your daughters

whom ye have left shall fall by the sword. And ye
shall do as I have done: ye shall not cover [your]
lips, nor eat the bread of men.
And your tires [shall be] upon your heads, and your
shoes upon your feet: ye shall not mourn nor weep;
but ye shall pine away for your iniquities, and mourn
one toward another. Thus Ezekiel is unto you a sign:
according to all that he hath done shall ye do: and
when this cometh, ye shall know that I [am] the Lord
GOD.

This is one of the most disturbing messages in scripture.
Great miracles and signs are nothing new for God and His
prophets. It is also not unusual for God to require great
sacrifice on the part of His prophets. The sign God brings
here requires an amazing sacrifice of Ezekiel. The life of
Ezekiel's wife is taken. We should realize that God was
taking care of the Jews in captivity in Babylon. If they had
publicly mourned the destruction of Jerusalem then it
would likely have been viewed by Nebuchadnezzar as an
indication of disloyalty bringing most certain reprisals.
There probably was nothing less dramatic that could have
been done to keep the people in the Babylonian captivity
from bringing such reprisals upon themselves. The point
we see here is that we ought to think of the sacrifice of
Ezekiel the next time we think God may be requiring too
much of us.

Ezekiel 25:6-7 For thus saith the Lord GOD; Because
thou hast clapped [thine] hands, and stamped with
the feet, and rejoiced in heart with all thy despite

against the land of Israel; Behold, therefore I will stretch out mine hand upon thee, and will deliver thee for a spoil to the heathen; and I will cut thee off from the people, and I will cause thee to perish out of the countries: I will destroy thee; and thou shalt know that I [am] the LORD.

God gives Ezekiel His pronouncements of judgment on Ammon, Moab, E dom, Philista, and Egypt. God will not do anything in the way of judgment except He first reveal His secret to His servants the prophets. (Amos 3:7) These people were celebrating the judgment of Israel being destroyed and going into captivity. It is important to remember that God takes no delight in judgment. Israel's rebellion against God forced God to judge them. God always wants to bless. God chose to reveal Himself to the world through Israel. They became a nation when God demonstrated His mighty power to the world in leading them out of bondage in Egypt. God wanted the Jews to be so blessed that all the world would be jealous to have Israel's God be their God. God gave Israel His law. Israel was to set the world's standards for righteousness. God blessed them mightily. As soon as they were blessed they became puffed up in self righteousness and rebelled against God and His law. In stead of setting the standards of righteousness they were setting the standards of unrighteousness. They made God ashamed to be identified as the God of Israel and forced God to judge them. However, when they were judged, it did not mean that God did not love them or that He had forgotten them. When the nations rejoiced over Israel's judgment they brought

judgment upon themselves. We should never rejoice over
the sufferings of anyone. All suffering is the result of sin.
Since Jesus Christ has opened the way for all mankind to
have direct access to God, we see that the law of God, which
no man could keep, has been replaced by the law of love and
God's grace. Today all suffering is still the result of sin.
However, today the people who are doing the suffering are
generally not the people who have done the sinning. When
we sin our adversary gets a license to cause suffering. Most
people do not want to hear this, but the highest calling of
God, today, is to be counted worthy of suffering for the
name of Jesus Christ. M ost people simply are not
spiritually strong enough to suffer.

**Ezekiel 29:14-16   And I will bring again the captivity
of Egypt, and will cause them to return [into] the land
of Pathros, into the land of their habitation; and they
shall be there a base kingdom. It shall be the basest
of the kingdoms; neither shall it exalt itself any more
above the nations: for I will diminish them, that they
shall no more rule over the nations. And it shall be
no more the confidence of the house of Israel, which
bringeth [their] iniquity to remembrance, when they
shall look after them: but they shall know that I [am]
the Lord GOD.**

Egypt was going to be conquered by Babylon. They would
never again have prominence as a nation. One simply
cannot avoid seeing God's truth in prophesy. One has to
wonder at the testimony of the pyramids and other grand
evidence of Egypt's prominence as a civilization. This great

civilization has remained a poor and lowly nation.

Ezekiel 28:2   Son of man, say unto the prince of Tyrus, Thus saith the Lord GOD; Because thine heart [is] lifted up, and thou hast said, I [am] a God, I sit [in] the seat of God, in the midst of the seas; yet thou [art] a man, and not God, though thou set thine heart as the heart of God:

In the description of the sins and judgment of Tyre, Ezekiel also uses the king of Tyre to personify and give us information about Satan. The Hebrew words translated god in verse 2 are Jehovah, el, Eloheim, el, and E loheim in the order in which they appear in the verse. Here is a situation where the NIV is helpful in separating the true God from the false gods. The 5 places where the word god is used in this verse should be as follows G,g,G,g,G. This was the sin of Satan when he said in his heart "I shall be like unto the Most High."   H ow stupid - How many Most High's can there be? An adaptation of the sin at the heart of Satan is the lie which he gave Adam and Eve in the garden. He has been putting new sugar coatings on the lie ever since. We must be hyper sensitive to recognize this lie of Satan in all its forms - "Ye shall be as god", is the lie designed to take all men to hell.

Ezekiel 28:3-5 Behold, thou [art] wiser than Daniel; there is no secret that they can hide from thee: With thy wisdom and with thine understanding thou hast gotten thee riches, and hast gotten gold and silver into thy treasures:

By thy great wisdom [and] by thy traffic hast thou
increased thy riches, and thine heart is lifted up
because of thy riches:

Ezekiel may be talking about Satan in verse 3. The king of
Tyre is likely the subject of 4-5. It is very easy for one's
heart to be lifted up with pride through wealth. We must
be careful to acknowledge that God is the source of every
good and perfect gift. God gives us wisdom. Every talent
we have is a gift from God.

Ezekiel 28:12-19 Son of man, take up a lamentation
upon the king of Tyrus, and say unto him, Thus saith
the Lord GOD; Thou sealest up the sum, full of
wisdom, and perfect in beauty. Thou hast been in
Eden the garden of God; every precious stone [was]
thy covering, the sardius, topaz, and the diamond,
the beryl, the onyx, and the jasper, the sapphire, the
emerald, and the carbuncle, and gold: the
workmanship of thy tabrets and of thy pipes was
prepared in thee in the day that thou wast created.
Thou [art] the anointed cherub that covereth; and I
have set thee [so]: thou wast upon the holy mountain
of God; thou hast walked up and down in the midst
of the stones of fire. Thou [wast] perfect in thy ways
from the day that thou wast created, till iniquity was
found in thee. By the multitude of thy merchandise
they have filled the midst of thee with violence, and
thou hast sinned: therefore I will cast thee as profane
out of the mountain of God: and I will destroy thee, O
covering cherub, from the midst of the stones of fire.

Thine heart was lifted up because of thy beauty, thou hast corrupted thy wisdom by reason of thy brightness: I will cast thee to the ground, I will lay thee before kings, that they may behold thee. Thou hast defiled thy sanctuaries by the multitude of thine iniquities, by the iniquity of thy traffic; therefore will I bring forth a fire from the midst of thee, it shall devour thee, and I will bring thee to ashes upon the earth in the sight of all them that behold thee. All they that know thee among the people shall be astonished at thee: thou shalt be a terror, and never [shalt] thou [be] any more.

There is no confusion here. Satan is definitely the subject. Compare this with Isaiah chapter 14. He was created perfect until iniquity was found in his heart. He was created to be the anointed cherub who delivered the gifts and praises of all the angels before the throne of God. He was created perfect in beauty and song and full of wisdom. Pride was his sin and he brought violence through his sin of pride to heaven and earth. He will be brought to ashes in the sight of all men. We are all subject to pride and vanity. We all need to carefully guard our hearts against this source of all sin and evil, which is pride. If we will humble ourselves, God will lift us up.

Ezekiel 28:25-26   Thus saith the Lord GOD; When I shall have gathered the house of Israel from the people among whom they are scattered, and shall be sanctified in them in the sight of the heathen, then shall they dwell in their land that I have given to my servant Jacob.

And they shall dwell safely therein, and shall build houses, and plant vineyards; yea, they shall dwell with confidence, when I have executed judgments upon all those that despise them round about them; and they shall know that I [am] the LORD their God.

We are quite likely to be the generation to witness the fulfillment of this prophesy. God is unquestionably regathering Israel from all over the world. Are they yet dwelling safely? Yes and no. We see how God is fighting with them in such things as their 92 to 0 air to air combat victory in 1982. Dwelling in safety probably will not occur until the Lord returns. It could be soon.

Ezekiel 29:14-16 And I will bring again the captivity of Egypt, and will cause them to return [into] the land of Pathros, into the land of their habitation; and they shall be there a base kingdom. It shall be the basest of the kingdoms; neither shall it exalt itself any more above the nations: for I will diminish them, that they shall no more rule over the nations. And it shall be no more the confidence of the house of Israel, which bringeth [their] iniquity to remembrance, when they shall look after them: but they shall know that I [am] the Lord GOD.

Egypt was going to be conquered by Babylon. They would never again have prominence as a nation. God's truth in prophesy is seen through the testimony of the pyramids and other grand evidence of Egypt's prominence as a civilization. Never again would Egypt have any greatness.

Ezekiel 37:1-3 The hand of the LORD was upon me, and carried me out in the spirit of the LORD, and set me down in the midst of the valley which [was] full of bones, And caused me to pass by them round about: and, behold, [there were] very many in the open valley; and, lo, [they were] very dry. And he said unto me, Son of man, can these bones live? And I answered, O Lord GOD, thou knowest.

This was a tough question for Ezekiel. Until Jesus rose again from the dead none of us could be certain of life after death. The resurrection of Jesus is one of the most accurately documented facts of ancient history.

I Corinthians 15:4-6 And that he was buried, and that he rose again the third day according to the scriptures: And that he was seen of Cephas, then of the twelve: After that, he was seen of above five hundred brethren at once; of whom the greater part remain unto this present, but some are fallen asleep.

There is no way 500 people could have the same hallucination at the same time.

Ezekiel 37:10 So I prophesied as he commanded me, and the breath came into them, and they lived, and stood up upon their feet, an exceeding great army.

Today Israel has the only invincible army in the world. God is on the side of Israel and they are not going to be defeated again.

Ezekiel 37:12-14 Therefore prophesy and say unto them, Thus saith the Lord GOD; Behold, O my

people, I will open your graves, and cause you to come up
out of your graves, and bring you into the land of Israel. And ye shall know that I [am] the LORD, when I have opened your graves, O my people, and brought you up out of your graves, And shall put my spirit in you, and ye shall live, and I shall place you in your own land: then shall ye know that I the LORD have spoken [it], and performed [it], saith the LORD.
God has indeed resurrected the nation of Israel. It is our generation which has seen Israel established and blossom as a nation. For 2500 years this prophesy remained in obscurity and in 1948 we see Israel as a nation again in the land that God gave them.

Ezekiel 38:1-6 And the word of the LORD came unto me, saying, Son of man, set thy face against Gog, the land of Magog, the chief prince of Meshech and Tubal, and prophesy against him, And say, Thus saith the Lord GOD; Behold, I [am] against thee, O Gog, the chief prince of Meshech and Tubal: And I will turn thee back, and put hooks into thy jaws, and I will bring thee forth, and all thine army, horses and horsemen, all of them clothed with all sorts [of armour, even] a great company [with] bucklers and shields, all of them handling swords: Persia, Ethiopia, and Libya with them; all of them with shield and helmet: Gomer, and all his bands; the house of Togarmah of the north quarters, and all his bands: [and] many people with thee.

These names Gog, Megog, M eshech, Tubal all point to a northern invasion of Israel by the chief prince (hebrew = roshe) or Russia. The break-up of the Soviet Union is a myth. Sooner or later Russia will invade I srael after the spoil of the Middle East oil.   Gog and Megog refer to the northern barbarous sons of Japheth. Some have thought Gog refers to a name of antichrist but it simply refers to Russia. Some have said Meshech is an ancient name of Moscow and Tubal is an ancient name of Tubalsk.

Ezekiel 38:10-12 Thus saith the Lord GOD; It shall also come to pass, [that] at the same time shall things come into thy mind, and thou shalt think an evil thought: And thou shalt say, I will go up to the land of unwalled villages; I will go to them that are at rest, that dwell safely, all of them dwelling without walls, and having neither bars nor gates, To take a spoil, and to take a prey; to turn thine hand upon the desolate places [that are now] inhabited, and upon the people [that are] gathered out of the nations, which have gotten cattle and goods, that dwell in the midst of the land.

Papers are often graded for spelling mistakes with the abbreviation sp.. What is the spoil for which Russia will invade Israel? Sp. oil, it is the oil of the M iddle East. Control of the Middle East oil means control of the industrialized nations. Russia will probably wait for chaos, collapse, or destruction of the U.S.A. before attacking Israel. This is all the more reason to be sure we are in right standing with God. The U nited States could go up in the smoke of a preemptive strategic nuclear attack at any time. For the Christian in right standing with the Lord the effect of the rapture and a nuclear blast is identical - instantly with the Lord. The situation should help us keep our priorities in line. Are our loved ones saved and walking with the Lord? Do we love our situation in this world so much that we are miserable when you face the possibility of a strategic nuclear attack? We need to break up our fallow ground and pull all the stops in our effort to spread the good news and hope of the gospel of Jesus Christ.

Ezekiel 38:14-16 Therefore, son of man, prophesy and say unto Gog, Thus saith the Lord GOD; In that day when my people of Israel dwelleth safely, shalt thou not know [it]? And thou shalt come from thy place out of the north parts, thou, and many people with thee, all of them riding upon horses, a great company, and a mighty army: And thou shalt come up against my people of Israel, as a cloud to cover the land; it shall be in the latter days, and I will bring thee against my land, that the heathen may know me, when I shall be sanctified in thee, O Gog, before their eyes.

God was glorified when Pharaoh hardened his heart. God demonstrated His power to the world as He plagued Egypt to deliver Israel. It will be the same thing as God Himself destroys the invading Russian armies. In the latter days God will demonstrate His mighty power to the world by destroying the Russian army to deliver Israel.

Ezekiel 38:18-23 And it shall come to pass at the same time when Gog shall come against the land of Israel, saith the Lord GOD, [that] my fury shall come up in my face. For in my jealousy [and] in the fire of my wrath have I spoken, Surely in that day there shall be a great shaking in the land of Israel; So that the fishes of the sea, and the fowls of the heaven, and the beasts of the field, and all creeping things that creep upon the earth, and all the men that [are] upon the face of the earth, shall shake at my presence, and the mountains shall be thrown down, and the steep places shall fall, and every wall shall fall to the ground.
And I will call for a sword against him throughout all my mountains, saith the Lord GOD: every man's sword shall be against his brother. And I will plead against him with pestilence and with blood; and I will rain upon him, and upon his bands, and upon the many people that [are] with him, an overflowing rain, and great hailstones, fire, and brimstone. Thus will I magnify myself, and sanctify myself; and I will be known in the eyes of many nations, and they shall know that I [am] the LORD.

God tells us here how He is going to destroy the invading Russian armies. There will be a great earthquake in Israel while Russia is invading. Much of the Russian army will be destroyed by this earthquake. The Russian troops will also kill each other and turn their weapons upon themselves much like the victory which God gave Gideon over the Midianites. God will also strike this massive invading

Russian army with pestilence. Great hailstorms and fire and brimstone destruction similar to the destruction of Sodom and Gamorah. Of all of the soldiers of the Russian empire over 83% will die in this attack on Israel. God will do it Himself and Israel may not even fire a shot. Many nations will then have to recognize the God of Israel as the one true mighty God of all.

Ezekiel 39:1-2 Therefore, thou son of man, prophesy against Gog, and say, Thus saith the Lord GOD; Behold, I [am] against thee, O Gog, the chief prince of Meshech and Tubal: And I will turn thee back, and leave but the sixth part of thee, and will cause thee to come up from the north parts, and will bring thee upon the mountains of Israel:

Has any army in modern history ever seen 83% of all their soldiers killed at one time?

Ezekiel 39:4-8 Thou shalt fall upon the mountains of Israel, thou, and all thy bands, and the people that [is] with thee: I will give thee unto the ravenous birds of every sort, and [to] the beasts of the field to be devoured. Thou shalt fall upon the open field: for I have spoken [it], saith the Lord GOD. And I will send a fire on Magog, and among them that dwell carelessly in the isles: and they shall know that I [am] the LORD. So will I make my holy name known in the midst of my people Israel; and I will not [let them] pollute my holy name any more: and the heathen shall know that I [am] the LORD, the Holy One in

Israel. Behold, it is come, and it is done, saith the
Lord GOD; this [is] the day whereof I have spoken.
All the world will fear the God of Israel when God finishes
with the destruction of the Russian army.

Ezekiel 39:10-17 So that they shall take no wood out
of the field, neither cut down [any] out of the forests;
for they shall burn the weapons with fire: and they
shall spoil those that spoiled them, and rob those
that robbed them, saith the Lord GOD. And it shall
come to pass in that day, [that] I will give unto Gog a
place there of graves in Israel, the valley of the
passengers on the east of the sea: and it shall stop
the [noses] of the passengers: and there shall they
bury Gog and all his multitude: and they shall call [it]
The valley of Hamon-gog. And seven months shall
the house of Israel be burying of them, that they may
cleanse the land. Yea, all the people of the land
shall bury [them]; and it shall be to them a renown
the day that I shall be glorified, saith the Lord GOD.
And they shall sever out men of continual
employment, passing through the land to bury with
the passengers those that remain upon the face of
the earth, to cleanse it: after the end of seven
months shall they search. And the passengers [that]
pass through the land, when [any] seeth a man's
bone, then shall he set up a sign by it, till the buriers
have buried it in the valley of Hamon-gog. And also
the name of the city [shall be] Hamonah. Thus shall
they cleanse the land.

And, thou son of man, thus saith the Lord GOD;
Speak unto every feathered fowl, and to every beast
of the field, Assemble yourselves, and come; gather
yourselves on every side to my sacrifice that I do
sacrifice for you, [even] a great sacrifice upon the
mountains of Israel, that ye may eat flesh, and drink
blood.

Hamon simply means multitude. This destruction is going
to be so massive that it will take 7 months to bury all the
dead soldiers in mass graves. People will be permanently
employed in the cleanup of the carnage of this destruction.
All the world will have to know the God of Israel is the only
true God. Some, with good reason, believe this is the battle
of Armageddon. It is more likely that this destruction of
Russia provides the power vacuum from which antichrist
comes to full power and control. No mention is made of the
involvement of the 200,000,000 man army of the kings of the
east. The more likely scenario is that Russia takes out the
U.S.A. with a preemptive strategic nuclear attack and then
follows with this attack of Israel. When God destroys them
then the power vacuum left by the destruction of both the
U.S.A. by Russia and the destruction of Russia by God
Himself, removes the super powers which could possibly
resist the increasing power of the antichrist. The antichrist
then moves out of the revived Roman empire to take full
control of all the world.

Ezekiel 39:21-23 And I will set my glory among the
heathen, and all the heathen shall see my judgment
that I have executed, and my hand that I have laid

upon them. So the house of Israel shall know that I
[am] the LORD their God from that day and forward.
And the heathen shall know that the house of Israel
went into captivity for their iniquity: because they
trespassed against me, therefore hid I my face from
them, and gave them into the hand of their enemies:
so fell they all by the sword.

At this time Israel will know the Lord Jesus Christ.

Ezekiel 39:25 Therefore thus saith the Lord GOD;
Now will I bring again the captivity of Jacob, and have
mercy upon the whole house of Israel, and will be
jealous for my holy name;

Through all of the judgments and trials of Israel they have
never been forsaken by God. God at this time will be
reveling Himself to the world through the nation of Israel.

Ezekiel 39:27-29 When I have brought them again
from the people, and gathered them out of their
enemies' lands, and am sanctified in them in the
sight of many nations; Then shall they know that I
[am] the LORD their God, which caused them to be
led into captivity among the heathen: but I have
gathered them unto their own land, and have left
none of them any more there. Neither will I hide my
face any more from them: for I have poured out my
spirit upon the house of Israel, saith the Lord GOD.

At this time Israel will be leading the church of Jesus
Christ. They will all know Messiah Jesus and have been
filled by the Holy Spirit of God.

HOSEA

Hosea ministered in the Northern kingdom of Israel at the same time that Isaiah was ministering in Judah. The time frame of Hosea's ministry was 750-725BC. His own personal experience with his unfaithful harlot wife Gomer pictured God's view of the unfaithfulness of Israel. Israel would go into captivity and separation for a time yet God's eternal love would ultimately bring restoration.

Hosea 2:18 And in that day will I make a covenant for them with the beasts of the field, and with the fowls of heaven, and [with] the creeping things of the ground: and I will break the bow and the sword and the battle out of the earth, and will make them to lie down safely.

Here is the great message of hope. Some time in the distant future, God would again make Israel His covenant people and give them everlasting peace. We are witnessing the beginning of the fulfillment of this promise. Israel is being regathered from the dispersion. The peace treaty with antichrist will come first. It will be broken in 3 1/2 years and 3 1/2 years later Christ will come to put down the armies of antichrist and set up His millennial kingdom here. Israel's army today is the only undefeatable army because God is on Israel's side again.

Hosea 2:23 And I will sow her unto me in the earth; and I will have mercy upon her that had not obtained

mercy; and I will say to [them which were] not my
people, Thou [art] my people; and they shall say,
[Thou art] my God.

Our generation is without question the generation which is
witnessing the fulfillment of this prophesy. We are
witnessing Israel being regathered in their homeland after
2000 years of dispersion.

**Hosea 4:1-2 Hear the word of the LORD, ye children
of Israel: for the LORD hath a controversy with the
inhabitants of the land, because [there is] no truth,
nor mercy, nor knowledge of God in the land. By
swearing, and lying, and killing, and stealing, and
committing adultery, they break out, and blood
toucheth blood.**

Is this also an accurate description of the conditions in our
land today as well?

**Hosea 4:6 <u>My people are destroyed for lack of
knowledge</u>: because thou hast rejected knowledge,
I will also reject thee, that thou shalt be no priest to
me: seeing thou hast forgotten the law of thy God, I
will also forget thy children.**

<u>This is the most important verse in the book of Hosea.</u>
God's people are destroyed for lack of knowledge. This is
the only reason that God's people are destroyed. What
knowledge is God talking about? The knowledge of God's
word. When God's people reject God's word, then they
have rejected God and they are destroyed. When one rejects
the knowledge of God's word and forgets the laws of God

then destruction will result.

Hosea 4:18 Their drink is sour: they have committed whoredom continually: her rulers [with] shame do love, Give ye.
It is sad to find the leaders of any nation promoting sodomites and abortion. Homosexuals are sodomites and sodomy is sin. Abortion is exactly the same as sacrificing children to Molech. According to what the word of God clearly teaches these are serious sins. When a nation's rulers dearly love shameful ways that nation will be swept away.

Hosea 5:4 They will not frame their doings to turn unto their God: for the spirit of whoredoms [is] in the midst of them, and they have not known the LORD.
Their deeds do not permit them to return to their God. A spirit of prostitution is in their heart and they do not acknowledge the Lord.

Hosea 6:6 For I desired mercy, and not sacrifice; and the knowledge of God more than burnt offerings.
God wants us to be merciful. We need to have forgiving and compassionate hearts. This is more important to God than any form of sacrifice. The pursuit of the knowledge of the word of God is more desirable to God than burnt offerings.

Hosea 7:3 They make the king glad with their wickedness, and the princes with their lies.
It is a lie to say that homosexuality is natural for anyone. It

is a lie to say that abortion does not kill a baby. Yet our president is glad to promote the rights of sodomites and the right of women to kill their unborn babies.

Hosea 7:13 Woe unto them! for they have fled from me: destruction unto them! because they have transgressed against me: though I have redeemed them, yet they have spoken lies against me.
Woe unto us! If this nation continues to forsake God it is headed for destruction. We must force ourselves to see the truth that destruction could come at any moment that Russia launches a first strike strategic nuclear attack. The "break-up" of the Soviet Union has no effect other than to increase the likelihood of a first strike strategic nuclear attack. This is not what we want to hear or think about but it is the truth that we must be told.

Hosea 8:7 For they have sown the wind, and they shall reap the whirlwind: it hath no stalk: the bud shall yield no meal: if so be it yield, the strangers shall swallow it up.
If you sow the wind, you shall reap the whirlwind.

Hosea 9:7 The days of visitation are come, the days of recompence are come; Israel shall know [it]: the prophet [is] a fool, the spiritual man [is] mad, for the multitude of thine iniquity, and the great hatred.
In our land today is the prophet considered a fool? Because of the way that wickedness has multiplied in this nation, and the rejection to the point of hatred of God and God's

principles, the spiritual man of God is considered crazy.

JOEL

It is unclear when Joel ministered. It was probably before the captivity in about 800BC. Joel's name means The Lord is God. The land was being devastated by drought and locusts. Joel is quoted by Peter (Acts 2) at his great Pentecost sermon in which thousands of Jews came to know their Messiah. Joel is a minor prophet with major importance in end time prophecy.

Joel 1:3   Tell ye your children of it, and [let] your children [tell] their children, and their children another generation.

Many times in the scriptures fathers are commanded to tell their children all of what the Lord has done and everything the Lord has said. According to God's commands we fathers are to tell the whole truth to our children. The many teachers of the end times will tickle the ears of their congregations with all God's promises of blessings. There will be little or no mention that with almost every promise of blessing from obedience there is a promise of cursing for sin and disobedience. We need to seek and share the whole truth. Emphasis must be placed on that hard truth that we are unlikely to hear just sitting in a congregation. It is not given to discourage or cause fear. It is given to encourage us to receive the blessings of obedience and to avoid the curses of sin. Everyone who only knows about blessings is much more likely to experience the curses due to ignorance of the curses.

Joel 1:15   Alas for the day! for the day of the LORD

[is] at hand, and as a destruction from the Almighty shall it come.

Has there ever been a generation which has more reasons to expect to see the day of the Lord? Obviously no. According to what Jesus said in Matthew 24, Luke 21, and Mark 13, the generation which would see Israel established and flourishing as a nation would be the generation that would see all end time events being fulfilled. We have every reason to believe that much of what Joel has written is for our generation.

Joel 2:1 Blow ye the trumpet in Zion, and sound an alarm in my holy mountain: let all the inhabitants of the land tremble: for the day of the LORD cometh, for [it is] nigh at hand;

The truth is that it is our generation which must be told that the day of the Lord is near at hand. We must be warned to get ready for the day is at hand.

Joel 2:11-13 And the LORD shall utter his voice before his army: for his camp [is] very great: for [he is] strong that executeth his word: for the day of the LORD [is] great and very terrible; and who can abide it? Therefore also now, saith the LORD, turn ye [even] to me with all your heart, and with fasting, and with weeping, and with mourning: And rend your heart, and not your garments, and turn unto the LORD your God: for he [is] gracious and merciful, slow to anger, and of great kindness, and repenteth him of the evil.

We must hear Joel speaking to us. Who can endure the day of the Lord? Only those whose heart is totally committed to the Lord. Is Jesus more important to you than your friends and family? We must turn to the Lord with all our heart. Outward shows won't be worth a rip. We need to rip our hearts in repentance. God is gracious, and merciful, and slow to anger, and great in kindness, and does not want any to perish. But we must hear Joel telling us that God will finally say enough and bring the evil of this world to an end in judgment. We must be told that the time is at hand. No one should be telling the day or the hour. But could it be less than 10 years? Could the 7 years of great tribulation already have begun? The great tribulation will be ushered in with such subtle gradual changes that no one will know the day or the hour in which the final 7 years of great tribulation will have started. Will we take the mark which our government will require us to take in order to buy or sell? It is time to get serious.

Joel 2:18-21 Then will the LORD be jealous for his land, and pity his people. Yea, the LORD will answer and say unto his people, Behold, I will send you corn, and wine, and oil, and ye shall be satisfied therewith: and I will no more make you a reproach among the heathen: But I will remove far off from you the northern [army], and will drive him into a land barren and desolate, with his face toward the east sea, and his hinder part toward the utmost sea, and his stink shall come up, and his ill savour shall come up, because he hath done great things. Fear not, O land;

be glad and rejoice: for the LORD will do great things.
We will see it if we are not taken out by a first strike nuclear
attack by Russia. The weakness of Russia is a myth. Their
strategic nuclear arsenal is intact. Prior to the lying
"break-up" of the Soviet Union there was only one finger on
the button. Now - who knows? Russia is very prominent in
end time prophesy. Russia is Joel's northern army. As long
as we have a 2nd amendment Russia knows that she can't
take the U.S.A.. If she can't take it she will likely destroy it.
Whoever strikes first in strategic nuclear war wins. Russia
grows more and more disparate every day. Is God putting
the hook in Russia's jaw to put her on the march to war?
Israel is Russia's final target but the U.S.A. is likely her first
target. Israel has nothing to fear because God Himself will
destroy Russia. Israel may not have to fire a shot and 83%
of all Russian soldiers will be killed so that the whole world
will know that the God of Israel is the only true God. The
Lord will do great things for Israel.

**Joel 2:25-27 And I will restore to you the years that
the locust hath eaten, the cankerworm, and the
caterpillar, and the palmerworm, my great army which
I sent among you. And ye shall eat in plenty, and be
satisfied, and praise the name of the LORD your God,
that hath dealt wondrously with you: and my people
shall never be ashamed. And ye shall know that I
[am] in the midst of Israel, and [that] I [am] the LORD
your God, and none else: and my people shall never
be ashamed.**

What a great promise of God - I will restore the years that

the locust and cankerworm have eaten. Israel is God's chosen people. The Jews rejection of M essiah Jesus is the only reason that we Gentiles have had the opportunity to become part of the family of God. But the times of the Gentiles will come to an end. The army of Israel is the only army in the world which cannot ever again be defeated. It took 6 days for the 3 million Jews to defeat the 20 million Arabs in 1963. They were even better in 1967. In the biggest air battle in history, Israel wiped out the entire Syrian air force equipped with the latest Russian migs. The results of the dog fight was 92 to 0 in favor of Israel. Somebody should have gotten off 1 lucky shot for Syria but God did not let it happen. Always be on the side of I srael. Otherwise God is not on your side. God will bless those who bless Israel and God will curse those who curse I srael.

Israel has been destroyed and dispersed but never again. Antichrist will make a peace treaty with Israel. Pay close attention to any peace talks involving Israel. N ever be against Israel or you will be against God.

Joel 2:28-32 And it shall come to pass afterward, [that] I will pour out my spirit upon all flesh; and your sons and your daughters shall prophesy, your old men shall dream dreams, your young men shall see visions: And also upon the servants and upon the handmaids in those days will I pour out my spirit. And I will shew wonders in the heavens and in the earth, blood, and fire, and pillars of smoke. The sun shall be turned into darkness, and the moon into blood, before the great and the terrible day of the LORD come.

And it shall come to pass, [that] whosoever shall call on the name of the LORD shall be delivered: for in mount Zion and in Jerusalem shall be deliverance, as the LORD hath said, and in the remnant whom the LORD shall call.

There cannot be any doubt about these passages. Peter explains them for us - Acts 2:14-24 But Peter, standing up with the eleven, lifted up his voice, and said unto them, Ye men of Judaea, and all [ye] that dwell at Jerusalem, be this known unto you, and hearken to my words: For these are not drunken, as ye suppose, seeing it is [but] the third hour of the day. But this is that which was spoken by the prophet Joel; And it shall come to pass in the last days, saith God, I will pour out of my Spirit upon all flesh: and your sons and your daughters shall prophesy, and your young men shall see visions, and your old men shall dream dreams: And on my servants and on my hand-maidens I will pour out in those days of my Spirit; and they shall prophesy: And I will shew wonders in heaven above, and signs in the earth beneath; blood, and fire, and vapour of smoke: The sun shall be turned into darkness, and the moon into blood, before that great and notable day of the Lord come: And it shall come to pass, [that] whosoever shall call on the name of the Lord shall be saved. Ye men of Israel, hear these words; Jesus of Nazareth, a man

approved of God among you by miracles and
wonders and signs, which God did by him in the
midst of you, as ye yourselves also know: Him,
being delivered by the determinate counsel and
foreknowledge of God, ye have taken, and by wicked
hands have crucified and slain: Whom God hath
raised up, having loosed the pains of death: because
it was not possible that he should be holden of it.

Was Peter telling them what they wanted to hear? No way!
He gave them the straight hard truth. It was at Pentecost.
Jesus had sent the Holy Spirit to indwell those who with all
their hearts had turned to the Lord Jesus Christ. Peter did
not hesitate to tell the truth that only those who call on the
name of the Lord Jesus Christ and have the indwelling Holy
Spirit would have any hope in the day of God's judgment.
Peter's explanation of Joel's prophesy should mean more to
us than it did when he spoke. Acts 2:37-38 Now when
they heard [this], they were pricked in their heart, and
said unto Peter and to the rest of the apostles, Men
[and] brethren, what shall we do? Then Peter said
unto them, Repent, and be baptized every one of you
in the name of Jesus Christ for the remission of sins,
and ye shall receive the gift of the Holy Ghost. Acts
2:41 Then they that gladly received his word were
baptized: and the same day there were added [unto
them] about three thousand souls.

Joel 3:12-17 Let the heathen be wakened, and come
up to the valley of Jehoshaphat: for there will I sit to

judge all the heathen round about. Put ye in the sickle, for the harvest is ripe: come, get you down; for the press is full, the vats overflow; for their wickedness [is] great. Multitudes, multitudes in the valley of decision: for the day of the LORD [is] near in the valley of decision. The sun and the moon shall be darkened, and the stars shall withdraw their shining. The LORD also shall roar out of Zion, and utter his voice from Jerusalem; and the heavens and the earth shall shake: but the LORD [will be] the hope of his people, and the strength of the children of Israel. So shall ye know that I [am] the LORD your God dwelling in Zion, my holy mountain: then shall Jerusalem be holy, and there shall no strangers pass through her any more.

We are likely to witness the gathering of the armies of antichrist to the valley of Jehoshaphat (Armageddon). The Lord shall roar out of Zion. Christ is coming back. This time not as the Lamb of God, but as the roaring Lion of Judah. The Lord is our only hope and strength. What priority does the Lord now have in our life?

An interesting point is that the prophet Joel wrote this prophesy about 2800 years ago. In the vocabulary of 3000 years ago how would one describe nuclear explosions? Blood and fire and pillars of smoke - fire & billowing pillars of smoke.

AMOS

Amos is the shepherd and sycamore dunger of Tekoa, near Bethlehem. God called this simple uneducated shepherd to prophesy against the kings, nobles, and priests of Israel. He boldly rebuked the hypocrisy of their religion. Jesus made it so clear that God wants to have a personal relationship with us through His Holy Spirit. Religion almost invariably will produce hypocrisy in the unregenerate human heart. We are not to be religious. We are to be real. This is the clear message which Amos brings us. Amos demonstrated how God's strength is made perfect in weakness.

Amos 1:1 The words of Amos, who was among the herdmen of Tekoa, which he saw concerning Israel in the days of Uzziah king of Judah, and in the days of Jeroboam the son of Joash king of Israel, two years before the earthquake.

Amos is a shepherd. Totally uneducated, he is called by God to rebuke the king and the religious leaders of Israel. Amos pronounces God's pending judgment on the nations for their specific national sins. Get set for some earthy language and Holy Spirit inspired boldness from the shepherd and sycamore pruner and dunger of Tekoa.

Amos 1:2 And he said, The LORD will roar from Zion, and utter his voice from Jerusalem; and the habitations of the shepherds shall mourn, and the top of Carmel shall wither.

We all need to be about our preparations to hear the Lord

roaring out of Zion. Messiah Jesus is soon to return as the
Lion of the tribe of Judah. Job 1 for all of us is - get ready!
He is coming again and everyone will recognize who He
really is this time. No lamb-like meekness and gentleness is
Jesus this time. The great roaring lion that none can
withstand is Jesus this time.

**Amos 1:3   Thus saith the LORD; For three
transgressions of Damascus, and for four, I will not
turn away [the punishment] thereof; because they
have threshed Gilead with threshing instruments of
iron:**
Thus saith the Lord; for three transgressions and for four, I
will not turn away the punishment. This is the message
which God called Amos to deliver against Syria,
Philistia, Tyre, Edom, Jordon, Moab, Judah and Israel.

**Amos 1:11   Thus saith the LORD; For three
transgressions of Edom, and for four, I will not turn
away [the punishment] thereof; because he did
pursue his brother with the sword, and did cast off
all pity, and his anger did tear perpetually, and
he kept his wrath for ever:**
When Amos gets to Edom, he gets personal. It is not
necessarily a sin to be angry. In fact, we should be angry
about the things that make God angry. Anger becomes sin
when it is not quenched. We are not to let the sun go down
on our anger. We are not to harbor anger. Harbored anger
will produce a deep strong root of bitterness. We are to be
quick to hear and slow to speak: quick to forgive, quick to

love, and slow to anger.

Amos 2:4 Thus saith the LORD; For three transgressions of Judah, and for four, I will not turn away [the punishment] thereof; because they have despised the law of the LORD, and have not kept his commandments, and their lies caused them to err, after the which their fathers have walked:
Even Judah was going to be judged by God for this. Even when Judah was judged it was not against the law in Judah to display the 10 commandments in any classroom in Judah. Is there any hope left for America? How can this nation so blessed by God, so utterly have rejected the law of the Lord? Only by wimpy Christian complacency. Love, love, love they say. It is really gutless baloney. Love takes courage. It was a message of love when Jesus, to their faces, told the scribes and Pharisees that they were hypocrites, a bunch of snakes. Christians must rise up in boldness and call this nation to repentance. The lies glorifying sodomy and infanticide must be boldly exposed. The lies glorifying global antichrist government must be boldly exposed. The lies of a global antichrist economic system musts be boldly exposed. The lies of a new age antichrist spiritualism and religious system must be boldly exposed.

Amos 3:7 Surely the Lord GOD will do nothing, but he revealeth his secret unto his servants the prophets. This is the most important verse in Amos. Surely the Lord God will do nothing, but He revealeth His secret unto H is servants the prophets.

Hear this - David Wilkerson - a mighty prophet of God in our time, has heard God reveal His secret regarding America. We don't want to hear it, but we must be told. America is going to go up in smoke. Russia will launch a strategic nuclear attack from which America will not survive. If you are not ready, get ready. God's secret has been revealed to His servants the prophets. Do not fear - get right with God. Your faith in Jesus Christ is all that really matters now. Tell your family. Tell your friends. Tell your government. Get bold now. Get ready now. Think logically for a moment, there is little or no difference to the true Believer between the rapture and being the target of a strategic nuclear attack. If Americans think there is a big difference between the rapture and strategic nuclear attack we must think again. Something is radically wrong with the faith of someone who sees a big difference between a strategic nuclear strike and the rapture. How real is the commitment to Christ?

Amos 4:1 hear this word, ye kine of bashan, that [are] in the mountain of samaria, which oppress the poor, which crush the needy, which say to their masters, bring, and let us drink.

Here is some of the most earthy language in the bible. Bashan was famous for its lush pasture land which produced the fattest cows of the world at that time. Here Amos speaks to the women of Israel. Hear this you fat cows, he says. You fat cows oppress the poor. You fat cows crush the needy. You fat cows order your husbands to fatten you.
Amos 5:5-6 But seek not Beth-el, nor enter into

Gilgal, and pass not to Beer-sheba: for Gilgal shall surely go into captivity, and Beth-el shall come to nought. Seek the LORD, and ye shall live; lest he break out like fire in the house of Joseph, and devour [it], and [there be] none to quench [it] in Beth-el. There is only one hope, only one way to avoid the destruction which is coming. Seek the Lord, and ye shall live. Even if your nation is the target of a strategic nuclear attack from which there is no escape for anyone - if you have sought God and found Him in MESSIAH, then you have eternal life. This eternal life in Jesus Christ makes the effect of a nuclear blast and the rapture exactly the same for the believer. Have you sought the Lord with your whole heart? Is anything in your life more important than Jesus?

Amos 5:14-15 Seek good, and not evil, that ye may live: and so the LORD, the God of hosts, shall be with you, as ye have spoken. Hate the evil, and love the good, and establish judgment in the gate: it may be that the LORD God of hosts will be gracious unto the remnant of Joseph.
God loves us. He wants to bless us. Only our sins separate us from God. God is a H oly God. Seeking God must involve turning away from our sins. We don't have the power in ourselves to hate evil and love the good. This is why Jesus told us that we must be born again. We are born sinners. It is the Holy Spirit that convicts us of our sins and gives the power we need to overcome our natural tendency to sin. We are born again when we make Jesus Christ Lord of our life. At that point Jesus baptizes us with the H oly

Spirit. The Holy Spirit provides the power we need to live a holy life and maintain unbroken fellowship with God.

Amos 5:18-20 Woe unto you that desire the day of the LORD! to what end [is] it for you? the day of the LORD [is] darkness, and not light. As if a man did flee from a lion, and a bear met him; or went into the house, and leaned his hand on the wall, and a serpent bit him. [Shall] not the day of the LORD [be] darkness, and not light? even very dark, and no brightness in it?

Woe unto those who desire the day of the Lord. The day of the Lord is not fun and games. The world has never seen such earthquakes, 100 pound hail stones, tremendous plagues, people will want to die and not be able.

Revelation 9:6 And in those days shall men seek death, and shall not find it; and shall desire to die, and death shall flee from them. Amos' question needs to be answered. The eternal destiny of our soul will be finalized at the day of the Lord or the day we die; which ever comes first. Amos' question demands an answer - where is our soul going to be?

Amos 6:1 Woe to them [that are] at ease in Zion, and trust in the mountain of Samaria, [which are] named chief of the nations, to whom the house of Israel came!

Are we at ease? Are we complacent? Is our government going to take care of us? Woe to those who like their life just as it is. **Luke 14:26 If any [man] come to me, and hate** not his father, and mother, and wife, and children, and brethren, and sisters, yea, and his own life also, he cannot be my disciple. Luke 16:13 No servant can serve two masters: for either he will hate the one, and love the other; or else he will hold to the one, and despise the other. Ye cannot serve God and mammon.

Amos 8:11-12 Behold, the days come, saith the Lord GOD, that I will send a famine in the land, not a famine of bread, nor a thirst for water, but of hearing the words of the LORD: And they shall wander from sea to sea, and from the north even to the east, they shall run to and fro to seek the word of the LORD, and shall not find [it].
In our land today, are we experiencing a famine for the word of God? There is coming a time when it will be hard to find the word of God being preached. That is why we need to memorize scripture. We need to be getting as much of the word of God stored securely in our minds before the famine occurs which Amos talks about here.

Amos 9:13-15 Behold, the days come, saith the LORD, that the plowman shall overtake the reaper, and the treader of grapes him that soweth seed; and the mountains shall drop sweet wine, and all the hills shall melt. And I will bring again the captivity of my people of Israel, and they shall build the waste cities, and inhabit [them]; and they shall plant vineyards, and drink the wine thereof; they shall also make

gardens, and eat the fruit of them. And I will plant
them upon their land, and they shall no more be
pulled up out of their land which I have given
them, saith the LORD thy God.

Israel would be judged. God never did forsake them. After
captivity, persecution, and dispersion God promised that He
would bring them back to their homeland again. We
are witnessing the regathering. God is doing a great work
in Israel that is not being reported in our media. Israel is
home again. God will not let them be removed again.

**Amos 7:12-13 Also Amaziah said unto Amos, O thou
seer, go, flee thee away into the land of Judah, and
there eat bread, and prophesy there: But prophesy
not again any more at Beth-el: for it [is] the king's
chapel, and it [is] the king's court.**

Amaziah the high priest told Amos to get out of town. They
did not want to hear the truth that God told Amos to give
them. Preachers of righteousness have always experienced
this treatment. In the last days they will heap to themselves
teachers having itching ears. If your preacher doesn't tickle
your ears and tries to give you the hard truth that God is a
Holy God and requires holiness from us, he will quite likely
be told to get out.

**Amos 7:14-15 Then answered Amos, and said to
Amaziah, I [was] no prophet, neither [was] I a
prophet's son; but I [was] an herdman, and a gatherer
of sycomore fruit: And the LORD took me as I
followed the flock, and the LORD said unto me, Go,**

prophesy unto my people Israel.

Amos tells the high priest that he is just a shepherd. The Lord told him where he had to go and what he had to say. This is what the preacher must tell those who do not want to hear the sobering truth that judgment awaits those who will not choose God's ways. Most people want the preacher to excuse their sins. Every year more and more preachers get more polished in delivering sermons to excuse and cover sins. God holds the preacher responsible to Him. The preacher and the parent must get their marching orders from God and faithfully preach righteousness, holiness, and judgment along with love and mercy.

JONAH

Jonah's name means dove. Jonah was called in the middle of Jeroboam II's reign in about 775BC. Nineveh represents the non-Jewish world which needs the awakening which only the true message of God can bring. Jonah illustrates the justice and mercy of God toward anyone who would repent from sin.

Jonah 1:1-3 Now the word of the LORD came unto Jonah the son of Amittai, saying, Arise, go to Nineveh, that great city, and cry against it; for their wickedness is come up before me. But Jonah rose up to flee unto Tarshish from the presence of the LORD, and went down to Joppa; and he found a ship going to Tarshish: so he paid the fare thereof, and went down into it, to go with them unto Tarshish from the presence of the LORD.

Nineveh was the capital of Syria. Syria was continually attacking Israel. Israel became weak because they had turned away from God. When we get weak from becoming a godless society the judgment of strategic nuclear attack could be the result in our time. Suppose we knew with absolute certainty that Russia was going to launch a first strike strategic nuclear war against us. Then suppose God told you to go to Moscow and tell them God was going to destroy them. This is exactly the situation of Jonah. He did not want to warn his country's mortal enemy that they were going to be destroyed by God. He wanted God to destroy his country's enemy. So instead of going to Nineveh he tries

to run away from God to the farthest part of the known
world of his day - Tarshish or Spain as we know it today.
We can not run away or hide from God. We only fool
ourselves.

**Jonah 1:11-12 & 15 Then said they unto him, What
shall we do unto thee, that the sea may be calm unto
us? for the sea wrought, and was tempestuous.
And he said unto them, Take me up, and cast me
forth into the sea; so shall the sea be calm unto you:
for I know that for my sake this great tempest [is]
upon you. So they took up Jonah, and cast him forth
into the sea: and the sea ceased from her raging.**
The Lord caused a tremendous storm on the sea. Jonah
told the sailors it was his fault because he was running
away from God. The only way any of them could avoid
drowning was to throw him overboard. That did the trick
the sea became calm.

**Jonah 1:16-17 Then the men feared the LORD
exceedingly, and offered a sacrifice unto the LORD,
and made vows. Now the LORD had prepared a
great fish to swallow up Jonah. And Jonah was in
the belly of the fish three days and three nights.**
At this point many say this is just a fable. It is not a fable,
it is an actual historical fact. About 10 years ago someone
survived being swallowed by a whale. Remember, whales
are air breathing mammals. It is not only possible but
probable. Is anything impossible for God? Remember
also, Jesus told us this is true. **Matthew 12:39, Matthew**

16:4, AND LUKE 11:29-30 And when the people were gathered thick together, he began to say, This is an evil generation: they seek a sign; and there shall no sign be given it, but the sign of Jonas the prophet. For as Jonas was a sign unto the Ninevites, so shall also the Son of man be to this generation.

Jonah 2:7-9 When my soul fainted within me I remembered the LORD: and my prayer came in unto thee, into thine holy temple. They that observe lying vanities forsake their own mercy. But I will sacrifice unto thee with the voice of thanksgiving; I will pay [that] that I have vowed. Salvation [is] of the LORD.
Have you ever gotten so low that your soul faints? Remember the Lord. Prayer changes things. No matter what our circumstances they could not be worse than the circumstance that Jonah was in while he prayed this great prayer. Salvation is of the Lord. Nobody can be good enough to merit anything but hell. God gives salvation as a demonstration of His mercy and grace through Jesus Christ. There is no other way of salvation.

Jonah 2:10   And the LORD spake unto the fish, and it vomited out Jonah upon the dry [land].
How would you like to be walking along the shore and here comes this great whale and - blaaahhh - there's Jonah. Get this picture straight. The whale deposits Jonah on shore and he walks into Nineveh bleached completely white by being in the whale's belly for 3 days. He walks up and says repent! What would you do? Just what they did in

Nineveh. They repented.

Jonah 3:3-6 So Jonah arose, and went unto Nineveh, according to the word of the LORD. Now Nineveh was an exceeding great city of three days' journey. And Jonah began to enter into the city a day's journey, and he cried, and said, Yet forty days, and Nineveh shall be overthrown. So the people of Nineveh believed God, and proclaimed a fast, and put on sackcloth, from the greatest of them even to the least of them. For word came unto the king of Nineveh, and he arose from his throne, and he laid his robe from him, and covered [him] with sackcloth, and sat in ashes.

When these people saw and heard Jonah they got serious about their repentance. Even the king fasted in sackcloth and ashes. He made a decree that they should quit their evil ways and their violence. No more attacking of Israel.

Jonah 3:9-10 Who can tell [if] God will turn and repent, and turn away from his fierce anger, that we perish not? And God saw their works, that they turned from their evil way; and God repented of the evil, that he had said that he would do unto them; and he did [it] not.

They repented and they were not destroyed.

Jonah 4:1-4 But it displeased Jonah exceedingly, and he was very angry. And he prayed unto the LORD, and said, I pray thee, O LORD, [was] not this my saying, when I was yet in my country? Therefore I fled before unto Tarshish: for I knew that thou [art] a gracious God, and merciful, slow to anger, and of great kindness, and repentest thee of the evil. Therefore now, O LORD, take, I beseech thee, my life from me; for [it is] better for me to die than to live. Then said the LORD, Doest thou well to be angry?

Jonah explains why he was fleeing to Tarshish. He knew how merciful God is. He wanted God to destroy Nineveh. If he had gone immediately, Nineveh may not have repented. The bleach job of his whole body by the whale no doubt made him much more believable.

Jonah 4:9-11 And God said to Jonah, Doest thou well to be angry for the gourd? And he said, I do well to be angry, [even] unto death. Then said the LORD, Thou hast had pity on the gourd, for the which thou hast not laboured, neither madest it grow; which came up in a night, and perished in a night: And should not I spare Nineveh, that great city, wherein are more than sixscore thousand persons that cannot discern between their right hand and their left hand; and [also] much cattle?

God told him there were more than 60,000 children who were too young to know their right from their left and therefore had to be innocent.

NAHUM

Nahum's name means consolation. He prophesied against Nineveh about 125 years after Jonah had brought the message of repentance to Asyria. The repentance of Nineveh did not last. By this time (about 650BC) they had become the world leaders in cruelty and ruthlessness. They were notorious for their atrocities, such as skinning their enemies alive. It is very easy to skip the application of this book to our land in our time. It can be applied to America today. The call to repentance is a call to real and lasting repentance.

Nahum 1:1 The burden of Nineveh. The book of the vision of Nahum the Elkoshite.
Nahum's little book is seldom given much consideration. It is a prophesy against Nineveh. Maybe it is time to take a serious look at this little book. Nineveh is the capitol of Babylon. Remember, in scripture, Babylon means tyranny and confusion. Suppose that the present capitol of tyranny and confusion is America. What country now is leading the way to the new world order of tyranny and confusion to be headed by the antichrist?

Nahum 1:2-3 God [is] jealous, and the LORD revengeth; the LORD revengeth, and [is] furious; the LORD will take vengeance on his adversaries, and he reserveth [wrath] for his enemies.
The LORD [is] slow to anger, and great in power, and will not at all acquit [the wicked]: the LORD hath his

way in the whirlwind and in the storm, and the clouds
[are] the dust of his feet.

Nahum says it thrice - the Lord revenges. The Lord will
have the last word. The Lord will take final vengeance. Do
you suppose the Lord is furious regarding the national sins
of America? Just because the Lord is so very much slower
to anger than we are, we cannot think His patience means
there will not be judgment.

**Nahum 1:7 The LORD [is] good, a strong hold in the
day of trouble; and he knoweth them that trust in him.**
When God's judgment falls only God can provide refuge.
Whatever else you trust will do you no good in judgment.

**Nahum 1:9 What do ye imagine against the LORD?
he will make an utter end: affliction shall not rise up
the second time.**
Are you against God in any area of your life or thoughts?

**Nahum 1:11 There is [one] come out of thee, that
imagineth evil against the LORD, a wicked
counsellor.**
In recent history we saw a man named Hitler who fit this
description. The world stage now is set for the antichrist.
His new world order is much more severe than Hitler's.
Know for sure that world government before the return of
Jesus Christ will be headed by Satan, the antichrist, and his
false prophet.

Nahum 3:4 Because of the multitude of the

whoredoms of the wellfavoured harlot, the mistress of witchcrafts, that selleth nations through her whoredoms, and families through her witchcrafts. Who is it that Nahum is talking about here? Today he could very well be speaking to America. This does not mean that we do not love our country. We are grieving over what it has become. The wellfavoured harlot, the richest nation in the world, founded for the glory of God which now holds the banner of antichrist higher than Russia. The mistress of witchcrafts, leading the world in wives rebelling against the God given authority of their husbands. Leading the world in the new age movement. Leading the world in the exultation of homosexuality. Leading the world in the philosophy of antichrist. Leading the world on the path to judgment and destruction. Selling nations through her whoredoms and families through her witchcrafts. Witchcraft is the attempt to control others by any means other than direct confrontation. Nahum's words are probably as applicable to America today as they were for Nineveh when he wrote them. America is leading the world in broken homes, in witchcraft, and the murder of unborn babies.

Nahum 3:19   [There is] no healing of thy bruise; thy wound is grievous: all that hear the bruit of thee shall clap the hands over thee: for upon whom hath not thy wickedness passed continually?
If Nahum is speaking of America today, then there is no escape of total destruction. How could this be?   The "break-up" of the Soviet Union is a myth. Is Russia paying

money to America or is America paying money to Russia? Have any first line strategic nuclear weapons of Russia been dismantled? Before the "break-up" there was only one finger on the button. How many fingers and whose fingers are now on Russia's strategic nuclear weapons? Russia has been preparing for strategic nuclear war for over 40 years. Russia is desperate. When she gets desperate enough, America goes up in smoke. The world has never seen strategic nuclear warfare.

<u>Now here is the Good News</u> - II Chronicles 7:14 **If my people, which are called by my name, shall humble themselves, and pray, and seek my face, and turn from their wicked ways; then will I hear from heaven, and will forgive their sin, and will heal their land.** Even if the land of America is not healed - even if it is destroyed by strategic nuclear weapons - for the Christian there is not one iota of difference in what happens to them when the nuclear strike occurs or when the rapture occurs. For the Christian who is in right standing with God the effect of either is identical - instantly with the Lord. The serious question - are you ready? We must get serious, and stay ready. <u>Be sure not to stop here with such sobering thoughts. Check the conclusions given in the next short little book of Habakkuk.</u>

HABAKKUK

One of the most difficult things that there is to do is to listen to the prophet who is warning of judgment. It is so difficult that most people will simply never look for personal application to their life, their time, and their country. If one does listen seriously to the prophet's message it can bring an unsettling nagging from deep within our souls. This is how Habakkuk is so helpful. He dares ask God that nagging question: How can a righteous and holy God use a wicked nation to bring judgment on God's own people? Even if these people are sinful and in rebellion and refusing to repent, how can God use a more wicked people to judge them? How can God permit the wicked to prosper at the expense of the righteous? How can God permit evil to exist at all? Habakkuk gets some answers. Evil always bears within itself the seeds of its own destruction. Dr. F. LaGard Smith explains it so well. "Only in righteousness is there life; sin always brings death."

Habakkuk 1:1-3 The burden which Habakkuk the prophet did see. O LORD, how long shall I cry, and thou wilt not hear! [even] cry out unto thee [of] violence, and thou wilt not save! Why dost thou shew me iniquity, and cause [me] to behold grievance? for spoiling and violence [are] before me: and there are [that] raise up strife and contention. Habakkuk asks some hard questions that we have probably all wondered about. How long shall I cry? Does God seem distant? Does He sometimes seem not to hear our prayers?

Why do we see such an increase of wickedness and violence? Why do we see strife and contention even in the church and in our family? These are good tough questions that God wants us to ask. Habakkuk comes to the right conclusion. Pay very close attention and even try to memorize the conclusion of Habakkuk's little book.

Habakkuk 1:5-6 Behold ye among the heathen, and regard, and wonder marvellously: for [I] will work a work in your days, [which] ye will not believe, though it be told [you]. For, lo, I raise up the Chaldeans, [that] bitter and hasty nation, which shall march through the breadth of the land, to possess the dwellingplaces [that are] not theirs.

Even if God told the people that it was His hand lifting up the Babylonians no one would believe it. These people were ruthless and the baddest of the bad. Everyone would think God could have nothing to do with such an evil bunch of people. But it was God's choice to use these wicked Babylonians as His instrument of judgment. If God were set against the powerful Babylonians they could not stand. The heathen could not believe this truth.

Habakkuk 1:13 [Thou art] of purer eyes than to behold evil, and canst not look on iniquity: wherefore lookest thou upon them that deal treacherously, [and] holdest thy tongue when the wicked devoureth [the man that is] more righteous than he?

Here is another of Habakkuk's hard questions. Why do the wicked seem to triumph over the righteous? Have you

reached any conclusions to this question? Habakkuk comes
to the right conclusion. We need to know it. Pay attention
to Habakkuk's conclusion.

**Habakkuk 2:1-4 I will stand upon my watch, and set
me upon the tower, and will watch to see what he will
say unto me, and what I shall answer when I am
reproved. And the LORD answered me, and said,
Write the vision, and make [it] plain upon tables, that
he may run that readeth it. For the vision [is] yet for
an appointed time, but at the end it shall speak, and
not lie: though it tarry, wait for it; because it will
surely come, it will not tarry. Behold, his soul
[which] is lifted up is not upright in him: but the just
shall live by his faith.**

Habakkuk has poured the questions of his soul to the Lord.
He says he is going to wait for God to answer him. He
expects to be reproved for his daring questions. But God
will always welcome our honest questions. We just must be
careful not to let our why's become a whine. Habakkuk has
asked God some very tough questions. God answers
Habakkuk with a vision. God says you just wait. God is
indeed always in control. Now get hold of this profound
answer - the just shall live by faith. Do you get it? The just
shall live by faith. This is not the full conclusion, but this is
where we must all start to ever find the answers. The just
shall live by faith.

**Habakkuk 2:12-16 Woe to him that buildeth a town
with blood, and stablisheth a city by iniquity!**

Behold, [is it] not of the LORD of hosts that the people shall labour in the very fire, and the people shall weary themselves for very vanity? For the earth shall be filled with the knowledge of the glory of the LORD, as the waters cover the sea. Woe unto him that giveth his neighbour drink, that puttest thy bottle to [him], and makest [him] drunken also, that thou mayest look on their nakedness! Thou art filled with shame for glory: drink thou also, and let thy foreskin be uncovered: the cup of the LORD'S right hand shall be turned unto thee, and shameful spewing [shall be] on thy glory.

God lets Habakkuk know that God is more keenly aware of and grieved by evil than we could ever be. God's kindness is meant to lead us to repentance. God will not allow evil to continue without God Himself bringing an end to evil. Some day the whole earth will be filled with the knowledge and glory of God. The smart people will seek God's knowledge and glory now even while the ungodly appear to prosper.

Habakkuk 2:20   But the LORD [is] in his holy temple: let all the earth keep silence before him.

Habakkuk is getting it figured out. The Lord is in His holy temple. The Lord is God. The Lord is in control. It doesn't make any difference how out of control we see the world to be. Only the one true God of Israel is God. God is in control. Let all the earth keep silence before Him. God will some day shut every vain and proud mouth. Get ready for Habakkuk's conclusion. Make it your conclusion and you will find peace for your soul.

Habakkuk 3:17-18 HABAKKUK'S CONCLUSION
Although the fig tree shall not blossom, neither
[shall] fruit [be] in the vines; the labour of the olive
shall fail, and the fields shall yield no meat; the flock
shall be cut off from the fold, and [there shall be] no
herd in the stalls: Yet I will rejoice in the LORD, I will
joy in the God of my salvation.

If the fig tree doesn't blossom,
if there is no fruit in the vines,
if the olive tree fails,
if all crops of the field fail,
if all the cattle are gone,
if I am starving to death - yet will I rejoice in the
Lord. I will joy in the God of my salvation.

Do we see it? The just shall live by faith. I will praise God
if I am starving to death. I will not take the scanner mark
tattoo of antichrist in my right hand or forehead. I will
praise the Lord. The Lord may let him appear to prosper
for seven years but the Lord is in
control. I will joy in the God of my salvation - no matter
what. If my family and friends hate me - I will rejoice in
the Lord. If my children turn against me - I will still joy in
the God of my salvation. If I am taken to be executed - I
will joy in the God of my salvation.
Habakkuk finishes his conclusion in verse 19.

Habakkuk 3:19 The LORD God [is] my strength, and

he will make my feet like hinds' [feet], and he will make me to walk upon mine high places. To the chief singer on my stringed instruments.

The Lord God is my strength. No matter what - the Lord God is my joy and strength. The Lord God will ultimately lift me up. No matter what.

ZEPHANIAH

Zephaniah's name means "the Lord has hidden." The time
of his ministry is during the reign of the young King Josiah
in about 630BC. Zephaniah's central theme is the coming
of the "day of the Lord." Today many parts of his message
are more applicable to America than to Israel. Much of the
message of Zephaniah ("the Lord has hidden") has been
hidden for our generation.

**Zephaniah 1:2-3 I will utterly consume all [things]
from off the land, saith the LORD.
I will consume man and beast; I will consume the
fowls of the heaven, and the fishes of the sea, and
the stumblingblocks with the wicked; and I will cut
off man from off the land, saith the LORD.**
Has this ever happened? No. It will indeed happen
because God has said that it will happen. Do you realize
that our generation is the first generation in history to
understand how such destruction could happen?
Zephaniah is talking about strategic nuclear weapons.

**Zephaniah 1:7-8 Hold thy peace at the presence of
the Lord GOD: for the day of the LORD [is] at hand:
for the LORD hath prepared a sacrifice, he hath bid
his guests. And it shall come to pass in the day of
the LORD'S sacrifice, that I will punish the princes,
and the king's children, and all such as are clothed
with strange apparel.**
This is the message of Zephaniah - the day of the Lord is at

hand. It was a message of obscurity until our generation.
Only the Jews are not clothed with strange apparel. God is
now on the side of Israel. All other nations are subject to
destruction except Israel. The destruction of which
Zephaniah speaks can apply to any nation except Israel.

**Zephaniah 1:14-18 The great day of the LORD [is]
near, [it is] near, and hasteth greatly, [even] the voice
of the day of the LORD: the mighty man shall cry
there bitterly. That day [is] a day of wrath, a day of
trouble and distress, a day of wasteness and
desolation, a day of darkness and gloominess, a day
of clouds and thick darkness, A day of the trumpet
and alarm against the fenced cities, and against the
high towers. And I will bring distress upon men, that
they shall walk like blind men, because they have
sinned against the LORD: and their blood shall be
poured out as dust, and their flesh as the dung.
Neither their silver nor their gold shall be able to
deliver them in the day of the LORD'S wrath; but the
whole land shall be devoured by the fire of his
jealousy: for he shall make even a speedy riddance
of all them that dwell in the land.**
We must hear this. The message of Zephaniah is for us.
The great day of the Lord is near, it is near, and hasteneth
greatly. The message is for us. When strategic nuclear
weapons are used kings and princes are destroyed along
with everything else. Nothing can protect or save you
except the Lord Jesus Christ. Only the Christian in right
standing with God can look at a nuclear explosion and see

it having the same effect on him as the rapture.
Are you ready? If we are nuked tomorrow - where will you
spend eternity? Will a nuclear explosion have the same
effect for you as the rapture?

**Zephaniah 2:3 Seek ye the LORD, all ye meek of the
earth, which have wrought his judgment; seek
righteousness, seek meekness: it may be ye shall be
hid in the day of the LORD'S anger.**
Meekness is not weakness. Meekness is strength and power
under control. Meek people are strong people. The proud
people are the weak people. Meek people are merciful
people. Meek people are forgiving people because they
know how much God has forgiven them. Meek people can
endure injury with patience and without resentment. How
do we seek meekness? We seek meekness by seeking to
forgive those who have injured us.

**Zephaniah 3:1-6 Woe to her that is filthy and
polluted, to the oppressing city! She obeyed not the
voice; she received not correction; she trusted not in
the LORD; she drew not near to her God. Her
princes within her [are] roaring lions; her judges
[are] evening wolves; they gnaw not the bones till
the morrow.
Her prophets [are] light [and] treacherous persons:
her priests have polluted the sanctuary, they have
done violence to the law.
The just LORD [is] in the midst thereof; he will not do
iniquity: every morning doth he bring his judgment**

to light, he faileth not; but the unjust knoweth no shame. I have cut off the nations: their towers are desolate; I made their streets waste, that none passeth by: their cities are destroyed, so that there is no man, that there is none inhabitant.

Who is Zephaniah talking about. It is more likely that he is talking about America than Israel. America, the other nation founded for the glory of God, has turned to antichrist. Nothing but true faith in Jesus Christ can protect anyone in this country from Russia's strategic nuclear attack. The S.D.I. "star wars" strategic defense initiative, which President Reagan wanted to develop was not deployed. The American progress on this moral and purely defensive weapon system had much to do with the mythical "break-up" of the Soviet Empire and the mythical end of the cold war. It is a farce how America's money says "In God we trust." This judgment is coming to America, not Israel. The towers of Israel can not fall for it is God who strengthens them. Israel can never again be destroyed because it is God who is regathering and protecting Israel. He is talking about that other nation, America, which was also founded for the glory of God.

Zephaniah 3:14-18 Sing, O daughter of Zion; shout, O Israel; be glad and rejoice with all the heart, O daughter of Jerusalem. The LORD hath taken away thy judgments, he hath cast out thine enemy: the king of Israel, [even] the LORD, [is] in the midst of thee: thou shalt not see evil any more.

In that day it shall be said to Jerusalem, Fear thou

not: [and to] Zion, Let not thine hands be slack.
The LORD thy God in the midst of thee [is] mighty;
he will save, he will rejoice over thee with joy; he will
rest in his love, he will joy over thee with singing.
Now Zephaniah is talking about Israel. The Lord thy God
in the midst of thee is mighty. This is Israel. I srael's king
Yeshua is coming soon to set up His everlasting kingdom.
Israel will soon recognize the Lord Yeshusa as their king,
as He comes in great power and glory to give them and all
the saints victory over the armies of antichrist.

HAGGAI

Haggai's name means "festive." He was a contemporary of the great minor end time Messianic prophet, Zechariah. They both minstered while the temple was being rebuilt by the exiles who were returning from the Babolonian captivity. While Haggai does not specifically address end time events his message is an important end time message. Keeping the main thing the main thing is his message. This message is most important to the generation which will witness the glorious powerful return of King Jesus.

Haggai 1:3-8 Then came the word of the LORD by Haggai the prophet, saying,[Is it] time for you, O ye, to dwell in your ceiled houses, and this house [lie] waste? Now therefore thus saith the LORD of hosts; Consider your ways. Ye have sown much, and bring in little; ye eat, but ye have not enough; ye drink, but ye are not filled with drink; ye clothe you, but there is none warm; and he that earneth wages earneth wages [to put it] into a bag with holes.
Thus saith the LORD of hosts; Consider your ways. Go up to the mountain, and bring wood, and build the house; and I will take pleasure in it, and I will be glorified, saith the LORD.

Consider your ways. The real reason that the temple construction project was dragging is because the people were much more concerned with building their own houses and farms than in building God's temple. They were sent to build the temple. They collected money from their friends in Babylon and from the king to build the temple and they were using these funds to build their own houses and farms. For this reason God would not allow their crops to prosper. They were robbing from God, their fellow Jews in Babylon, and the king. God is the source of every good thing we have. God expects us to put a minimum of 10% of our increase into the spread of the gospel. If we don't we are robbing from God. It is not smart to steal from God. If we are giving at least 10% of our increase to God then we may trust Him to prosper us. Otherwise we will have a difficult time with all financial aspects of our life. We earn wages and they fall through holes in our pockets faster than we can earn it.

Haggai 2:4-9 Yet now be strong, O Zerubbabel, saith the LORD; and be strong, O Joshua, son of Josedech, the high priest; and be strong, all ye people of the land, saith the LORD, and work: for I [am] with you, saith the LORD of hosts: [According to] the word that I covenanted with you when ye came out of Egypt, so my spirit remaineth among you: fear ye not.
For thus saith the LORD of hosts; Yet once, it [is] a little while, and I will shake the heavens, and the earth, and the sea, and the dry [land];
And I will shake all nations, and the desire of all nations shall come: and I will fill this house with glory, saith the LORD of hosts.
The silver [is] mine, and the gold [is] mine, saith the LORD of hosts. The glory of this latter house shall

be greater than of the former, saith the LORD of
hosts: and in this place will I give peace, saith the
LORD of hosts.

Be strong, be strong says the Lord and work, for God is
with you. Because the almighty power of God's Holy Spirit
is within us we are strong and we should have no fear. We
can choose not to believe this and be weak wimps from
whom Satan will steal, kill and destroy. What will you do?
Will you be strong in the Lord and choose to live a life
without fear? Our body is the temple of the Holy Spirit.
Are we reading the word of God every day and growing in
grace, knowledge, understanding, and faith. Is the Holy
Spirit's temple of our body stronger and more glorious in
faith today than it was yesterday? Are we neglecting God's
word and allowing the glorious faith in God to diminish,
and wither?

Haggai 2:15 And now, I pray you, consider from this
day and upward, from before a stone was laid upon a
stone in the temple of the LORD:

Think about it every day. We have a choice of faith or fear.
Our faith will grow if we feed it. Faith comes by hearing
and hearing by the word of God. Faith may grow by
testimonies, preaching, prayer and miracles. In the long
run there is no true easy short cut. Faith comes by hearing
and hearing by the word of God. Prayer is important.
When we pray we talk to God. Yet God talks to us when
we read His word. It is so important to keep the
conversation a 2 way conversation. What can we tell God
that He doesn't already know? It is more important for us

to hear from God than for God to hear from us. It needs top priority in our life to read God's word every day.

Haggai 2:17-19 I smote you with blasting and with mildew and with hail in all the labours of your hands; yet ye [turned] not to me, saith the LORD. Consider now from this day and upward, from the four and twentieth day of the ninth [month, even] from the day that the foundation of the LORD'S temple was laid, consider [it]. Is the seed yet in the barn? yea, as yet the vine, and the fig tree, and the pomegranate, and the olive tree, hath not brought forth: from this day will I bless [you].

From this day and from now on out God promises to bless you. Is there any condition associated with this promise of blessing? They were putting their money in purses with holes in them. They were loosing it faster than they could make it because their own personal priorities were more important than God's priorities. Obedience is the condition of blessing. God deserves top priority in our life. Does He have top priority in our life? We need to think about this every day. Will we give Him a chance to talk to us every day by reading His word? God only wants to bless us. We can not turn our backs on God and expect to be blessed. This does not mean our life will be totally free of any problems or trials. It does mean that God will bless us even in the middle of our loss, our grief, and our trials. He will be with us and bring us through the trial.

ZECHARIAH

Zechariah's name means "the Lord remembers." He
ministered at the same time of Haggai in about 520BC.
Zechariah was a priest as well as a prophet. This is quite
unusual. Most of God's prophets were not priests and
generally rebuked the hypocrisy of the priests. No prophet
gives more specific predictions than Zechariah.

**Zechariah 1:14-16 So the angel that communed with
me said unto me, Cry thou, saying, Thus saith the
LORD of hosts; I am jealous for Jerusalem and for
Zion with a great jealousy. And I am very sore
displeased with the heathen [that are] at ease: for I
was but a little displeased, and they helped forward
the affliction.
Therefore thus saith the LORD; I am returned to
Jerusalem with mercies: my house shall be built in it,
saith the LORD of hosts, and a line shall be
stretched forth upon Jerusalem.**

God loves the Jews. The Jews are God's chosen people.
God choose to reveal Himself to the world through the
Jews. Jesus is a Jew. God always will bless those who
bless the Jews and curse those who curse the Jews. God is
again with the nation of Israel to fight their battles. If we
don't have a tender heart toward the Jews, we should pray
and ask God to heal us. Jesus will rule the world in
righteousness for a 1000 years from His throne in
Jerusalem.

Zechariah 2:4-5 And said unto him, Run, speak to

this young man, saying, Jerusalem shall be inhabited [as] towns without walls for the multitude of men and cattle therein: For I, saith the LORD, will be unto her a wall of fire round about, and will be the glory in the midst of her.

God is defending and prospering Israel. Israel's army is the only undefeatable army in the world today. God is on the side of Israel and if we are against Israel we are going against God.

Zechariah 2:7-11 Deliver thyself, O Zion, that dwellest [with] the daughter of Babylon. For thus saith the LORD of hosts; After the glory hath he sent me unto the nations which spoiled you: for he that toucheth you toucheth the apple of his eye. For, behold, I will shake mine hand upon them, and they shall be a spoil to their servants: and ye shall know that the LORD of hosts hath sent me. Sing and rejoice, O daughter of Zion: for, lo, I come, and I will dwell in the midst of thee, saith the LORD. And many nations shall be joined to the LORD in that day, and shall be my people: and I will dwell in the midst of thee, and thou shalt know that the LORD of hosts hath sent me unto thee.

Who ever goes against Israel goes against the apple of God's eye. God tells His people to flee Babylon and return to their homeland. Remember the word Babylon means tyranny and confusion. If we look carefully at the political correctness of America's national leadership today we see the tyranny and confusion of Babylon. Woe to America if this nation ever fails to continue supporting Israel. Israel is America's best and only significant ally.

Zechariah 3:1-2 And he shewed me Joshua the high priest standing before the angel of the LORD, and Satan standing at his right hand to resist him. And the LORD said unto Satan, The LORD rebuke thee, O Satan; even the LORD that hath chosen Jerusalem rebuke thee: [is] not this a brand plucked out of the fire?

It is not coincidence that Joshua was high priest. The name Joshua in Hebrew means Jehovah saves. The name Jesus in Hebrew is Yeshua or Joshua. Jehovah saves us. We cannot save ourselves. This is Messianic prophesy. Jesus Christ the anointed high priest Messiah is still being opposed by Satan. Israel had been saved out of the fire of the Babylonian captivity. Jesus has rescued us from the tyranny and confusion that we would have without having Jesus Christ as Lord of our life! Satan is the accuser of the brethren. All of his accusation becomes null and void when we are covered by the blood of Jesus and God will pass over us in judgment and show us His infinite mercy. Praise the Lord!

Zechariah 3:8-9 Hear now, O Joshua the high priest, thou, and thy fellows that sit before thee: for they [are] men wondered at: for, behold, I will bring forth my servant the BRANCH. For behold the stone that I have laid before Joshua; upon one stone [shall be] seven eyes: behold, I will

engrave the graving thereof, saith the LORD of hosts, and I will remove the iniquity of that land in one day.
Joshua (Jesus) is the great high priest and king. Jesus is the BRANCH of David. Isaiah 11:1 And there shall come forth a rod out of the stem of Jesse, and a Branch shall grow out of his roots: Jeremiah 23:5-6 Behold, the days come, saith the LORD, that I will raise unto David a righteous Branch, and a King shall reign and prosper, and shall execute judgment and justice in the earth. In his days Judah shall be saved, and Israel shall dwell safely: and this [is] his name whereby he shall be called, THE LORD OUR RIGHTEOUSNESS. Jeremiah 33:15 In those days, and at that time, will I cause the Branch of righteousness to grow up unto David; and he shall execute judgment and righteousness in the land.
Jesus is the BRANCH. In one day all Israel will be saved. They will be saved the same way that everyone else gets saved - by accepting Jesus as Savior and Lord of their life. Jesus is the precious corner stone, the stumbling stone, the rock of offense, the great stone cut without hands to come down from heaven to smash the world government and religious system of antichrist.

Zechariah 4:6 Then he answered and spake unto me, saying, This [is] the word of the LORD unto Zerubbabel, saying, Not by might, nor by power, but by my spirit, saith the LORD of hosts.
If we want to be strong and if we want to have power, never forget that it will not be accomplished by our own might or

by our own power. Remember that it will be accomplished
by the awesome power of the Holy Spirit of God.

**Zechariah 5:7 & 10 - 11 And, behold, there was lifted
up a talent of lead: and this [is] a woman that sitteth
in the midst of the ephah. Then said I to the angel
that talked with me, Whither do these bear the
ephah? And he said unto me, To build it an house in
the land of Shinar: and it shall be established, and
set there upon her own base.**
Wickedness is personified as a woman in a basket, mystery
Babylon, the whore who caused people to turn away from
the true God to the false gods of self and/or antichrist.

**Zechariah 6:11-13 Then take silver and gold, and
make crowns, and set [them] upon the head of
Joshua the son of Josedech, the high priest;
And speak unto him, saying, Thus speaketh the
LORD of hosts, saying, Behold the man whose name
[is] The BRANCH; and he shall grow up out of his
place, and he shall build the temple of the LORD:
Even he shall build the temple of the LORD; and he
shall bear the glory, and shall sit and rule upon his
throne; and he shall be a priest upon his throne: and
the counsel of peace shall be between them both.**
Joshua (Jesus) the high priest will also be crowned King of
Kings. Jesus is the man whose name is the BRANCH.
Jesus established His church which is the body of Christ.
Some day all Jews will become part of the body of Christ.
Individually and collectively we are the temple of God's

Holy Spirit. Jesus will set up His throne in awesome power and glory as the Great High P riest and King of Kings to bring everlasting peace and j oy.

Zechariah 7:9-10 Thus speaketh the LORD of hosts, saying, Execute true j udgment, and shew mercy and compassions every man to his brother: And oppress not the widow, nor the fatherless, the stranger, nor the poor; and let none of you imagine evil against his brother in your heart.

What does God want us to do? D o not imagine evil in your heart against your brother. Do unto others as you would have them do unto you. As God is merciful and compassionate to you, being godly means that we are merciful and compassionate to our brothers. Helping the poor, widows and orphans greatly pleases God.

Zechariah 7:12-13 Yea, they made their hearts [as] an adamant stone, lest they should hear the law, and the words which the LORD of hosts hath sent in his spirit by the former prophets: therefore came a great wrath from the LORD of hosts. Therefore it is come to pass, [that] as he cried, and they would not hear; so they cried, and I would not hear, saith the LORD of hosts:

When we harden our hearts against God's word and refuse to listen to Him we are asking for big trouble. There can even come a time when we cry to Him and He chooses not to hear us. Nothing could be worse. That sounds like hell.

Zechariah 8:7-8 Thus saith the LORD of hosts;

Behold, I will save my people from the east country, and from the west country; And I will bring them, and they shall dwell in the midst of Jerusalem: and they shall be my people, and I will be their God, in truth and in righteousness.

We are watching this prophesy being fulfilled before us. God is regathering Jews from their dispersion to their homeland. They are dwelling again in Jerusalem after almost 2000 years of dispersion.

Zechariah 8:16-17 These [are] the things that ye shall do; Speak ye every man the truth to his neighbour; execute the judgment of truth and peace in your gates: And let none of you imagine evil in your hearts against his neighbour; and love no false oath: for all these [are things] that I hate, saith the LORD.

Speak the truth. Love peace and truth. Think good things about others. God hates false witnesses and stinking thinking about our brothers and sisters.

Zechariah 9:9 Rejoice greatly, O daughter of Zion; shout, O daughter of Jerusalem: behold, thy King cometh unto thee: he [is] just, and having salvation; lowly, and riding upon an ass, and upon a colt the foal of an ass.

What is Zechariah talking about? H e is talking about the first Palm Sunday. John 12:12-15 On the next day much people that were come to the feast, when they heard that Jesus was coming to Jerusalem, Took branches of palm trees, and went forth to meet him, and cried, Hosanna: Blessed [is] the King of Israel that cometh in the name of the Lord. Jesus, when he had found a young ass, sat thereon; as it is written, Fear not, daughter of Sion: behold, thy King cometh, sitting on an ass's colt.

The people of Jerusalem were receiving their King as He entered the city riding on the foal of an ass. They were rejoicing greatly. The religious people, who should have known better, told Jesus to rebuke the people who were rejoicing over Him as their King. Luke 19:39-40 And some of the Pharisees from among the multitude said unto him, Master, rebuke thy disciples. And he answered and said unto them, I tell you that, if these should hold their peace, the stones would immediately cry out. The prophet Zechariah had said Messiah would cause the people of Jerusalem to greatly rejoice when they saw their King entering the city riding on the foal of an ass. Because the word of God is always true, Jesus tells them that even if the people would not be rejoicing at that time, the very rocks would immediately take up the rejoicing. The word of God is always true.

Zechariah 10:3-4 Mine anger was kindled against the shepherds, and I punished the goats: for the LORD of hosts hath visited his flock the house of Judah, and hath made them as his goodly horse in the battle. Out of him came forth the corner, out of him the nail, out of him the battle bow, out of him every oppressor together.

Those who are charged with the care of the children of God
had better take such work most seriously. Many times we
see in scripture how God's anger is kindled against
pastors who do not genuinely care for their flock. We also
see more Messianic prophesy which Jesus will fulfill. J esus
is the chieftain (corner) who will destroy all of Israel's
oppressors and the armies of antichrist with the brightness
of His glorious return as King of K ings and Lord of Lords.

**Zechariah 11:4-5 Thus saith the LORD my God;
Feed the flock of the slaughter; Whose possessors
slay them, and hold themselves not guilty: and they
that sell them say, Blessed [be] the LORD; for I am
rich: and their own shepherds pity them not.**
The Jews have been dispersed for over 2000 years. Other
people have possessed them and killed them and made them
slaves. Even their own shepherds have not had pity on
them. There is a warning here against anyone who would
mistreat or fail to help the Jews. There is also another
warning to pastors that they must be genuinely concerned
with the welfare of their flock.

**Zechariah 11:12-13 And I said unto them, If ye think
good, give [me] my price; and if not, forbear. So they
weighed for my price thirty [pieces] of silver. And
the LORD said unto me, Cast it unto the potter: a
goodly price that I was prised at of them. And I took
the thirty [pieces] of silver, and cast them to the
potter in the house of the LORD.**
The price Judas was paid for Judas to deliver J esus to be

killed was 30 pieces of silver. **Matthew 26:14-15 Then
one of the twelve, called Judas Iscariot, went unto
the chief priests, And said [unto them], What will ye
give me, and I will deliver him unto you? And they
covenanted with him for thirty pieces of silver.
Matthew 27:3-10 Then Judas, which had betrayed
him, when he saw that he was condemned, repented
himself, and brought again the thirty pieces of silver
to the chief priests and elders, Saying, I have sinned
in that I have betrayed the innocent blood. And they
said, What [is that] to us? see thou [to that]. And
he cast down the pieces of silver in the temple, and
departed, and went and hanged himself. And the
chief priests took the silver pieces, and said, It is not
lawful for to put them into the treasury, because it is
the price of blood. And they took counsel, and
bought with them the Potter's field, to bury strangers
in. Wherefore that field was called, The field of
blood, unto this day. Then was fulfilled that which
was spoken by Jeremy the prophet, saying, And they
took the thirty pieces of silver, the price of him that
was valued, whom they of the children of Israel did
value; And gave them for the Potter's field, as the
Lord appointed me.**

One has to wonder how Jesus remains a stumbling block to
the Jews with such scriptures as these.

**Zechariah 11:17 Woe to the idol shepherd that
leaveth the flock! the sword [shall be] upon his arm,
and upon his right eye: his arm shall be clean dried**

up, and his right eye shall be utterly darkened.

When the Lord says woe it is very serious. Pastors have a very serious responsibility to care for the flock God places in their hands.

Zechariah 12:2-5 Behold, I will make Jerusalem a cup of trembling unto all the people round about, when they shall be in the siege both against Judah [and] against Jerusalem. And in that day will I make Jerusalem a burdensome stone for all people: all that burden themselves with it shall be cut in pieces, though all the people of the earth be gathered together against it.

In that day, saith the LORD, I will smite every horse with astonishment, and his rider with madness: and I will open mine eyes upon the house of Judah, and will smite every horse of the people with blindness. And the governors of Judah shall say in their heart, The inhabitants of Jerusalem [shall be] my strength in the LORD of hosts their God.

God said that when Russia and all of her vast army invades Israel that God Himself would wipe out 5 of 6 of every one of their soldiers. This supernatural destruction would be so that the world would know that the God of Israel is Almighty God. These verses may give insight into the type of destruction which God will use. It will be a cavalry invasion. Russia has been buying horses for years. The horses will be struck with blindness and the riders with madness. They will likely kill each other. It will take 7 months to bury them all.

Zechariah 12:10   And I will pour upon the house of David, and upon the inhabitants of Jerusalem, the spirit of grace and of supplications: and they shall look upon me whom they have pierced, and they shall mourn for him, as one mourn for [his] only [son], and shall be in bitterness for him, as one that is in bitterness for [his] firstborn.

Here is perhaps the most blessed of the promises to Israel. In one day all Israel will be saved as they look upon Jesus whom they have pierced and mourn for Him as one that is in bitterness for his firstborn.

Zechariah 13:1   In that day there shall be a fountain opened to the house of David and to the inhabitants of Jerusalem for sin and for uncleanness.

In that day they shall all be cleansed from their sins as we all are cleansed from our sins. What is this amazing fountain? Nothing other than the precious blood of Jesus which has already been shed to cleanse everyone who will only receive this pardon from Jesus.

Zechariah 13:9   And I will bring the third part through the fire, and will refine them as silver is refined, and will try them as gold is tried: they shall call on my name, and I will hear them: I will say, It [is] my people: and they shall say, The LORD [is] my God.

What do you suppose is referred to in this verse? This is the purpose of tribulation. To refine the saints as gold and silver are refined by the fires so are the saints refined by the fires of tribulation.

Zechariah 14:3-7 Then shall the LORD go forth, and fight against those nations, as when he fought in the day of battle. And his feet shall stand in that day upon the mount of Olives, which [is] before Jerusalem on the east, and the mount of Olives shall cleave in the midst thereof toward the east and toward the west, [and there shall be] a very great valley; and half of the mountain shall remove toward the north, and half of it toward the south. And ye shall flee [to] the valley of the mountains; for the valley of the mountains shall reach unto Azal: yea, ye shall flee, like as ye fled from before the earthquake in the days of Uzziah king of Judah: and the LORD my God shall come, [and] all the saints with thee.

And it shall come to pass in that day, [that] the light shall not be clear, [nor] dark: But it shall be one day which shall be known to the LORD, not day, nor night: but it shall come to pass, [that] at evening time it shall be light.

The Lord Jesus Christ will return in great power and glory and with his words will totally destroy the armies of antichrist assembled in the valley of Megeddo. He shall touch the earth on the Mount of Olives which will be split by a great earthquake. The day of the Lord will be a day like no other ever. His glory shall light up the darkness of the thick clouds that day.

Zechariah 14:9 And the LORD shall be king over all the earth: in that day shall there be one LORD, and his name one.
Jesus will then begin his reign as King over all the earth.

Zechariah 14:12-13 And this shall be the plague wherewith the LORD will smite all the people that have fought against Jerusalem; Their flesh shall consume away while they stand upon their feet, and their eyes shall consume away in their holes, and their tongue shall consume away in their mouth. And it shall come to pass in that day, [that] a great tumult from the LORD shall be among them; and they shall lay hold every one on the hand of his neighbour, and his hand shall rise up against the hand of his neighbour.
It would be difficult for a nuclear physicist to give a more graphic description of how a human body can be consumed by nuclear radiation. This was not possible to understand until our generation.

Zechariah 14:16-17 And it shall come to pass, [that] every one that is left of all the nations which came against Jerusalem shall even go up from year to year to worship the King, the LORD of hosts, and to keep the feast of tabernacles.
And it shall be, [that] whoso will not come up of [all] the families of the earth unto Jerusalem to worship the King, the LORD of hosts, even upon them shall

be no rain.

All nations will come to worship the Lord in Jerusalem.

PETER

Peter has some important things to say to us regarding end time prophecy. Reviewing Peter's end time prophecy provides a good way to conclude this work. Only Peter tells us that, even within the church, at the time of the end, they all will be mocking "where is the promise of His coming." Most importantly, "It is not God's will that any should perish; but that all should come to repentance." Peter makes it quite clear that we are called to patient endurance of tribulation in true holiness. You will notice that there are no comments on the few verses selected from Peter's second epistle. These verses form an ideal conclusion to this work. May I encourage you to read these concluding verses several times allowing the Holy Spirit of Truth to quicken them for you. Memorizing some of these verses will help maintain Great Joy in Great Tribulation.

I Peter 1:2-4 Elect according to the foreknowledge of God the Father, through sanctification of the Spirit, unto obedience and sprinkling of the blood of Jesus Christ: Grace unto you, and peace, be multiplied. Blessed [be] the God and Father of our Lord Jesus Christ, which according to his abundant mercy hath begotten us again unto a lively hope by the resurrection of Jesus Christ from the dead, To an inheritance incorruptible, and undefiled, and that fadeth not away, reserved in heaven for you,
We are called to obedience. We are set apart for the glory of God by having our sins covered by the blood of Jesus Christ.

We are not called to be free of trials and tribulation, but to glorify God by the peace we have in the middle of tribulation.

I Peter 1:5-7 Who are kept by the power of God through faith unto salvation ready to be revealed in the last time.
Wherein ye greatly rejoice, though now for a season, if need be, ye are in heaviness through manifold temptations:
That the trial of your faith, being much more precious than of gold that perisheth, though it be tried with fire, might be found unto praise and honour and glory at the appearing of Jesus Christ:

Our salvation is ready to be revealed in the last time. Nothing is said about this salvation being revealed 7 years before the last time. We are to find great joy in great tribulation. We glorify God by our faithfulness in tribulation. At the appearing of Jesus Christ our faith in tribulation will become great joy indeed. Even those on the side of Antichrist in the war on the saints will be joyful when things are going well for their side in the 7 years before the last time. We will be kept by the power of God through faith during great tribulation.

I Peter 1:8-13 Whom having not seen, ye love; in whom, though now ye see [him] not, yet believing, ye rejoice with joy unspeakable and full of glory:
Receiving the end of your faith, [even] the salvation of [your] souls.

Of which salvation the prophets have inquired and searched diligently, who prophesied of the grace [that should come] unto you:
Searching what, or what manner of time the Spirit of Christ which was in them did signify, when it testified beforehand the sufferings of Christ, and the glory that should follow.
Unto whom it was revealed, that not unto themselves, but unto us they did minister the things, which are now reported unto you by them that have preached the gospel unto you with the Holy Ghost sent down from heaven; which things the angels desire to look into.
Wherefore gird up the loins of your mind, be sober, and hope to the end for the grace that is to be brought unto you at the revelation of Jesus Christ;

There is nothing in scripture describing a secret second coming of Jesus Christ. Everything that is said about the revelation of Jesus Christ is that His second coming will be with great power and glory. Every eye shall see Him. In the mean time, we should be getting prepared for the war with Antichrist. This is the meaning of "gird up the loins." We are to be strong in faith. God is with us now in the presence and power of His Holy Spirit.

I Peter 1:15-16 But as he which hath called you is holy, so be ye holy in all manner of conversation;
Because it is written, Be ye holy; for I am holy.

The secret of victory is holiness. The power of the Holy Spirit is unlimited in the life of the believer who is walking in holiness. We must become hypersensitive to the convicting work of the Holy Spirit. We need to take our sins to the cross immediately. There is no condemnation. God only wants us to be in agreement with Him to maintain that unbroken fellowship with Him through His Holy Spirit. If God is for us, who can be against us?

I Peter 1:18-21 Forasmuch as ye know that ye were not redeemed with corruptible things, [as] silver and gold, from your vain conversation [received] by tradition from your fathers;
But with the precious blood of Christ, as of a lamb without blemish and without spot:
Who verily was foreordained before the foundation of the world, but was manifest in these last times for you,
Who by him do believe in God, that raised him up from the dead, and gave him glory; that your faith and hope might be in God.
Our hope is in God and His integrity. We place our hope and trust in the integrity of His Word. We are not trusting ourselves our anyone else. Our trust and hope is solidly based on God's integrity.

I Peter 1:22-25 Seeing ye have purified your souls in obeying the truth through the Spirit unto unfeigned love of the brethren, [see that ye] love one another with a pure heart fervently:
Being born again, not of corruptible seed, but of incorruptible, by the word of God, which liveth and

abideth for ever.

For all flesh [is] as grass, and all the glory of man as the flower of grass. The grass withereth, and the flower thereof falleth away:

But the word of the Lord endureth for ever. And this is the word which by the gospel is preached unto you.

Where the rubber meets the road in relation to holiness is the unfeigned love for the brethren in great tribulation. One of the reasons the God allows Antichrist to wage war on the saints is to disclose those who have feigned love for the brethren. Those who love one another with a pure heart fervently will shine in great tribulation.

I Peter 2:1-3 Wherefore laying aside all malice, and all guile, and hypocrisies, and envies, and all evil speakings,

As newborn babes, desire the sincere milk of the word, that ye may grow thereby:

If so be ye have tasted that the Lord [is] gracious.

This is great preparation for great tribulation. Lay aside all malice. Lay aside all lies, and hypocrisies, and envies, and all evil speaking. Desire to know more and more of God's absolute truth by reading and studying our bibles every day. This is the right response to the grace of God, that we may grow mighty in faith.

I Peter 2:5-12 Ye also, as lively stones, are built up a spiritual house, an holy priesthood, to offer up spiritual sacrifices, acceptable to God by Jesus

Christ.

Wherefore also it is contained in the scripture,
Behold, I lay in Sion a chief corner stone, elect,
precious: and he that believeth on him shall not be
confounded.

Unto you therefore which believe [he is] precious:
but unto them which be disobedient, the stone which
the builders disallowed, the same is made the head
of the corner,

And a stone of stumbling, and a rock of offence,
[even to them] which stumble at the word, being
disobedient: whereunto also they were appointed.

But ye [are] a chosen generation, a royal priesthood,
an holy nation, a peculiar people; that ye should
shew forth the praises of him who hath called you
out of darkness into his marvellous light:

Which in time past [were] not a people, but [are] now
the people of God: which had not obtained mercy,
but now have obtained mercy.

Dearly beloved, I beseech [you] as strangers and
pilgrims, abstain from fleshly lusts, which war
against the soul;

Having your conversation honest among the
Gentiles: that, whereas they speak against you as
evildoers, they may by [your] good works, which they
shall behold, glorify God in the day of visitation.

It all comes to a great shakedown in the great tribulation.
Everyone will make a firmly and finally committed choice
of following Jesus Christ or Antichrist. Many today can
have a token faith and feigned affection. Today it is

possible to hold a cheap grace void of holiness, commitment, and free of trial and tribulation. It is the trying of our faith which produces steadfastness. It will not be possible to have feigned faith or feigned affection in great tribulation. Everyone will either passionately love or hate Jesus Christ and His saints in great tribulation.

I Peter 2:19-25 For this [is] thankworthy, if a man for conscience toward God endure grief, suffering wrongfully.
For what glory [is it], if, when ye be buffeted for your faults, ye shall take it patiently? but if, when ye do well, and suffer [for it], ye take it patiently, this [is] acceptable with God.
For even hereunto were ye called: because Christ also suffered for us, leaving us an example, that ye should follow his steps:
Who did no sin, neither was guile found in his mouth: Who, when he was reviled, reviled not again; when he suffered, he threatened not; but committed [himself] to him that judgeth righteously:
Who his own self bare our sins in his own body on the tree, that we, being dead to sins, should live unto righteousness: by whose stripes ye were healed.
For ye were as sheep going astray; but are now returned unto the Shepherd and Bishop of your souls.

Many will not want to hear such truth. Peter is speaking with the same sort of Holy Spirit inspired hard hitting truth that brought 3000 souls to repentance and faith

in Jesus Christ in his first sermon on Pentecost. Peter tells us
that we are called to _____. Nobody wants to suffer and
few will ever even hear this message. Most want to hear the
no suffering, no trials, "no tribulation for me,"
"I have faith in my faith," message so popular in this time
of strong delusion. It is easy to find the preacher who will
scratch itching ears. Few teachers will have the courage to
box those itching ears with the truth of the call to suffering
with Christ. Christ is our example.

**I Peter 3:8-12 Finally, [be ye] all of one mind, having
compassion one of another, love as brethren, [be]
pitiful, [be] courteous:
Not rendering evil for evil, or railing for railing: but
contrariwise blessing; knowing that ye are thereunto
called, that ye should inherit a blessing.
For he that will love life, and see good days, let him
refrain his tongue from evil, and his lips that they
speak no guile:
Let him eschew evil, and do good; let him seek
peace, and ensue it.
For the eyes of the Lord [are] over the righteous,
and his ears [are open] unto their prayers: but the
face of the Lord [is] against them that do evil.**

Finally be of one mind. In looking at the power of God
demonstrated in the book of acts, over and over we see that
they were of "one accord." We must have unity in the
Body of Christ. The unity must not compromise the truth.
Look at Peter's sermon in Acts 2. The truth cannot be
compromised for the sake of unity. Peter and Paul

withstood each other, toe to toe, face to face until they came to one accord in the truth. Compassion, love, pity and even courtesy all require the foundation of truth. Love of the truth is paramount.

I Peter 3:14-17 But and if ye suffer for righteousness' sake, happy [are ye]: and be not afraid of their terror, neither be troubled;
But sanctify the Lord God in your hearts: and [be] ready always to [give] an answer to every man that asketh you a reason of the hope that is in you with meekness and fear:
Having a good conscience; that, whereas they speak evil of you, as of evildoers, they may be ashamed that falsely accuse your good conversation in Christ.
For [it is] better, if the will of God be so, that ye suffer for well doing, than for evil doing.
We are not to be afraid or troubled of the terror of Antichrist. We are to find great joy in great tribulation so that we may be giving answers to those who will be asking for the reason for the hope that is in us. The great tribulation will be the greatest opportunity for glory and evangelism ever in the history of the Church.

I Peter 4:1-4 Forasmuch then as Christ hath suffered for us in the flesh, arm yourselves likewise with the same mind: for he that hath suffered in the flesh hath ceased from sin;
That he no longer should live the rest of [his] time in the flesh to the lusts of men, but to the will of God.

For the time past of [our] life may suffice us to have wrought the will of the Gentiles, when we walked in lasciviousness, lusts, excess of wine, revellings, banquetings, and abominable idolatries:
Wherein they think it strange that ye run not with [them] to the same excess of riot, speaking evil of [you]:

Peter encourages us to arm ourselves with the mind of Christ. Paul also said "Let this mind be in you which was also in Christ Jesus." Philippians 2:3-7 gives us more detail about acquiring the mind of Christ. Let nothing be done through strife or vanity. In lowliness of mind esteem others better than yourself. Christ being in the form of God, did not allow His equality with God to prevent him from lowering Himself and was obedient in suffering that is beyond human understanding.

I Peter 4:7-10 But the end of all things is at hand: be ye therefore sober, and watch unto prayer.
And above all things have fervent charity among yourselves: for charity shall cover the multitude of sins.
I Peter 4:9 Use hospitality one to another without grudging.
I Peter 4:10 As every man hath received the gift, [even so] minister the same one to another, as good stewards of the manifold grace of God.

Now we come to the practical outworking of this great preparation for great tribulation. We are told to be watching soberly as the end approaches and above all things to have fervent love for all those for whom Christ paid such a great price. We are to practice hospitality without murmuring and share whatever we have with our brothers and sisters in Christ.

I Peter 4:12-19 Beloved, think it not strange concerning the fiery trial which is to try you, as though some strange thing happened unto you: But rejoice, inasmuch as ye are partakers of Christ's sufferings; that, when his glory shall be revealed, ye may be glad also with exceeding joy.
If ye be reproached for the name of Christ, happy [are ye]; for the spirit of glory and of God resteth upon you: on their part he is evil spoken of, but on your part he is glorified.
But let none of you suffer as a murderer, or [as] a thief, or [as] an evildoer, or as a busybody in other men's matters.
Yet if [any man suffer] as a Christian, let him not be ashamed; but let him glorify God on this behalf.
For the time [is come] that judgment must begin at the house of God: and if [it] first [begin] at us, what shall the end [be] of them that obey not the gospel of God?
And if the righteous scarcely be saved, where shall the ungodly and the sinner appear?
Wherefore let them that suffer according to the will of God commit the keeping of their souls [to him] in well doing, as unto a faithful Creator.
Peter tells us that we are not to think it is strange that we

are going to be tried by the fiery trial of Antichrist's war on the saints. We are to rejoice that we are partakers of Christ's sufferings so that we will be glad with exceeding joy when His glory is revealed. He returns to win the war for us in great power and glory. Judgment begins with the house of God. The house of God, the Church of Jesus Christ, stands against Antichrist in the great tribulation war on the saints. The Church of Jesus Christ needs to quit playing ostrich with the pre-tribulation rapture doctrine as we see the forces of Antichrist's New World Order coming to power. It seems that very few, in the name it and claim it Church in America, are prepared to take heed and to stand and endure to the end. Peter will not scratch the itching ears of those who refuse to consider the call to endure to the end.

I Peter 5:4-7 And when the chief Shepherd shall appear, ye shall receive a crown of glory that fadeth not away.
Likewise, ye younger, submit yourselves unto the elder. Yea, all [of you] be subject one to another, and be clothed with humility: for God resisteth the proud, and giveth grace to the humble.
Humble yourselves therefore under the mighty hand of God, that he may exalt you in due time:
Casting all your care upon him; for he careth for you.
We are called to endure to the end. When Jesus shall appear we will receive a crown of glory that will last forever. We must humble ourselves because God resists the proud but gives grace to the humble. He cares for us and

we can trust Him to be with us in great power in great
tribulation.

I Peter 5:8-11 Be sober, be vigilant; because your
adversary the devil, as a roaring lion, walketh about,
seeking whom he may devour:
Whom resist stedfast in the faith, knowing that the
same afflictions are accomplished in your brethren
that are in the world.
But the God of all grace, who hath called us unto his
eternal glory by Christ Jesus, after that ye have
suffered a while, make you perfect, stablish,
strengthen, settle [you].
To him [be] glory and dominion for ever and ever.
Amen.

The armor of God has no protection on the back side. We
are not to retreat or run away from the threat of great
tribulation. We are not to refuse to think about it. Satan
has already been defeated. The roaring lion is the oldest
toothless lion in the pride. This old toothless lion has a
great roar and that is all. This old lion will roar from the
opposite side of the herd of prey. If the lion's prey would
run right at the sound of the roar they would trample the
roaring lion. Unfortunately they become gripped with fear
and run away from the roar to where the young lions are
waiting in ambush. We may have to suffer for a while to
make us perfect, firmly established, strengthened, and
settled in our faith in Jesus Christ. We need to prepare for
the war on the saints and quit thinking the war on the
saints is of no concern to us. If we are saints and we know

the war is fixing to become total war, let us put on the full armor of God. We have the greatest opportunity for evangelism and giving glory to God of any generation in history.

II Peter 1:2 Grace and peace be multiplied unto you through the knowledge of God, and of Jesus our Lord,

II Peter 1:3 According as his divine power hath given unto us all things that [pertain] unto life and godliness, through the knowledge of him that hath called us to glory and virtue:

II Peter 1:4 Whereby are given unto us exceeding great and precious promises: that by these ye might be partakers of the divine nature, having escaped the corruption that is in the world through lust.

II Peter 1:5 And beside this, giving all diligence, add to your faith virtue; and to virtue knowledge;

II Peter 1:6 And to knowledge temperance; and to temperance patience; and to patience godliness;

II Peter 1:7 And to godliness brotherly kindness; and to brotherly kindness charity.

II Peter 1:16 For we have not followed cunningly devised fables, when we made known unto you the power and coming of our Lord Jesus Christ, but were eyewitnesses of his majesty.

II Peter 1:20 Knowing this first, that no prophecy of the scripture is of any private interpretation.

II Peter 1:21 For the prophecy came not in old time by the will of man: but holy men of God spake [as they were] moved by the Holy Ghost.

II Peter 2:1 But there were false prophets also among the people, even as there shall be false teachers among you, who privily shall bring in damnable heresies, even denying the Lord that bought them, and bring upon themselves swift destruction.
II Peter 2:2 And many shall follow their pernicious ways; by reason of whom the way of truth shall be evil spoken of.

II Peter 2:4 For if God spared not the angels that sinned, but cast [them] down to hell, and delivered [them] into chains of darkness, to be reserved unto judgment;
II Peter 2:5 And spared not the old world, but saved Noah the eighth [person], a preacher of righteousness, bringing in the flood upon the world of the ungodly;
II Peter 2:6 And turning the cities of Sodom and Gomorrha into ashes condemned [them] with an overthrow, making [them] an ensample unto those that after should live ungodly;
II Peter 2:7 And delivered just Lot, vexed with the filthy conversation of the wicked:
II Peter 2:8 (For that righteous man dwelling among them, in seeing and hearing, vexed [his] righteous soul from day to day with [their] unlawful deeds;)

II Peter 2:9 The Lord knoweth how to deliver the godly out of temptations, and to reserve the unjust unto the day of judgment to be punished:

II Peter 2:10 But chiefly them that walk after the flesh in the lust of uncleanness, and despise government. Presumptuous [are they], selfwilled, they are not afraid to speak evil of dignities.
II Peter 2:11 Whereas angels, which are greater in power and might, bring not railing accusation against them before the Lord.
II Peter 2:12 But these, as natural brute beasts, made to be taken and destroyed, speak evil of the things that they understand not; and shall utterly perish in their own corruption;

II Peter 2:20 For if after they have escaped the pollutions of the world through the knowledge of the Lord and Saviour Jesus Christ, they are again entangled therein, and overcome, the latter end is worse with them than the beginning.
II Peter 2:21 For it had been better for them not to have known the way of righteousness, than, after they have known [it], to turn from the holy commandment delivered unto them.
II Peter 2:22 But it is happened unto them according to the true proverb, The dog [is] turned to his own vomit again; and the sow that was washed to her wallowing in the mire.

II Peter 3:3 Knowing this first, that there shall come in the last days scoffers, walking after their own lusts,

II Peter 3:4 And saying, Where is the promise of his coming? for since the fathers fell asleep, all things continue as [they were] from the beginning of the creation.

II Peter 3:5 For this they willingly are ignorant of, that by the word of God the heavens were of old, and the earth standing out of the water and in the water:

II Peter 3:6 Whereby the world that then was, being overflowed with water, perished:

II Peter 3:7 But the heavens and the earth, which are now, by the same word are kept in store, reserved unto fire against the day of judgment and perdition of ungodly men.

II Peter 3:8 But, beloved, be not ignorant of this one thing, that one day [is] with the Lord as a thousand years, and a thousand years as one day.

II Peter 3:9 The Lord is not slack concerning his promise, as some men count slackness; but is longsuffering to us-ward, not willing that any should perish, but that all should come to repentance.

II Peter 3:10 But the day of the Lord will come as a thief in the night; in the which the heavens shall pass away with a great noise, and the elements shall melt with fervent heat, the earth also and the works that are therein shall be burned up.

II Peter 3:11 [Seeing] then [that] all these things shall

be dissolved, what manner [of persons] ought ye to
be in [all] holy conversation and godliness,
II Peter 3:12 Looking for and hasting unto the coming
of the day of God, wherein the heavens being on fire
shall be dissolved, and the elements shall melt with
fervent heat?

II Peter 3:13 Nevertheless we, according to his
promise, look for new heavens and a new earth,
wherein dwelleth righteousness.
II Peter 3:14 Wherefore, beloved, seeing that ye look
for such things, be diligent that ye may be found of
him in peace, without spot, and blameless.
II Peter 3:17 Ye therefore, beloved, seeing ye know
[these things] before, beware lest ye also, being led
away with the error of the wicked, fall from your own
stedfastness.
II Peter 3:18 But grow in grace, and [in] the
knowledge of our Lord and Saviour Jesus Christ.
To him [be] glory both now and for ever.

Amen.

LAST DAYS? END TIMES?
DAY OF THE LORD?
ARE THESE THINGS CONFUSING?

Will we witness the glorious return of the Messiah, the true King of Kings, who will destroy the false messiah, antichrist, with the brightness of His coming?

What does the Bible tell us? From Genesis to Revelation, God has told us to Watch, Take Heed, and be prepared.

This book is not deep theology. This book is a simple summary of end times scriptures. It is a call to joyful anticipation of the most spectacular event of all history. It is a call to look up with joy.

We have a joyful blessed hope and calling to be more than conquerors in a world coming apart at the seams in confusion and tyranny.

This book is a simple study of the scriptures from Genesis to Revelation to clear up the confusion of the many unbiblical teachings concerning the end times.

"The scriptural compendium on the tribulation is excellent.."
Dr. Daniel C. Juster
President, Messiah Biblical Institute
& Graduate School of Theology

"This book will be considered too controversial by many in the Church because it is such Christ centered, simple, straight forward, strong meat."
Rev. Terry Chupp
Minister to the B.A.S.S. Touring Pros

(QUESTIONS, COMMENTS, ORDERS 1-800-731-7545)